Modern French Classics

CAMILLE LE FOLL

Modern French Classics

photographs by David Japy | styling by Delphine de Montalier

HACHETTE Illustrated

PRICE GUIDE

○ INEXPENSIVE

○○ MODERATELY EXPENSIVE

○○○ EXPENSIVE

CONTENTS

SOUPS

BASIC STOCKS

THE FOLLOWING STOCK RECIPES EACH HAVE A SLIGHTLY DIFFERENT FLAVOUR, SO USE THE STOCK THAT SUITS THE TYPE OF SOUP YOU ARE MAKING. FOR EXAMPLE, CHICKEN STOCK IS BEST FOR CLEAR AND CREAMY SOUPS, VEGETABLE STOCK FOR SOUPS THICKENED WITH OATMEAL OR CONTAINING CEREALS (VERMICELLI, CHINESE NOODLES), ALTHOUGH CHICKEN STOCK CAN ALSO BE USED. BEEF STOCK IS IDEAL FOR CERTAIN REGIONAL DISHES AND RISOTTOS.

HOWEVER, IF YOU HAVE SOME LEFTOVER STOCK FROM A BEEF, FISH OR CHICKEN STEW, OR A FEW BONES FROM A SHOULDER OF LAMB OR A POULTRY CARCASS, DON'T THROW THEM AWAY. USE THEM TO MAKE STOCK AND FREEZE IT – IT'S MUCH BETTER THAN USING A STOCK CUBE.

CHICKEN STOCK
(make the day before)

Makes about 1.5 litres/2$\frac{1}{2}$ pints/6 cups

Bring 2 litres/3$\frac{1}{2}$ pints/8 cups water to the boil in a large pan or stockpot. Add an uncooked chicken carcass with neck and giblets (or the leftover carcass from a roast chicken), 1 carrot (peeled and cut into chunks), 1 onion (peeled and quartered) and 1 bouquet garni (see recipe below). Leave to simmer gently for 1 hour if using a cooked carcass, 1$\frac{1}{2}$-2 hours if uncooked. (Do not let the stock boil or it will become cloudy.) Remove any scum as it forms.

Remove the bouquet garni and leave the stock to cool. Refrigerate overnight.

Next day remove any solidified surface fat – this will make the stock tastier and more digestible.

BOUQUET GARNI

Wrap 1 bay leaf, 1 thyme sprig, a few parsley sprigs and celery leaves in the green part of a leek leaf and tie with kitchen string.

VEGETABLE STOCK

Makes about 1.5 litres/2$\frac{1}{2}$ pints/6 cups

Bring 2 litres/3$\frac{1}{2}$ pints/8 cups water to the boil in a large pan or stockpot and add 1 celery stalk (chopped) or a large piece of celeriac (peeled and cut into chunks), 2 carrots (peeled and cut into chunks), 2 leeks (peeled and sliced), 1-2 small onions (peeled and stuck with a clove), 1 peeled garlic clove (optional), 2-3 tomatoes (chopped) and any other vegetables you have to hand. Add 1 bouquet garni and leave to simmer gently (do not let boil) for 50 minutes. Remove any scum as it forms.

Strain the stock (there's no fat to be skimmed off). It can be used immediately.

QUICK BEEF STOCK

Makes about 1.5 litres/2$\frac{1}{2}$ pints/6 cups

Put a chopped oxtail (or some beef bones) in a cooking pot or stockpot and add 2 litres/ 3$\frac{1}{2}$ pints/8 cups cold water. Bring to the boil, skim off any scum and add 1 carrot (peeled and cut into chunks), 1 celery stalk (chopped), 1 leek (peeled and sliced) and 1 bouquet garni.

Leave to simmer gently for 1 hour and then leave to cool. Add 250 g/8 oz/1 cup lean minced (ground) steak to the cold stock, bring back to the boil then remove from the heat and strain immediately. Leave to cool. If desired, refrigerate overnight and next day remove any solidified surface fat.

GAZPACHO

Serves 6

1.25 kg/2½ lb tomatoes

1 red (bell) pepper

1 cucumber

3 salad onions

1 garlic clove

750 ml/1¼ pints/3 cups water

3 tablespoons olive oil

2 tablespoons wine vinegar

2 slices bread, crusts removed

salt and freshly ground black pepper

To serve: **12 crushed ice cubes**

Peel the tomatoes and pepper by plunging into boiling water for 2 minutes to loosen the skins.

Peel the cucumber, onions and garlic.

Remove the seeds from the tomatoes, pepper and cucumber, cutting one third of each vegetable into small dice and processing the rest in an electric blender with the onions, garlic, measured water, olive oil, wine vinegar and bread. Season with salt and pepper.

Pour into a soup tureen, add the diced vegetables and chill in the refrigerator for at least 4 hours.

Just before serving, mix the crushed ice cubes into the soup.

menu idea | grilled king prawns (shrimp) | raspberry delight

serve with | white rioja or a dry rosé

CRAB SOUP
(SOUPE D'ÉTRILLES)

Serves 6

1 onion

2 carrots

1 leek

1 bouquet garni (thyme, bay, celery)

330 ml/11 fl oz/1½ cups dry white wine

1.5 litres/2½ pints/6 cups water

1.5 kg/3 lb small soft-shell or velvet crabs

5 tablespoons rice flour

salt and freshly ground black pepper

To serve: 6 slices baguette or crusty bread

Peel and dice the vegetables and place in a covered cooking pot or stock pot with the bouquet garni, white wine and measured water. Bring to the boil and leave to simmer gently for 15 minutes.

Add the crabs to the pot and cook for a further 10 minutes. Remove the bouquet garni and strain through a small-mesh sieve, keeping the cooking liquid. Process the contents of the sieve in an electric blender, diluting with a little of the stock if necessary, and then strain again through the small-mesh sieve into the cooking pot, pressing hard to extract all the juices.

Add the rest of the stock to the cooking and thicken with the rice flour mixed with a little warm soup. Season with salt and pepper and leave to simmer for 3-4 minutes. While the soup is simmering, toast the bread ready to serve.

menu idea | fish and prawn (shrimp) kebabs | prune quiche

serve with | muscadet or chenin blanc

PUMPKIN SOUP
(SOUPE À LA CITROUILLE)

Serves 6

2 onions

20 g/³⁄₄ oz butter

1 pumpkin, weighing about 1.5 kg/3 lb

1 litre/1³⁄₄ pints/4 cups water

1 bay leaf

freshly grated nutmeg

125 ml/4 fl oz/¹⁄₂ cup crème fraîche, or single (light) cream or yogurt

salt and freshly ground black pepper

Peel and thinly slice the onions. Melt the butter in a pan and lightly fry the onions until transparent.

While the onions are cooking, remove the flesh from the pumpkin and cut into chunks, discarding the seeds.

Add the pumpkin to the pan, along with the measured water and bay leaf. Season with salt and pepper, and leave to simmer for 30 minutes.

Remove the bay leaf and add a pinch of freshly grated nutmeg. Process in an electric blender and then reheat the soup in the pan. Pour into a soup tureen and add the crème fraîche, cream or yogurt.

menu idea | rabbit with garlic and rosemary | caramel pear cake

serve with | sancerre rosé, cabernet sauvignon, or any light dry red

SPLIT-PEA SOUP
(SOUPE DE POIS CASSÉS)

Serves 6

300 g/10½ oz/1½ cups
split peas

1 large carrot

1 onion

2 litres/3½ pints/8 cups
water

1 bouquet garni

salt and freshly ground
black pepper

To serve: single (light)
cream or croutons

Rinse the split peas under running water. Peel and thinly slice the carrot and onion. Put the vegetables and peas in a large pan and cover with the measured water. Add the bouquet garni but do not add seasoning yet.

Bring to the boil, lower the heat and leave to simmer gently for about 1¼ hours. Season with salt and pepper only after the peas are cooked. Remove the bouquet garni and process the soup in an electric blender to obtain a smooth, creamy consistency, diluting with a little water if necessary.

Serve with a swirl of single (light) cream, or croutons lightly browned in olive oil.

menu idea | rolled beef | spiced fruit crumble

serve with | nuits-saint-georges, côtes du rhône, any full-bodied red

WHITE BEAN SOUP
(SOUPE À COCOS DE PAIMPOL)

Serves 6

750 g/1½ lb large white haricot beans (Great Northern or navy beans)

2 onions

1 thyme sprig

1 bay leaf

5 sprigs flat-leaf parsley, 4 finely chopped

3 litres/5¼ pints/12 cups cold water

10 sprigs chervil, finely chopped

2 tablespoons olive oil

salt and freshly ground black pepper

Rinse the beans under running water and soak for 48 hours, changing the water at regular intervals (this makes the beans more digestible).

Peel and chop the onions. Tie the thyme, bay leaf and 1 sprig parsley together with kitchen string to make a bouquet garni.

Drain the beans and put into a large pan with the onions and bouquet garni. Add the measured water, bring to the boil, lower the heat and cook for 2 hours. Season with salt and continue cooking for a further 30 minutes.

Test the beans to make sure they are well cooked, remove the herbs and process the soup in an electric blender – you can also strain it through a small-meshed sieve if you want a really smooth consistency. Reheat the soup, adding a little water if necessary, and pour into a soup tureen. Sprinkle with finely chopped chervil and parsley and drizzle with olive oil.

menu idea | steak with green peppercorns | poached pears with blackcurrants

serve with | a good bordeaux, or burgundy

SORREL SOUP
(SOUPE À L'OSEILLE)

Serves 6

300 g/10½ oz sorrel

600 g/1¼ lb potatoes

25 g/1 oz butter, chilled

1.5 litres/2½ pints/6 cups water

salt

To serve: crème fraîche or cream

Rinse the sorrel and discard the stalks.

Peel and roughly chop the potatoes. Put the butter into a large pan with the sorrel and potatoes. Cover and leave to sweat over a low heat for 10-15 minutes.

Remove the lid from the pan – the contents should be well softened – add the measured water and season with salt to taste. Increase the heat and continue cooking for a further 15-20 minutes or until the potatoes are cooked.

Process in an electric blender to obtain a smooth, creamy texture. Check the seasoning and consistency. Just before serving, add 2 large tablespoons crème fraîche or cream, or serve separately if preferred.

menu idea | lemon sole fillets with creamed broccoli | rhubarb tart

serve with | riesling or muscadet

WATERCRESS SOUP
(SOUPE AU CRESSON)

Serves 6

1 large bunch watercress

600 g/1 lb 5 oz potatoes

25 g/1 oz butter, chilled

1.5 litres/2½ pints/6 cups water

salt

To serve: crème fraîche or single (light) cream

Rinse the watercress and discard the stalks.

Peel and roughly chop the potatoes. Put the butter into a pan with the cress and potatoes. Cover and leave to sweat over a low heat for 10-15 minutes.

Remove the lid from the pan – the contents should be well softened – add the measured water and season with salt to taste. Increase the heat and continue cooking for a further 15-20 minutes or until the potatoes are cooked.

Process in an electric blender to obtain a smooth, creamy texture. Check the seasoning and consistency. Just before serving, add 2 large tablespoons crème fraîche or cream, or serve separately.

menu idea | French onion tart | crémets

serve with | white hermitage, or any alsace

CABBAGE AND BACON SOUP
(SOUPE AU CHOU ET AU LARD)

Serves 6

½ green cabbage

2 carrots

2 leeks

400 g/14 oz potatoes

1.5 litres/2½ pints/6 cups water

1 thyme sprig

1 bay leaf

6 rashers smoked bacon, thinly sliced

salt and freshly ground black pepper

To serve: chilled butter (optional)

Discard the coarse outer leaves and stalk of the cabbage. Peel and thinly slice the carrots and leeks, peel the potatoes and cut into medium-sized dice. Shred the cabbage, blanch in boiling water for 2 minutes and drain.

Bring the measured water to the boil in a large pan and add the carrots, leeks, potatoes, thyme, bay leaf and sliced bacon rashers. Leave to simmer for 15 minutes or until the vegetables are tender. Add the shredded cabbage and cook for a further 5-7 minutes.

Season to taste with salt and pepper and serve immediately. You can add a knob of chilled butter to each bowl to serve.

menu idea | goat's cheese tart | crème brûlée

serve with | beaujolais, or cabernet sauvignon

PROVENÇAL TOMATO SOUP
(SOUPE DE TOMATES À LA PROVENÇALE)

Serves 6

2 onions

8 large, ripe tomatoes

2 tablespoons olive oil

1 garlic clove, peeled

1 thyme sprig

1 bay leaf

1 small rosemary sprig

1.5 litres/2½ pints/6 cups water

salt

To serve: grated cheese or 6 slices of crusty bread

Peel and thinly slice the onions. Peel the tomatoes by plunging into boiling water for 2 minutes to loosen the skins, remove the seeds and chop roughly. Put the onions and oil in a large pan and fry lightly over a low heat until the onions are transparent. Add the tomatoes, garlic and herbs.

Leave to simmer gently for 15 minutes and then add the measured water. Increase the heat and continue cooking for a further 10 minutes.

Remove the herbs and garlic and mash the tomatoes with a fork or potato masher. Season only with salt.

Serve hot with grated cheese or, if you prefer, a slice of toasted, crusty bread rubbed with garlic and drizzled with olive oil.

menu idea | squid tourte | chilled pears with redcurrant syrup

serve with | rosé, pinot grigio

VICHYSSOISE

Serves 6

1 kg/2 lb leeks

500 g/1 lb white potatoes

20 g/1 oz unsalted butter

1 litre/1³/₄ pints/4 cups water

200 ml/7 fl oz/³/₄ cup single (light) cream

salt

To serve: **chives finely snipped with scissors**

Only the white part of the leeks is used for classic vichyssoise, keep the green parts for your stockpot. Slice the white parts from top to not quite the bottom. Hold firmly at the bottom and fan out under cold running water to rinse out any soil. Shake dry and slice thinly. Peel and dice the potatoes.

Put the butter, leeks and potatoes in a pan, cover and cook for 7-8 minutes over a very low heat, shaking or stirring occasionally so that all the vegetables come into contact with the heat. Add the measured water and cook for a further 20 minutes. Season only with salt.

Leave the soup to cool, add the cream and then process in an electric blender until it has a perfectly smooth, fluid consistency. Chill in the refrigerator for at least 4 hours.

Just before serving, check the seasoning and consistency of the soup, adding a little iced water if necessary. Sprinkle with snipped chives to serve.

menu idea | grilled mullet with three (bell) pepper purée | almond blancmange

serve with | sauvignon blanc

CREAM OF CAULIFLOWER SOUP
(CRÈME DE CHOU-FLEUR)

Serves 6

1 large cauliflower

1 white onion

1.5 litres/2½ pints/6 cups water

4 tablespoons ground rice or pudding rice

150 ml/5 fl oz/⅔ cup single (light) cream

freshly ground nutmeg

salt and pepper

Discard the leaves and stalk of the cauliflower, remove the florets and rinse under running water. Peel and chop the onion.

Bring the measured water to the boil in a large pan and add the cauliflower, onion and ground (or pudding) rice. Leave to simmer for 30 minutes.

Process the soup in an electric blender until smooth and creamy. If necessary, thin with water to the desired consistency, add the cream, stir in a pinch of nutmeg, and season with salt and pepper. Return to the pan to reheat and serve immediately.

menu idea | poached smoked haddock | sugar tart

serve with | white burgundy or a mâcon

CREAM OF COURGETTE (ZUCCHINI) SOUP WITH PARSLEY (CRÈME DE COURGETTES AU PERSIL)

Serves 6

1 kg/2 lb courgettes (zucchini)

1 tablespoon olive oil

2 tablespoons ground rice

1.5 litres/2½ pints/6 cups water

125 g/4 oz fresh goat's cheese

a few sprigs flat-leaf parsley

salt and freshly ground black pepper

Peel, or just rinse if you prefer to keep the skin on, and roughly chop the courgettes (zucchini), place in a large pan with the olive oil, cover, and leave to sweat over a very low heat for 10 minutes. Add the ground rice, season with salt and pepper and cover with the measured water. Leave to simmer for 25 minutes.

Process the contents of the pan with the goat's cheese and parsley leaves in an electric blender. Reheat the soup, but don't let it boil, check the seasoning and serve immediately.

menu idea | scrambled eggs with truffles | rhubarb and orange compote

serve with | pinot blanc, white rioja

GREEN PEA SOUP
(POTAGE SAINT-GERMAIN)

Serves 6

3 small salad onions

1.5-2 kg/3 lb-4 lb fresh unshelled peas, yielding about 1 kg/2 lb peas when shelled

60 g/2½ oz butter

1.5 litres/2½ pints/6 cups water

1 thyme sprig

1 bay leaf

125 g/4 oz smoked bacon, thinly sliced

salt

Peel the onions, place in a pan with the shelled peas and half the butter, cover and leave to sweat over a very low heat for 10 minutes, shaking the pan now and again. Add the measured water, thyme and bay leaf, bring to the boil, lower the heat and leave to simmer for 15-20 minutes. Remove the herbs and season with salt.

Cut the bacon into matchstick-sized pieces and brown lightly by dry-frying in a non-stick frying pan.

Process the contents of the pan in an electric blender, reserving a few peas for the garnish. Reheat the soup, adding the bacon, whole peas and knobs of the remaining butter. Check the seasoning and serve immediately.

menu idea | St-Jean-de-Luz tuna with onions| lemon tartlets

serve with | sauvignon blanc or oaked chardonnay

CHILLED TOMATO SOUP
(POTAGE GLACÉ À LA TOMATE)

Serves 6

1.5 kg/3 lb ripe tomatoes

2 salad onions

1 celery stalk

1 unwaxed lemon, sliced

600 ml/1 pint/2½ cups cold water

2 tablespoons olive oil

1 small carton thick, creamy yogurt

3 sprigs fresh mint, finely chopped

2 sprigs dill, finely chopped

salt and freshly ground black pepper

Peel the tomatoes by plunging into boiling water for 1–2 minutes to loosen the skins, remove the seeds and chop roughly. Peel and roughly chop the onions and chop the celery. Process the vegetables and lemon slices in an electric blender, gradually adding sufficient of the measured water to obtain a fine, smooth consistency.

Pass through a sieve, season with salt and pepper, and add the olive oil, yogurt and chopped herbs. Chill in the refrigerator for at least 4 hours.

menu idea | squid tourte | strawberry charlotte

serve with | rosé, pinot grigio, white côtes du rhône

MINESTRONE

Serves 6

300 g/10 oz/1½ cups white haricot beans (Great Northern or navy beans)

1 bay leaf

2 onions

6 tablespoons olive oil

1 carrot

2 small courgettes (zucchini)

2 stalks celery, washed

250 g/8 oz French beans (green beans)

1.5 litres/2½ pints/6 cups water

1 thyme sprig

1 rosemary sprig

4 tomatoes

6 garlic cloves, peeled

1 large bunch basil

salt and pepper

To serve: 125 g/4 oz/1 cup freshly grated Parmesan

Soak the haricot beans in cold water overnight.

Drain and place the beans and bay leaf in a pan of boiling water and leave to cook for 1 hour. While the beans are cooking, peel and chop the onions and soften in a high-sided cooking pot or flameproof casserole, in 2 tablespoons of the olive oil.

Peel and dice the carrot and courgettes (zucchini), rinse and chop the celery and French beans, and add to the onions. Cover with the measured water, season only with salt and add the thyme and rosemary. Cover and leave to simmer gently for 1½ hours.

Peel the tomatoes by plunging into boiling water for 2 minutes to loosen the skins, remove the seeds and chop roughly.

When the haricot beans are cooked, remove the bay leaf and process half the beans, with the cooking liquid, in an electric blender. Add to the soup, along with the rest of the beans and the tomatoes. Leave to simmer for a further 10 minutes, check the seasoning and add pepper to taste.

Make a pesto sauce by crushing the garlic cloves and basil leaves by pestle and mortar, and stirring in the rest of the olive oil. Add to the piping hot soup and serve with freshly grated Parmesan cheese.

menu idea | risotto milanaise | plum crumble tart

serve with | valpolicella, cabernet sauvignon

FRENCH ONION SOUP
(GRATINÉE LYONNAISE)

Serves 6

500 g/1 lb onions

60 g/2½ oz butter

30 g/1 oz plain (all-purpose) flour

2 litres/3½ pints/8 cups water or vegetable stock

1 thyme sprig

1 bay leaf

6 slices of day-old baguette or crusty bread

200 g/7 oz/1¾ cups freshly grated Gruyère cheese

salt and freshly ground black pepper

Peel and thinly slice the onions and then fry lightly in a high-sided cooking pot or flameproof casserole with 50 g/2 oz of the butter until golden brown. Sprinkle with the flour and cook for 1 minute.

Add the measured water or stock, season with salt and pepper and add the thyme and bay leaf. Leave to simmer gently for 30 minutes and then remove the herbs.

Toast the bread and pour the soup into a tureen or individual heatproof bowls. Add the toasted bread, sprinkle with grated cheese and place under a preheated grill for 10 minutes or until crusty and golden.

menu idea | chicken with tarragon | dark chocolate mousse

serve with | white mâcon, sauvignon blanc

BÉARNAISE STEW
(GARBURE BÉARNAISE)

Serves 6

1 kg/2 lb potatoes

3 carrots

3 small leeks

1 onion

1 garlic clove

2 litres/3½ pints/8 cups cold water

1 bouquet garni

1 end slice of lightly smoked, cured ham

½ teaspoon mildly hot chilli pepper

1 green cabbage

450-500 g/1 lb drained weight canned flageolet beans

400 g/14 oz confit of duck breast (preserved duck breast) with some of the fat removed (available in jars)

salt

To serve: 6 thick slices baguette or crusty bread

Peel and chop the potatoes, carrots, leeks, onion and garlic, and place in a large flameproof cooking pot or casserole. Cover with the measured water and add the bouquet garni, ham and chilli pepper. Season with a little salt. Bring to the boil, lower the heat, cover, and leave to simmer for about 30 minutes.

Discard the stalk and outer leaves of the cabbage and shred finely. Add to vegetables after 30 minutes and leave to simmer for a further 15-20 minutes.

Add the drained flageolet beans and the confit of duck breast and cook for another 30 minutes, adding more water if necessary. Taste to check the seasoning.

To serve, arrange the bread in the bottom of a soup tureen and soak with a little of the stock. Place the duck breast and ham on a serving dish and pour the soup into the tureen.

Note The soup is usually served before the meat but there's nothing to stop you serving them at the same time.

menu idea | tôt-fait with plum brandy

serve with | dry rosé, pink zinfandel

ONION SOUP WITH GARLIC
(TOURIN À L'AIL)

Serves 6

500 g/1 lb onions

8 garlic cloves

2 tablespoons olive oil

2 tablespoons plain (all-purpose) flour

1.5 litres/2½ pints/6 cups water

1 bouquet garni (bay leaf, thyme, parsley)

4 eggs, separated

2 tablespoons wine vinegar

salt and freshly ground black pepper

To serve: croutons

Peel and thinly slice the onions and garlic. Lightly fry the onions with the olive oil in a cast-iron cooking pot or flame-proof casserole. When the onions are a light golden colour, add the garlic, sprinkle with flour and cook over a low heat for 1 minute.

Add the measured water and bouquet garni. Season with salt and pepper and leave to cook over a low heat for 30 minutes.

Remove the bouquet garni, process in an electric blender, and then reheat to produce a thick broth. Remove from the heat and briskly whisk in the egg whites. Beat the yolks in a separate bowl with the wine vinegar. Pour the soup into a tureen and add the beaten egg mixture. Serve with croutons.

menu idea | tagliatelle with mussels | soft cheese tart

serve with | pinot grigio, or any crisp dry white

CREAM OF BROAD (FAVA) BEAN SOUP
(VELOUTÉ DE FÈVES FRAÎCHES)

Serves 6

1.5 kg/3 lb fresh (or frozen) broad beans (fava or lima beans), shelled and skinned

1.5 litres/2½ pints/6 cups chicken stock

pinch of sugar

1 teaspoon rice flour

40 g/1½ oz butter

salt and freshly ground black pepper

To serve: 1 marjoram sprig, chopped

Cook the fresh beans in boiling salted water for 8 minutes. (If using frozen beans, follow the cooking instructions on the packaging.)

Drain and process in an electric blender, gradually adding the chicken stock. When you have a smooth, creamy consistency add the sugar and rice flour, and season with salt and pepper.

Reheat the soup over a low heat and allow to thicken for a few minutes.

Place knobs of butter in the bottom of a soup tureen and pour in the soup. Sprinkle with chopped marjoram.

menu idea | chicken with tarragon | clafoutis with black cherries

serve with | any dry white burgundy

CREAM OF CARROT SOUP
(VELOUTÉ DE CAROTTES)

Serves 6

1 kg/2 lb carrots

2 onions

50 g/2 oz butter

1.5 litres/2½ pints/6 cups
home-made vegetable or
chicken stock, or 3 stock
cubes dissolved in 1.5 litres/
2½ pints/6 cups boiling
water

4 tablespoons rice

1 teaspoon sugar

salt and pepper

Peel and finely chop the carrots and onions. Place in a large pan with half the butter, cover and leave to sweat over a low heat until the vegetables begin to soften. Add the stock, rice, sugar and season with a little salt.

Leave to simmer for 20 minutes and then process in an electric blender or mash with a potato masher, adding a little water if the purée is too thick. Reheat the soup with the remaining butter and serve immediately.

menu idea | baked eggs with tarragon | rhubarb and orange compote

serve with | white or pink zinfandel, chardonnay

CREAM OF MUSSEL SOUP WITH SAFFRON (VELOUTÉ DE MOULES AU SAFRAN)

Serves 6

1.5 kg/3 lb fresh mussels

2 shallots

40 g/1½ oz butter

2 carrots

1 leek

1 celery stalk, washed

1.5 litres/2½ pints/6 cups water

1 bouquet garni

a few saffron threads

2 egg yolks

200 ml/7 fl oz/¾ cup crème fraîche, or double (heavy) cream, or thick yogurt

salt and pepper

Scrape and clean the mussels. Peel and finely chop the shallots, and place in a high-sided cooking pot or flameproof casserole with half the butter. Leave to soften over a very low heat for 5 minutes. Add the mussels, cover and cook for 7-8 minutes, stirring occasionally, until all the mussels are open. Remove from the heat and leave to cool.

While the mussels are cooking, prepare and finely shred the carrots and leek, and finely chop the celery. Leave to sweat in a large covered pan with the rest of the butter over low heat, until they begin to soften. Add the measured water and bouquet garni, bring to the boil, lower the heat, and leave to simmer for 15 minutes.

Shell the mussels, discarding any that have not opened, strain the cooking liquid through a sieve lined with muslin to catch any sand and add to the pan of vegetable stock.

Mix the saffron with a little warm stock, then beat the egg yolks with the crème fraîche or cream and saffron. Add the egg mixture to the pan and allow the soup to thicken without letting it boil. Add the mussels to the soup, heat through, and serve immediately.

menu idea | skate with capers | fig tart

serve with | white bordeaux or oaked chardonnay

SALADS

ALWAYS TRY AND BUY SALAD GREENS IN SEASON.
DON'T REMOVE THEIR OUTER LEAVES OR PICK THEM OVER UNTIL YOU NEED THEM, OR UNLESS THEY WILL DEFINITELY BE USED WITHIN THE NEXT 24 HOURS. WHEN THE OUTER LEAVES HAVE BEEN REMOVED, SALAD GREENS CAN BE KEPT IN AN AIRTIGHT PLASTIC CONTAINER OR BAG, OR PLACED DIRECTLY IN THE SALAD COMPARTMENT OF THE REFRIGERATOR. WILTED GREENS CAN BE REVIVED IN A BOWL OF ICED SUGAR WATER OR VINEGAR WATER – VINEGAR HAS THE ADVANTAGE OF KILLING ANY PARASITES. AFTER DRYING WITH A SALAD SPINNER, KEEP IN THE REFRIGERATOR FOR A FEW HOURS UNTIL READY TO SERVE.

STORAGE

• Some salad greens need to be washed more thoroughly than others. For example, corn salad (lambs' tongues or mache) should be rinsed several times to get rid of any soil or sand, whereas rocket (arugula) needs only a quick rinse.

• Herbs should be rinsed and blotted gently with kitchen paper (paper towels). They can then be stored in a plastic container, separated by kitchen paper that is replaced every 2 days.

Basil can't be refrigerated, so buy fresh growing in a pot and it should keep for several months. Don't worry about mixing different types of salad greens.

Handy hints

• Don't over-dry salad greens. They will be lighter and need less seasoning.

• Similarly, potato salad absorbs less oil if you pour a glass of white wine over the sliced potato while it is still warm.

SEASONING

• You can vary seasonings and dressings by making sure you always have an aged wine vinegar, sherry vinegar, lemon juice, olive oil (one mild, one full flavoured), walnut or hazelnut oil, and a milder oil (e.g. groundnut, grapeseed) for mayonnaise.

• If you use sea salt, always add just before serving.

• Remember that thick, creamy yogurts make excellent sauces and are also ideal for lightening or "slackening" a mayonnaise.

• Always add dressings just before serving to prevent the leaves "cooking" on contact with the vinaigrette.

BASIC VINAIGRETTE

(VINAIGRETTE DE BASE)

1 part (e.g. 1 tablespoon) vinegar

4 parts (e.g. 4 tablespoons) oil

salt and pepper

Dissolve the salt in the vinegar, add the pepper and then gradually stir in the oil of your choice.

This vinaigrette can be made with lemon juice instead of vinegar.

MUSTARD VINAIGRETTE

(VINAIGRETTE À LA MOUTARDE)

1 part (e.g. 1 tablespoon) vinegar

1 part (e.g. ½ tablespoon) mustard, any kind will do

4 parts (e.g. 4 tablespoons) oil

salt and pepper

Dissolve the salt in the vinegar, mix in the mustard and pepper, and then gradually stir in the oil.

This vinaigrette can be made with lemon juice instead of vinegar.

CREAM OR YOGURT DRESSING

(SAUCE À LA CRÈME OU AU YAOURT)

200 ml/7 fl oz/¾ cup soured cream, or yogurt (or a mixture of the two)

a few drops of lemon juice

spices

a mixture of fresh herbs, depending on the recipe

salt and pepper

Chop the herbs and mix with the rest of the ingredients.

PASTA SALAD WITH VEGETABLE GARNISH
(SALADE DE COQUILLETTES À LA PARISIENNE)

Serves 6

300 g/10 oz/2–2½ cups small pasta shells

1 tablespoon white wine vinegar

1 teaspoon mustard

4 tablespoons olive oil

2 slices cooked ham, about 1 cm/½ inch thick

200 g/7 oz Gruyère cheese

20 black olives, pitted

a few sprigs flat-leaf parsley, chopped

salt and freshly ground black pepper

Cook the pasta in plenty of boiling salted water, according to the cooking instructions on the packet.

While the pasta is cooking, prepare a vinaigrette by mixing (in the following order) the vinegar, salt, pepper, mustard and oil.

Drain the pasta and rinse quickly under the cold tap so that it remains firm and doesn't stick together. Turn into a salad bowl, season immediately with the vinaigrette and leave to cool.

Cut the ham and cheese into small dice and add to the pasta with the olives. Mix well, sprinkle with chopped parsley and serve at room temperature.

menu idea | monkfish (anglerfish) à la Armoricaine | egg custard
serve with | white pinot, pinot grigio

SALADE NIÇOISE

Serves 6

12 canned anchovy fillets in brine

3 eggs

6 small salad onions

2 green (bell) peppers

1 celery heart

100 g/3½ oz Provençal mesclun (mixed herbs and small salad leaves)

6 medium tomatoes

150 g/5 oz small broad beans, shelled (fava or lima beans)

1 garlic clove

2 tablespoons wine vinegar

12 basil leaves, chopped

6 tablespoons olive oil

100 g/3½ oz small black olives

salt and pepper

Rinse the anchovy fillets under cold running water to wash off the salt.

Boil the eggs for 8 minutes and then cool under running water to prevent them discolouring. Remove the shells and put the eggs in the refrigerator.

Peel the onions, rinse the peppers and celery, and remove the seeds from the peppers. Slice the vegetables thinly. Wash the mesclun and dry in a salad spinner. Slice and remove the seeds from the tomatoes and skin the broad beans. Chill all the ingredients in the refrigerator.

When ready to serve, rub the garlic clove around the inside of a large serving dish and arrange the mesclun and vegetables on the dish. Cut the eggs into quarters and decorate the salad with egg quarters and anchovies.

Prepare a vinaigrette by mixing the vinegar, chopped basil, salt, pepper and olive oil. Pour over the salad and top with black olives.

menu idea | rabbit with mustard | redcurrant meringue tart
serve with | rosé, or white zinfandel

DANDELION LEAF AND BACON SALAD
(SALADE DE PISSENLIT AU LARD)

Serves 6

400 g/14 oz young
dandelion leaves

200 g/7 oz smoked bacon,
thickly sliced

1 tablespoon oil,
for cooking

3 tablespoons aged wine
vinegar

salt and freshly ground
black pepper

Wash the dandelion leaves carefully, discarding any that are tough or damaged. Dry in a salad spinner and turn into a salad bowl.

Blanch the bacon rashers in boiling water and cut into diced pieces. Heat the oil in a frying pan, fry the bacon pieces until they are crisp and golden, and add to the salad bowl. Deglaze the pan with the wine vinegar, bring to the boil and pour over the salad. Season with salt and pepper and toss before serving.

Note Do not gather your dandelion leaves from roadsides or near fields that may have been crop-sprayed.

menu idea | Lemon sole fillets with creamed broccoli | tôt-fait with plum brandy
serve with | riesling or muscadet

SPINACH SALAD WITH GOAT'S CHEESE (SALADE D'ÉPINARDS CRUS AU CHÈVRE)

Serves 6

300 g/10½ oz tender baby spinach

3 tablespoons sherry vinegar

6 tablespoons walnut oil

3 small, round goat's cheeses

75 g/2¾ oz chopped walnuts

salt and freshly ground black pepper

Pick over and rinse the spinach under cold running water. Dry in a salad spinner and then blot dry with a cloth or kitchen paper.

Make a vinaigrette dressing in a salad bowl with the salt, pepper, vinegar and walnut oil.

Shred the spinach and place in the salad bowl. Thinly slice the cheeses and arrange over the spinach.

Sprinkle with walnuts and serve immediately.

menu idea | seared salmon steaks | peaches in red wine
serve with | a very light, red or white burgundy

RICE AND COCKLE SALAD
(SALADE DE RIZ AUX COQUES)

Serves 6

2 litres/3½ pints fresh cockles, or small clams

250 g/8 oz/1¼ cups brown rice

4 tablespoons lemon juice

1 small carton thick, creamy yogurt

3 tablespoons olive oil

150 g/5 oz mushrooms

1 bunch mixed herbs (tarragon, chervil, chives)

salt and freshly ground black pepper

Leave the cockles in salted water for 12 hours before cooking, to clear any residual sand from their shells.

Place the rice in a pan, cover with 3 times its own volume of water, and cook until the water has been completely absorbed. Leave to cool.

Wash and scrub the cockles and cook in a covered pan for about 5 minutes, giving a shake now and again, until all the cockles have opened (discard any that have not). Strain 3 tablespoons of the cooking juices through a piece of muslin to catch any sand.

Prepare a dressing by mixing the strained cooking juices with the lemon juice, yogurt, olive oil, salt and pepper.

Wipe the mushrooms and peel if necessary. Thinly slice the mushrooms and mix carefully in a salad bowl with the cold rice and cockles. Add the dressing and sprinkle with chopped herbs. Mix well and serve chilled.

menu idea | eggs à l'andalouse | cheesecake
serve with | chablis, sancerre, or other fruity wine

MUSSEL SALAD WITH CURRY SAUCE
(SALADE DE MOULES AU CURRY)

Serves 6

2 litres/3½ pints fresh mussels

6 salad onions

1 shallot

100 ml/3½ fl oz white wine

1 large crisphead lettuce (e.g. Webb's Wonder, Iceberg, Butterhead)

3 medium tomatoes

1 teaspoon curry powder

2 tablespoons crème fraîche, or yogurt

½ lemon

½ bunch chives, chopped

salt and pepper

Scrape and clean the mussels. Peel and finely chop the onions and shallot and bring to the boil in a pan with the white wine. Add the mussels, cover and leave to cook until the shells have opened. Drain through a sieve lined with a piece of muslin to catch any sand and retain 200 ml/7 fl oz/¾ cup of the filtered cooking liquid.

Shell the mussels, discarding any that have not opened. Discard the outer leaves of the lettuce. Peel the tomatoes by plunging into boiling water for 2 minutes to loosen the skins, remove the seeds and cut into small diced pieces.

Put the cooking liquid, curry powder and crème fraîche or yogurt in a small pan and allow to reduce for a few minutes. Add the mussels and reheat for 30 seconds. Remove from the heat and leave to cool.

Arrange a few lettuce leaves on each individual plate and top with mussels in curry sauce and a few pieces of diced tomato. Season with salt and pepper, add a squeeze of lemon juice and sprinkle with chopped chives. Serve warm or chilled.

menu idea | oven-baked chicken with garlic | quick ice-cream
serve with | cabernet sauvignon

RICE SALAD À LA ROMAINE
(SALADE DE RIZ À LA ROMAINE)

Serves 6

200 g/7 oz/1 cup
long-grain rice

150 g/5 oz/1 cup fresh
(shelled) or frozen peas

150 g/5 oz Parma ham

1 red (bell) pepper

100 g/3½ oz Parmesan
cheese, in a piece

1 tablespoons wine vinegar

4 tablespoons olive oil

salt and freshly ground
black pepper

Cook the rice in a large pan of boiling salted water for
10 minutes. Add the peas and cook for a further 5 minutes.
Drain and leave to cool.

While the rice is cooking, cut the Parma ham into thin strips.
Rinse the red pepper, remove the seeds and cut into diced
pieces. Pare fine shavings of Parmesan cheese with a
vegetable peeler.

Make a vinaigrette in a salad bowl with the vinegar, oil, salt
and pepper. Add the warm rice and peas, and mix well. Then
add the diced pepper, strips of Parma ham and Parmesan
shavings. Serve at room temperature.

menu idea | aubergine mould (eggplant mold) | chocolate refrigerator cake
serve with | dry rosé, or white rioja

WARM CHESTNUT SALAD
(SALADE TIÈDE AUX CHÂTAIGNES)

Serves 6

200 g/7 oz corn salad
(lambs' tongues or mache)

6 large shallots

3 tablespoons olive oil

1 teaspoon granulated
sugar

100 ml/3½ fl oz/½ cup
white wine vinegar

600 g/1 lb 5 oz chestnuts,
vacuum packed

salt and freshly ground
black pepper

Wash and pick over the corn salad and dry in a salad spinner. Peel and quarter the shallots lengthways and soften in the olive oil over a very low heat – they should remain tender and not be allowed to brown. When they are almost transparent, add the sugar and mix well.

Add the vinegar, boil for 1-2 minutes and then add the chestnuts. Season with salt and pepper, cover and leave to cook for 5 minutes.

Arrange the corn salad in a salad bowl. Remove the chestnuts from the heat and leave to cool for a few minutes before adding to the salad bowl. Mix carefully, check the seasoning and serve immediately.

menu idea | salmon trout fillets with mushrooms | egg custard
serve with | strong white burgundy or oaked chardonnay

MUSHROOM SALAD WITH YOGURT
(SALADE DE CHAMPIGNONS AU YAOURT)

Serves 6

500 g/1 lb mushrooms

1 lemon

2 garlic cloves, finely chopped

1 tablespoon crushed coriander seeds

2 tablespoons olive oil

300 g/¹/₂ pint//1¹/₄ cups thick, creamy yogurt

salt and pepper

Wipe, peel and thinly slice the mushrooms. A few squeezes of lemon juice will prevent them discolouring.

Mix the chopped garlic, crushed coriander seeds, olive oil and yogurt together in a salad bowl and season with salt and pepper, add the mushrooms and mix carefully so as not to break them up. Serve immediately.

Note If you don't like raw garlic, use chopped chives instead. Don't prepare this salad too far in advance, as the salt tends to soften the mushrooms.

menu idea | lamb casserole à la normande | tiramisu
serve with | merlot, valpolicella, cabernet

SCANDINAVIAN SALAD
(SALADE NORDIQUE)

Serves 6

1 kg/2 lb waxy, salad potatoes

100 ml/3½ fl oz/½ cup crème fraîche, or sour cream

1 small pot thick, creamy yogurt

a few sprigs dill, finely chopped

100 g/3½ oz salmon roe

4 medium pickled dill cucumbers, sliced

salt and freshly ground black pepper

Scrub the potatoes and boil in their skins in a covered pot for 20-30 minutes, or until cooked through, but not overcooked – test by inserting the blade of a knife. Drain, peel and slice thinly while still warm.

Mix the crème fraîche with the yogurt and dill. Season with salt and pepper and carefully mix in the sliced potatoes, salmon roe and sliced pickled cucumbers. Serve warm.

menu idea | poached smoked haddock | soft cheese tart
serve with | riesling or chardonnay

AUTUMN SALAD
(SALADE D'AUTOMNE)

Serves 6

1 small celeriac (celery root)

2 tablespoons lemon juice

2 chicken breasts, about 180 g/6 oz each

5 tablespoons walnut oil

1 radicchio (Treviso variety)

1 bunch red or green seedless grapes

2 tablespoons wine vinegar

1 tablespoon coarse-grain mustard (Meaux is good)

salt and pepper

Peel and rinse the celeriac, cut into quarters and slice thinly. Cook in boiling salted water, with the lemon juice, for about 15 minutes, or until cooked through but not mushy. Drain and leave to cool.

Lightly brown the chicken breasts in 1 tablespoon of the oil for 10 minutes and leave to cool. Discard the outer leaves of the radicchio, rinse and dry in a salad spinner. Remove the grapes from their stalks. Prepare the vinaigrette by mixing (in the following order) the vinegar, salt, pepper, mustard and remaining oil.

Cut the chicken breasts into thin slices and then arrange on the serving dish, or individual plates, interleaved with the celeriac. Add the radicchio and grapes, dress with the vinaigrette and serve immediately.

menu idea | John Dory fillets with mushrooms | spiced fruit crumble
serve with | red sancerre, red zinfandel or other light dry red

CRUNCHY VEGETABLE SALAD
(SALADE CROQUANTE)

Serves 6

200 g/7 oz fine green beans

100 g/3½ oz mangetout (snow peas, or sugar snap peas, if preferred)

3 large carrots

100 g/3½ oz mushrooms

4 tablespoons of lemon juice

5 tablespoons olive oil

1 small bunch fresh mixed herbs

2 tablespoons sesame seeds

salt and pepper

Top and tail the green beans and mangetout or snow peas. Peel and slice the carrots. Cook the vegetables in boiling salted water for about 10 minutes – they should remain crunchy – then drain and plunge into a bowl of iced water.

While the vegetables are cooking, wipe, peel and thinly slice the mushrooms.

Prepare a lemon vinaigrette by mixing salt, lemon juice (to taste), pepper and the olive oil. Arrange the raw and cooked vegetables in a salad bowl, drizzle with the vinaigrette and sprinkle with the chopped herbs and sesame seeds.

menu idea | rabbit with garlic and rosemary| apple crumble
serve with | rosé, merlot, or any light dry red

MOUNTAIN SALAD
(SALADE DES MONTAGNES)

Serves 6

300 g/10½ oz/3½ cups large pasta shells

200 ml/7 fl oz/¾ cup single (light) cream

1 teaspoon wine vinegar

2 courgettes (zucchini)

2 tomatoes

250 g/8oz tasty smoked ham, thinly sliced (Grisons mountain ham from France would be ideal)

100 g/3½ oz walnuts, chopped

a few sprigs chervil, or flat-leaf parsley

salt and pepper

Cook the pasta in plenty of boiling salted water, according to the cooking instructions on the packet.

While the pasta is cooking, whisk the cream with the vinegar, salt and pepper. Drain the pasta and rinse quickly under the cold tap so that it remains firm and doesn't stick together. Turn into a salad bowl, add the cream sauce and leave to cool.

Rinse and thinly slice the courgettes (zucchini). Peel the tomatoes by plunging into boiling water for 2 minutes to loosen the skins, remove the seeds and cut into dice. Cut the ham into thin strips.

Add the courgettes (zucchini), tomatoes, walnuts, chervil leaves or parsley and strips of ham to the salad bowl. Mix carefully and serve immediately.

menu idea | honey and walnut tart

serve with | any light dry red

BLACK PUDDING AND APPLE SALAD
(SALADE DE BOUDIN NOIR)

Serves 6

1 large loose-leaf lettuce

4 crisp, slightly sharp apples (e.g. Granny Smith or Braeburn)

2 black puddings, about 15 cm/6 inches long

1 tablespoon oil for frying

40 g/1½ oz butter

a few sprigs chervil or flat-leaf parsley

100 ml/3½ fl oz/½ cup cider vinegar

salt and pepper

Discard the outer leaves of the lettuce, rinse and dry in a salad spinner. Rinse but do not peel the apples and cut each one into twelve sections.

Prick the black puddings with a pin (to prevent them bursting), heat the oil in a frying pan and fry the puddings lightly to cook through. Melt the butter in another pan and lightly brown the apple pieces.

Cut each pudding into 12 slices. Arrange the lettuce and chopped chervil or parsley leaves on a serving dish and add the apple pieces and sliced black puddings.

Deglaze the black pudding pan with the cider vinegar over a high heat, scraping the sides so as not to waste any of the tasty cooking residue. Season with salt and pepper, pour over the salad and serve immediately.

Note If preferred, the black puddings can be first sliced and the slices lightly fried.

menu idea | baked lasagne | floating islands
serve with | merlot, beaujolais, valpolicella

MARINATED FISH SALAD
(SALADE DE POISSON CRU MARINÉ)

Serves 6

400 g/14 oz very fresh white fish fillets

juice of 3 limes

1 green (bell) pepper

4 stalks celery

2 avocados

¼ bunch chives, chopped

¼ bunch coriander (cilantro), chopped

4 tablespoons olive oil

salt and pepper

To serve: **crushed ice**

Remove any remaining bones from the fish and cut into thin strips. Place in a large bowl and add the lime juice. Cover and leave to marinate in the refrigerator for 4-6 hours, or until the fish has turned opaque.

Rinse the green pepper, remove the seeds and cut into small sticks or dice. Rinse the celery and also cut into small sticks or dice. Peel and dice the avocados.

Add the vegetables to the bowl containing the marinated fish and season with the chopped herbs, olive oil, salt and pepper. Serve on a bed of crushed ice.

menu idea | piperade | gâteau battu
serve with | sauvignon blanc, pinot grigio

CARROT AND CUMIN SALAD
(SALADE DE CAROTTES AU CUMIN)

Serves 6

1 kg/2 lb carrots

2 salad onions or 1 garlic clove

juice of 1 orange

2 tablespoons of lemon juice

3 tablespoons olive oil

½ teaspoon cumin

salt and pepper

To serve: ½ bunch fresh coriander (cilantro)

Peel the carrots and onions (or garlic). Slice thinly and put in a pan with the orange juice. Season with salt, cover and cook over a low heat for 15-20 minutes, stirring occasionally to make sure the vegetables don't stick and adding a little water if necessary. Remove the lid a few minutes before the carrots are cooked to reduce any remaining liquid.

Leave to cool in the pan and then turn the cooked vegetables onto a serving dish. Add the lemon juice and olive oil, season with pepper and cumin, and mix well.

Serve well chilled, sprinkled with chopped coriander leaves.

menu idea | rabbit with garlic and rosemary | lemon mousse
serve with | sauvignon blanc, white rioja

PURPLE SALAD
(SALADE VIOLETTE)

Serves 6

1 small radicchio
(Treviso variety)

1 head Chinese leaves

9 ripe figs

9 very thin slices Parma
ham

2 teaspoons mustard
(Brive purple Mustard,
if possible)

1 tablespoon sherry
vinegar

4 tablespoons olive oil

salt and pepper

To serve: 2 tablespoons
shelled pistachios

Discard the outer leaves of the radicchio and Chinese leaves, separate the inner leaves, rinse and dry in a salad spinner. Rinse the figs in cold water, cut off the thick pointed end and cut into quarters. Cut the Parma ham into thin strips.

Arrange the salad leaves, ham and figs on a serving dish. Make a vinaigrette with the mustard, vinegar, olive oil, salt and pepper; and drizzle over the salad. Serve immediately, sprinkled with pistachios.

menu idea | blue trout | mocha biscuit cake
serve with | rosé, riesling, white bordeaux

FRUITY DUCK SALAD
(SALADE DE MAGRET FRUITÉE)

Serves 6

4–5 small radicchio
(Treviso variety)

4 nectarines

200 g/7 oz smoked duck
breast

125 g/4 oz raspberries

1 tablespoon raspberry
vinegar

4 tablespoons rich, fruity
olive oil

a few tarragon leaves

salt and pepper

Discard the outer leaves of the radicchio, separate the inner leaves, rinse and dry with a salad spinner. Wash the nectarines, remove the pits and cut into thin slices.

Cut the duck breast into very thin strips.

Process half the raspberries with the vinegar, salt, pepper and oil in an electric blender, and then strain through a small-mesh sieve to catch the seeds.

Toss the radicchio with the raspberry vinaigrette and tarragon leaves and place on a serving dish. Arrange the nectarines, the rest of the raspberries and the thin strips of duck breast on the salad and serve immediately.

menu idea | blanquette de veau | apple rabotes
serve with | any crisp light red

LANDES-STYLE SMOKED DUCK SALAD
(SALADE À LA LANDAISE)

Serves 6

300 g/10 oz baby spinach

300 g/10 oz purslane
(or a mixture of flat-leaf
parsley and watercress)

2 x 200 g/7 oz smoked
duck breasts

1 tablespoon wine vinegar

4 tablespoons walnut oil

1 bunch chervil

salt and pepper

Pick over and rinse the spinach and purslane, and dry with a salad spinner.

Slice the duck breasts.

Make a vinaigrette by mixing (in the following order) the vinegar, salt, pepper and walnut oil. Pour the vinaigrette into a salad bowl or serving dish and add the salad greens and chopped chervil leaves. Add the sliced duck breasts to the salad and mix thoroughly before serving.

menu idea | escalopes of foie gras with apples | Yule log
serve with | bergerac, merlot

ARTICHOKES À LA GRECQUE
(ARTICHAUTS POIVRADE À LA GRECQUE)

Serves 6

24 small artichokes

6-8 tablespoons lemon juice

6 small salad onions

2 stalks celery

½ teaspoon each peppercorns, fennel seeds, coriander seeds

2 sprigs fresh thyme

1 bay leaf

200 ml/7 fl oz/¾ cup water

200 ml/7 fl oz/¾ cup dry white wine

4 tablespoons olive oil

salt

To serve: fresh or dried oregano

Rinse the artichokes and discard the outer leaves. Cut off the top quarter and stem of each artichoke (removing the stem enables them to stand upright). Blanch in boiling water with half the lemon juice for 5 minutes, and drain. Peel the salad onions, rinse and cut the celery into small dice.

Place the artichokes, onions and celery in a large frying pan with the spices, thyme and bay leaf. Add the measured water along with the rest of the lemon juice, the wine and olive oil, and season with salt.

Cover and cook over a low heat for 35-40 minutes and then leave to cool in the cooking liquid. Remove the thyme and bay leaf and sprinkle with a little chopped oregano.

Serve chilled.

menu idea | quails roasted in muscat | crêpes Suzette
serve with | sauvignon blanc, oaked chardonnay

GORGONZOLA PEARS
(POIRES FARCIES AU GORGONZOLA)

Serves 6

6 ripe pears (Williams, Comice, Bartlett)

1 lemon

125 g/4 oz Gorgonzola

2 tablespoons crème fraîche, or yogurt

pepper

To serve: **walnut bread and 12 very thin slices Parma ham**

Peel and halve the pears, remove the core and scoop out a hollow in the centre about 1 cm/¹/₂ inch across. A squeeze of lemon juice will prevent the pears discolouring. Place in the refrigerator.

Mix the Gorgonzola with the crème fraîche or yogurt, season generously with pepper and fill the pears with the mixture. Chill in the refrigerator for 30 minutes.

Serve with the Parma ham and slices of lightly toasted, buttered walnut bread.

menu idea | blanquette de veau | apple upside-down tart
serve with | sauternes

96

MELON SURPRISE
(MELONS-SURPRISES)

Serves 6

6 small melons

150 g/5 oz strawberries

1 small cucumber

4 tablespoons lemon juice

3 tablespoons olive oil

1/2 bunch fresh coriander (cilantro), chopped

salt and pepper

To serve, crushed ice

Cut off the top $\frac{1}{3}$ of each melon (keep the tops for another dessert), remove the seeds and then use a melon scoop to scoop out melon balls.

Rinse the strawberries and cut into four or more pieces, depending on their size. Peel and dice the cucumber.

Mix the lemon juice, olive oil, salt and pepper in a salad bowl, and then carefully mix in the melon balls, strawberries and diced cucumber. Finally, add the chopped coriander (cilantro). Fill each hollow melon with the salad and serve well chilled on a bed of crushed ice.

menu idea | red mullet à la nicoise | chocolate fondant

serve with | any crisp dry white

EGGS

TRY AND BUY ORGANIC FREE-RANGE EGGS (LAID BY FREE-RANGE HENS FED ON AN ORGANIC DIET). THEY MAY BE MORE EXPENSIVE AND HAVE THE DATE STAMPED ON THEIR SHELLS – NOT PARTICULARLY ATTRACTIVE, BUT AT LEAST YOU KNOW THEY ARE FRESH. EGGS KEEP FOR ABOUT 2-3 WEEKS FROM THE DATE THEY ARE LAID.

REMEMBER TO TAKE THEM OUT OF THE REFRIGERATOR BEFORE YOU START PREPARING ANY OF THE FOLLOWING DISHES, ESPECIALLY IF THEY ARE TO BE BOILED, OTHERWISE THEY MAY CRACK. IT WILL ALSO PREVENT PROBLEMS CAUSED BY SUDDEN TEMPERATURE DIFFERENTIALS WHEN YOU ADD THEM TO CREAMED BUTTER AND SUGAR FOR A CAKE, OR TRY TO BEAT THE WHITES INTO STIFF PEAKS...

BOILED EGGS, SOFT- AND HARD-BOILED

(OEUFS À LA COQUE, MOLLETS ET DURS)

Place the eggs in a pan and cover them over by 1 cm ($\frac{1}{2}$ inch) of cold water. Bring to the boil over high heat, reduce to a simmer and allow 4 minutes (timed) for a soft-boiled egg, 5 minutes for eggs that are well set but with the centre of the yolk still moist and 8 minutes for hard-boiled.

EGGS MIMOSA (OEUFS MIMOSA)

Serves 6

10 eggs + 1 yolk

1 teaspoon mustard

200 ml/7 fl oz/^{3}/$_4$ cup grapeseed oil

3$\frac{1}{2}$ tablespoons olive oil

1 tablespoon aged wine vinegar

a few sprigs fresh chives, chervil and parsley, finely chopped

salt and freshly ground black pepper

Hard boil the eggs for 8-10 minutes, rinse under the cold tap to prevent discolouration, and leave to cool completely before shelling. Cut them in half lengthways, remove the yolks with a teaspoon and mash with a fork.

Make a mayonnaise (see recipe below) with the raw egg yolk, mustard, both oils, and wine vinegar. Mix in the mashed yolks and fresh herbs, and season to taste. Fill 18 of the halved egg whites with the mixture and sprinkle with the remaining whites, finely chopped.

102

PAN-GLAZED EGGS (OEUFS MIROIRS)

For each person:

2 eggs

butter, for cooking

salt and freshly ground black pepper

Preheat the oven to 240ºC (475ºF), gas mark 9. Break 2 eggs onto a plate. Melt a knob of butter in a shallow flameproof egg dish on the hob until it sizzles. Slide the eggs carefully into the melted butter. Season the white with salt, and top the yolk with a small knob of softened butter. Place in the oven until the white is set. Serve hot while the yolk is shiny.

BAKED EGGS WITH TARRAGON

(OEUFS COCOTTE À L'ESTRAGON)

Serves 6

20 g/^{3}/$_4$ oz butter

12 eggs

6 tablespoons crème fraîche, or double (heavy) cream

2 sprigs tarragon or chervil, or a few chive stems, or fine strips of mushroom or ham

salt and freshly ground black pepper

To serve: slices of toast

Preheat the oven to 150ºC (300ºF), gas mark 2. Butter 6 ramekins, season the bases with salt and pepper and break 2 eggs into each dish. Cover with the crème fraîche or cream and top with chopped herbs (or strips of mushroom or bacon). Put the ramekins in a bain-marie and bake for 8 minutes until the whites have set. Serve immediately with toast.

SCRAMBLED EGGS WITH TRUFFLES (OEUFS BROUILLÉS AUX TRUFFES)

Serves 6

14 eggs

25 g/1 oz butter

2 large, fresh truffles

mushrooms, cheese, or bacon (optional), cut into fine strips

salt and freshly ground black pepper

For added flavour, keep the eggs in a large screw-top jar with the truffles for 2-3 days.

Shave the truffles finely. Melt the butter in a high-sided frying pan and break in the eggs. Season with salt and pepper and cook over a very low heat, stirring continuously. When the eggs begin to thicken, add the truffles (mushrooms, cheese, or bacon, if using) and cook until the mixture is thick and creamy.

MAYONNAISE

Put 2 egg yolks in a bowl and season with salt and pepper. Add 300 ml/$\frac{1}{2}$ pint/1$\frac{1}{4}$ cups oil (olive, groundnut, grapeseed), INITIALLY ONE DROP AT A TIME, stirring continuously with an electric whisk until each drop of oil blends with the yolks. As the mixture begins to thicken, add larger drops. When half the oil has been added, add 1 teaspoon white wine vinegar or lemon juice to thin the mixture. Then add the remaining oil in a steady trickle whisking constantly. If it curdles, put a yolk in a bowl and whisk in the curdled mayonnaise, drop by drop. Home-made mayonnaise will keep for 2 days.

EGGS IN ASPIC (OEUFS EN GELÉE)

Serves 6

6 fresh eggs

2 tomatoes

2 dozen fine green beans

a handful of peas

1/4 bunch chervil

600 ml/1 pint/2½ cups home-made chicken or vegetable stock

4 x 3 g gelatine leaves, or 1 x 11g sachet powdered gelatine

Prepare 6 poached eggs by breaking each egg into a cup and carefully sliding it into a pan of gently simmering salted water to which a little vinegar has been added. Don't poach more than 4 eggs at a time.

After 2 minutes, turn the eggs carefully using 2 spoons, and continue cooking for a further 2 minutes. Keep warm in a pan of water at a temperature of 70°C (160°F) while poaching the remaining eggs. Drain the eggs on a plate lined with a clean tea towel, removing any white "threads" so that the eggs have a "clean" edge.

Peel the tomatoes by plunging into boiling water for 2 minutes to loosen the skins, remove the seeds and cut into small diced pieces. Cook the beans and peas in lightly salted boiling water for 8 minutes, drain and cut the beans into small sticks. Rinse the chervil, remove and chop the leaves.

Heat the stock, add the gelatine, stirring to dissolve, and leave to cool. Quickly rinse 6 ramekins (oval if possible) and pour a thin layer of cooled stock into each dish. Decorate with the diced tomato and some of the chopped chervil, and leave to set in the refrigerator. Add the rest of the vegetables and chervil to the remaining stock.

When the stock in the ramekins has set, place an egg in the centre of each dish and half-fill with the remaining stock and return to the refrigerator to set. Top up the ramekins with the rest of the stock and leave in the refrigerator for 5-6 hours. Turn the eggs out of the ramekins when ready to serve.

menu idea | braised leg of lamb with mushrooms | poached pears with blackcurrants
serve with | rosé, pink zinfandel

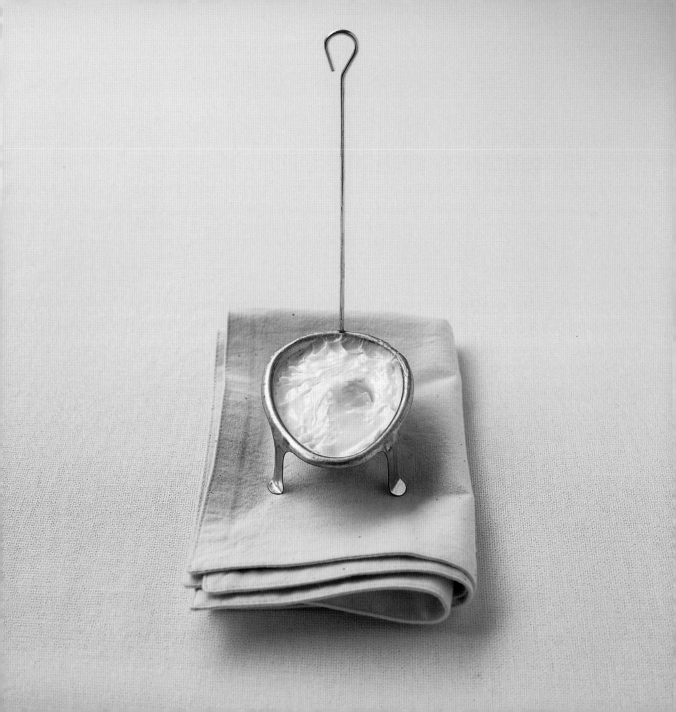

OMELETTE WITH GOAT'S CHEESE AND FRESH MINT (OMELETTE AU BROCCIU ET À LA MENTHE)

Serves 6

200 g/7 oz goat's cheese

12 eggs

5 sprigs fresh mint, finely chopped

2 tablespoons olive oil

salt and freshly ground black pepper

Roughly chop, or crumble, the goat's cheese. Break the eggs into a bowl and add the chopped mint leaves. Season with salt and pepper and beat the eggs, but not too vigorously.

Heat the oil in a large frying pan and pour in the eggs. Use a spatula to push the eggs from the edge of the pan toward the centre, allowing the unset mixture to run to the edges. When the eggs are almost set, sprinkle the goat's cheese on top of the omelette and cover for 1 minute to allow the cheese to heat through. Fold the omelette in half and slide onto a serving dish.

Note For a really successful omelette, don't over-beat the eggs or the mixture will dry out. Season when the eggs are almost cooked and use oil or clarified butter to seal the omelette over a high heat.

The authentic version of this Corsican recipe uses Brocciu, an unsalted cheese made from ewe's or goat's milk but you can make it with other fresh goat's cheeses, or Ricotta, and garnish it in a variety of ways.

menu idea | lamb stew garnished with spring vegetables | poached pears with blackcurrants
serve with | any alsace

EGGS À L'ANDALOUSE
(OEUFS À L'ANDALOUSE)

Serves 6

1 kg/2 lb ripe tomatoes

2 onions

1 garlic clove

3 small green (bell) peppers

2 tablespoons olive oil

150 g/5 oz/1 cup shelled peas

½ (fairly dry) chorizo sausage, sliced

6 eggs

salt and freshly ground black pepper

Peel the tomatoes by plunging into boiling water for 2 minutes to loosen the skins, remove the seeds and chop roughly.

Peel and thinly slice the onions, peel and crush the garlic. Rinse the peppers, remove the seeds and cut into fine strips. Heat the oil in a high-sided frying pan and lightly fry the garlic and onions until transparent. Add the peppers and, after 5 minutes, the tomatoes. Leave to simmer for 5 minutes over a fairly high heat and then add the peas and sliced chorizo. Cook for a further 5 minutes.

Preheat the oven to 180°C (350°F), gas mark 4.

Divide the mixture between 6 individual ovenproof dishes and crack 1 egg in the centre of each dish. Season with salt and pepper and cook in the preheated oven for 5 minutes or until the whites have set.

menu idea | paella | crème catalane

serve with | rioja, merlot, cabernet sauvignon

LIGHT BITES

THERE'S NO POINT IN BAKING BLIND IN A TIN BAKING DISH TO ENSURE THAT THE BASE OF YOUR QUICHE OR TART IS PROPERLY COOKED. BAKING BLIND HAS AN ANNOYING TENDENCY TO SHRINK THE PASTRY CASE BEFORE THE FILLING IS ADDED. ALL YOU NEED DO IS PLACE THE QUICHE DISH OR BAKING PAN ON THE LOWEST SHELF IN THE OVEN AND, IF THE TOPPING IS NOT CRUSTY AND GOLDEN ENOUGH AT THE END OF THE COOKING TIME, SIMPLY RAISE THE SHELF AND INCREASE THE TEMPERATURE BY 30–50ºC (85º–120ºF). IF YOU ARE WORRIED THAT YOUR FILLING MAY BE TOO "SOGGY", SPRINKLE THE BASE OF THE PASTRY CASE WITH A LITTLE FINE SEMOLINA. SOME QUICHES AND SAVOURY TARTS HAVE MORE FLAVOUR IF YOU ALLOW THEM TO REST FOR 10-15 MINUTES AT ROOM TEMPERATURE RATHER THAN SERVING IMMEDIATELY.

SHORTCRUST PASTRY

(PÂTE BRISÉE)

Makes 300 g/10½ oz pastry dough, or to fit a 25-cm/10-inch pastry case

200 g/7 oz/1½ cups plain (all-purpose) flour

125 g/4 oz butter, well chilled

3½ tablespoons chilled water

pinch of salt

Put the flour into a mixing bowl, add a little salt and then rub in the butter with your fingertips until you have a coarse, crumbly texture and the fat has been evenly dispersed. Gradually mix in the water and then use your hands to bring the dough together in a ball. Leave to rest in the refrigerator for at least 1 hour. Allow to thaw out a bit before attempting to roll out to use.

PUFF PASTRY

(PÂTE FEUILLETÉE)

Makes 450 g/1 lb pastry

250 g/9 oz/2 cups plain (all-purpose) flour

1 tablespoon melted butter

100 ml/3½ fl oz/½ cup chilled water

1 teaspoon white wine vinegar

200 g/7 oz butter, well-chilled

pinch of salt

The above quantities will make two tarts or quiches. You can always make one and freeze the other half of the pastry.

Mix all the ingredients (except the chilled butter) by hand, or in a food processor. When you have a smooth and elastic dough, use your hands to bring it together in a ball and cut a cross in the surface with a knife.

Put the dough in a freezer bag and chill in the refrigerator for 3 hours. Dust your work surface with flour, and roll out each quarter of the cross so that the pastry looks like a four-pointed star. Soften the chilled butter by hitting it several times with the rolling pin, and spread it over the central part of the "star". Then bring the 4 points into the centre, folding them over the butter, to form a square. Chill in the refrigerator for 30 minutes so that the butter and pastry reach the same temperature.

Flour the work surface again and roll out the pastry as evenly as possible into the shape of a rectangle. Fold one third over to the centre, and then the other third over that. Give the pastry a quarter turn and roll it out into the same size rectangle as before. Fold into three once more, put it back in the freezer bag and chill in the refrigerator for 30 minutes. Repeat the process twice more with a 30-minute chilling period after each stage. The pastry is then ready to use but allow it to thaw out before attempting to roll it out to use.

Don't worry about over-flouring the work surface, you can always use a pastry brush to remove any excess flour when folding the pastry in three. Make sure the layers adhere well and that the dough has an even consistency.

PIZZA/BREAD DOUGH

(PÂTE À PIZZA/PAIN)

Makes 250 g/9 oz dough

225 g/8 oz plain (all-purpose) flour

1 teaspoon salt

1 x 7 g /¼ oz sachet easy-blend yeast

150 ml/¼ pint hand-hot water

2 tablespoons olive oil

Put the flour into a mixing bowl with the salt and yeast and gradually stir in the hand-hot water. When the dough is pliable, add the oil and knead for 5 minutes until the dough is soft and smooth and leaves the bowl clean. Cover with a clean, damp cloth and leave to rise for at least 1 hour in a warm place. When the dough has doubled in size, knead again for about 5 minutes. The dough will keep in the refrigerator for several hours, but take it out 45 minutes before you want to use it.

BÉCHAMEL SAUCE (SAUCE BÉCHAMEL)

Makes about 750 ml/1¼ pints/3 cups

Melt 50 g/2 oz butter in a small pan over a low heat. Add 50 g/2 oz plain flour and stir to a smooth paste. Cook over a medium heat for a few minutes then gradually add 600 ml/ 1 pint/2½ cups milk, stirring briskly with a balloon whisk. Allow to thicken, stirring constantly, for 5-7 minutes. Season with salt and pepper and a pinch of fresh nutmeg.

For a Mornay sauce, simply add an egg yolk and grated Gruyère to the Béchamel sauce.

CHEESE PUFFS
(GOUGÈRES AU FROMAGE)

Serves 6

250 ml/9 fl oz/1 cup water

75 g/3 oz butter

250 g/9 oz/2 cups plain (all-purpose) flour

4 eggs + 1 yolk, mixed with a little water

100 g/3½ oz/1 cup grated Gruyère cheese

salt and freshly ground black pepper

Preheat the oven to 180°C (350°F), gas mark 4.

Put the water, butter and a little salt into a pan and bring to the boil. When the butter has melted, add all the flour, remove from the heat and beat well.

Return the pan to the heat and add the 4 whole eggs, one at a time, mixing each one well in before adding the next. Remove the pan from the heat, add 2/3 of the grated cheese and season with a little pepper.

Grease a baking sheet and use a tablespoon to spoon balls of mixture onto the sheet, each one lightly touching the next, to form a ring. Brush the top with the egg yolk and sprinkle with the remaining cheese.

Bake in the preheated oven for 20 minutes. Increase the temperature to 200°C (400°F), gas mark 6 and bake for a further 20 minutes. Turn off the oven, open the door slightly and leave the puffs to cool and dry out for a few minutes.

menu idea | vegetable pancakes | chilled pears with redcurrant syrup
serve with | mâcon blanc, white rioja

LEEK FLAMICHE
(FLAMICHE AUX POIREAUX)

Serves 6

250 g/9 oz ready-made puff pastry

10 medium-sized leeks

30 g/1 oz butter

200 ml/7 fl oz/¾ cup crème fraîche or single (light) cream

2 egg yolks

1 tablespoon finely chopped chives

salt and freshly ground black pepper

Roll out the puff pastry and use to line a quiche dish or baking pan. Chill in the refrigerator.

Preheat the oven to 180°C (350°F), gas mark 4.

Peel and slice the leeks from top to not quite the bottom. Hold firmly at the bottom and fan out under cold running water to rinse out any soil. Shake dry and slice thinly. Fry lightly in the butter, without letting them brown, for 20 minutes until all the liquid released has evaporated. Remove from the heat and add the crème fraîche or cream, egg yolks and chopped chives. Season with salt and pepper.

Pour the filling into the chilled flan case and bake in the preheated oven – on the lowest shelf to prevent the base becoming soggy – for about 35 minutes.

menu idea | stuffed tomatoes | egg custard
serve with | any alsace or muscat

PISSALADIÈRE

Serves 6

1.5 kg/3 lb onions

2 garlic cloves

6 tablespoons olive oil

1 sprig chopped fresh thyme

300 g/10 oz pizza/bread dough (see recipe p. 112)

10 anchovy fillets canned in oil

20 black olives

salt and freshly ground black pepper

Peel and thinly slice the onions and garlic, and put into a high-sided cooking pot or flameproof casserole with 3 tablespoons olive oil and half the thyme. Season with salt and pepper, and cook over a low heat for about 1 hour until the onions become transparent – don't let them brown.

Roll out the dough on a well-oiled baking sheet and leave to rise in a warm place, (e.g an airing cupboard) for 15 minutes.

Preheat the oven to 220°C (425°F), gas mark 7.

Spread the onion mixture over the dough, arrange the anchovy fillets in a lattice pattern, top with black olives and sprinkle with the remaining thyme. Drizzle with the rest of the olive oil and season generously with pepper. Cook in the preheated oven for 20 minutes.

Note Pissaladière is best served warm rather than hot.

menu idea | lamb casserole à la normande | apricots in ginger

serve with | light dry red

QUICHE LORRAINE

Serves 6

300 g/10 oz shortcrust
pastry (see recipe p. 112)

200 g/7 oz smoked bacon,
diced

3 eggs

200 ml/7 fl oz/³/₄ cup
crème fraîche or single
(light) cream

salt and freshly ground
black pepper

Roll out the pastry and use to line a greased quiche dish or baking pan. Sprinkle the diced bacon over the base of the pastry case and bake in a preheated oven at 180°C (350°F), gas mark 4, for 10 minutes.

Beat the eggs and crème fraîche or cream together, but not too vigorously, and season with salt and pepper. Pour the egg mixture into the pastry case and cook for a further 30 minutes. Serve immediately.

menu idea | cream of cauliflower soup | autumn-fruit compote
serve with | riesling

FRENCH ONION TART
(TARTE À L'OIGNON À L'ALSACIENNE)

Serves 6

300 g/10 oz shortcrust
pastry (see recipe p. 112)

40 g/1½ oz/5 tablespoons
plain (all-purpose) flour

40 g/1½ oz/3 tablespoons
butter

1 litre/1¾ pints/4 cups milk

freshly grated nutmeg

500 g/1 lb onions

1 tablespoon oil or butter,
for cooking

1 tablespoons fine
semolina

150 g/5 oz smoked bacon,
diced

4 eggs, beaten

salt and freshly ground
black pepper

Roll out the pastry and use to line a lightly greased quiche dish or baking pan. Prepare a Béchamel sauce using the flour, butter and milk (see recipe p. 112). Season with salt and pepper and a pinch of freshly grated nutmeg.

Peel and thinly slice the onions and soften in the oil or butter over a very low heat for 20 minutes. Then add the semolina and leave to swell for a few seconds. Blanch the diced bacon in boiling water and drain well.

Preheat the oven to 180°C (350°F), gas mark 4.

Mix the beaten eggs, Béchamel sauce, diced bacon and onions together in a large mixing bowl, pour into the pastry case and bake in the preheated oven for 45 minutes.

menu idea | aubergine mould (eggplant mold) | dark chocolate mousse
serve with | gewurztraminer

POTATO PIE À LA BERRICHONNE
(PÂTE DU BERRY AUX POMMES DE TERRE)

Serves 6

500 g/1 lb ready-made puff pastry (see recipe p. 112)

1.5 kg/3 lb potatoes

2 onions, thinly sliced

freshly grated nutmeg

1 egg, beaten

150 g/5 oz/²/₃ cup crème fraîche or single (light) cream

2 tablespoons mixed finely chopped chives, tarragon and chervil

salt and freshly ground black pepper

Preheat the oven to 180°C (350°F), gas mark 4.

Roll out half the pastry and use to line a high-sided baking pan.

Peel and thinly slice the potatoes and onions. Blanch the potatoes in boiling water for 5 minutes, drain well and use half to line the base of the pastry case. Season with salt and pepper and a pinch of freshly grated nutmeg. Cover with a layer of thinly sliced onions and top with another layer of potatoes. Cover with the rest of the pastry, sealing the edges well with some of the beaten egg.

Make a hole in the centre of the pastry crust and insert a pie chimney to allow the steam to escape during cooking. Brush the pastry with the rest of the beaten egg and bake in the preheated oven for 1 hour.

Season the crème fraîche or cream with salt and pepper, add the chopped herbs and mix well. Take the pie out of the oven, remove the chimney and pour the cream mixture into the hole. Return to the oven and bake on the floor of the oven or the lowest shelf for a further 10 minutes.

menu idea | dandelion leaf and bacon salad | peaches in red wine
serve with | chinon blanc, white rioja, pinot grigio

SQUID TOURTE (TIELLE SÉTOISE)

Serves 6

For the pastry:

250 g/9 oz/2 cups plain
(all-purpose) flour

125 g/4 oz butter

50 g/2 oz sugar

muscat wine

salt

For the filling:

750 g/1½ lb small squid
(buy ready-prepared from
a supermarket or ask your
fish shop to prepare them
for you)

2 onions

2 garlic cloves

3 tablespoons olive oil

200 ml/7 fl oz muscat wine

3 tomatoes

1 red (bell) pepper

1 sprig fresh marjoram,
finely chopped

1 egg, beaten

salt and freshly ground
black pepper

Use the pastry ingredients to make a pliable shortcrust pastry
(see recipe p. 112).

Rinse the squid and cut into fine rings. Peel and thinly slice the
onions, peel and crush the garlic, and fry lightly in the olive oil,
in a high-sided frying pan, for a few minutes before adding the
squid and the wine.

Peel the tomatoes by first plunging into boiling water for
2 minutes to loosen the skins, remove the seeds, and chop
roughly. Rinse the red pepper, remove the seeds and cut into
thin strips. Add the tomatoes, pepper and chopped marjoram
to the pan, season to taste and leave to simmer over a low
heat for 20 minutes or until all the cooking juices have
evaporated.

Preheat the oven to 180°C (350°F), gas mark 4.

Roll out half the pastry and use it to cover a greased baking
sheet, or line a quiche dish or baking pan. Add the squid and
vegetable filling. Roll out the remaining pastry and cover
the tourte, sealing the edges with some of the beaten egg
and pinching them firmly together. Brush the top with the
rest of the beaten egg and bake in the preheated oven for
30 minutes.

menu idea | Provençal tomato soup | chilled pears with redcurrant syrup
serve with | dry white muscat, white zinfandel

GOAT'S CHEESE TART
(TARTE AU CHÈVRE)

Serves 6

For the pastry:

125 g/4 oz butter

200 g/7 oz/1½ cups plain
(all-purpose) flour

salt

For the filling:

1 tablespoon fine semolina

600 g/1¼ lb fresh goat's
cheese

4 eggs

5 sprigs fresh flowering
thyme, finely chopped

2 sprigs fresh (or a pinch
dried) oregano, finely
chopped

salt and freshly ground
black pepper

Use the pastry ingredients to make shortcrust pastry
(see recipe p. 112), and chill in the refrigerator for ½ hour.

Preheat the oven to 180°C (350°F), gas mark 4.

Roll out the pastry and use to line a greased quiche dish or
baking pan. Sprinkle the base with the semolina.

Mash the goat's cheese with a fork and then add the eggs,
one at a time. Season with salt and pepper, and add the
chopped herbs.

Pour the filling into the pastry case and bake in the preheated
oven for 30-40 minutes until the filling has risen and the top
is crisp and golden.

Turn off the heat and stand the dish or baking pan on the floor
of the oven for 10 minutes to allow the base to cook through.

menu idea | cream of carrot soup | currant cramique
serve with | sauvignon blanc, white rioja

RATATOUILLE TART
(TARTE À LA RATATOUILLE)

Serves 6

For the pastry:

200 g/7 oz/1½ cups plain (all-purpose) flour

125 g/4 oz butter

chilled water

salt

For the filling:

1 onion

1 garlic clove

2 tablespoons olive oil

1 aubergine (eggplant)

1 red and 1 green (bell) pepper

2 small, firm courgettes (zucchini)

3 ripe tomatoes

2 eggs

250 ml/9 fl oz/1 cup crème fraîche or single (light) cream

4 sprigs fresh basil, finely chopped

Use the pastry ingredients to make shortcrust pastry (see recipe p. 112), and chill in the refrigerator for ½ hour.

Roll out the pastry and use to line a greased quiche dish or baking pan. Chill in the refrigerator.

Peel and thinly slice the onion and garlic, rinse and cut the aubergine (eggplant) into small diced pieces, and rinse and cut the peppers into fine strips. Heat the olive oil in a high-sided frying pan and lightly fry the onions and garlic for 10 minutes. Add the aubergine and cook for a further 10 minutes, then add the peppers. Cover, if necessary, and leave to simmer. Rinse but do not peel the courgettes (zucchini) and cut into even-sized pieces. When the vegetables start to break down, add the courgettes, stir with a spatula and continue cooking. Peel the tomatoes by plunging into boiling water for 2 minutes to loosen the skins remove the seeds and chop roughly. Add to the pan, increase the heat and continue cooking until the liquid has evaporated.

Preheat the oven to 180°C (350°F), gas mark 4.

Beat the eggs (but not too vigorously) together with the crème fraîche or cream and chopped basil, and stir in the ratatouille. Pour the mixture into the pastry case and bake in the preheated oven for about 40 minutes. Turn off the heat and stand the dish or baking pan on the floor of the oven for 10 minutes to allow the base to cook through. Serve immediately.

menu idea | mocha biscuit cake
serve with | rosé

SPINACH TART
(TOURTE AUX ÉPINARDS)

Serves 6

250 g/8 oz ready-made puff pastry

600 g/1¼ lb fresh spinach

1 tablespoon olive oil

2 large tomatoes

3 eggs, beaten

150 ml/¼ pint/⅔ cup full-fat crème fraîche or double (heavy) cream

125 g/4 oz/1 cup freshly grated Parmesan cheese

pinch of freshly grated nutmeg

salt and freshly ground black pepper

Roll out the pastry and use to line a quiche dish or baking pan. Chill in the refrigerator.

Pick over and rinse the spinach under running water. Drain well and soften in the olive oil over a low heat. Slice the tomatoes, removing the seeds.

Preheat the oven to 200°C (400°F), gas mark 6.

When the spinach has released all its water, drain through a sieve or colander, pressing hard to extract all the liquid. Turn into a bowl and add the eggs, crème fraîche or cream, Parmesan, and nutmeg. Mix well, season to taste with salt and pepper and turn into the pastry-lined dish. Cover with the sliced tomato, season to taste, and drizzle with a little olive oil. Bake in the preheated oven for about 30 minutes.

menu idea | quick ice-cream
serve with | beaujolais, merlot

ASPARAGUS À LA FLAMANDE
(ASPERGES À LA FLAMANDE)

Serves 6

1 kg/2 lb green asparagus

2 eggs

125 g/4 oz butter

a few fresh chervil leaves

salt

Cut off the tough bases of the asparagus, wash in plenty of water (but do not soak) and drain. Asparagus is best sprinkled with a little coarse salt and steamed for 10-15 minutes, depending on the size. While the asparagus is cooking, hard boil the eggs for 10 minutes (see p. 102), rinse in cold water to prevent them discolouring and shell.

Melt the butter in a small pan, mash the eggs with a fork and add to the melted butter without mixing too much. Season with salt.

Arrange the asparagus on a dish, cover the tips with the melted butter and egg mixture and decorate with chervil leaves. Serve immediately.

menu idea | rolled beef | strawberry charlotte
serve with | sauvignon blanc

BIBBELSKÄSE

Serves 6

1 large or 2 medium baking
potatoes, per person

½ bunch chives

5 sprigs flat-leaf parsley

½ bunch chervil

3 tarragon sprigs

2 shallots

creamed horseradish

500 g/1 lb cream cheese

Preheat the oven to 180°C (350°F), gas mark 4.

Choose potatoes of a similar size so that they have the same cooking time. Scrub the potatoes well, dry with kitchen paper and prick each one several times with a fork. Wrap each potato in foil and bake in the preheated oven for 40-60 minutes, depending on their size.

Rinse, dry and chop but don't mix the herbs and place in small individual dishes. Peel and chop the shallots and also place in small individual dishes. Put the creamed horseradish in a separate dish and turn the cheese into a serving dish.

When the potatoes are baked through (i.e. when you can insert the blade of a knife easily), remove from the oven and place in a basket, covered with a serviette to keep them warm. (Leave wrapped in the foil if preferred.)

Serve with the cheese, shallots, horseradish and herbs, so that your guests can choose their own flavouring.

Note Bibbelskäse also goes well with sautéed potatoes.

menu idea | plum crumble tart
serve with | riesling

CHEESE SOUFFLÉ
(SOUFFLÉ AU FROMAGE)

Serves 6

50 g/2 oz butter

50 g/2 oz/scant ½ cup plain (all-purpose) flour

500 ml/17 fl oz/2 cups milk

150 g/5 oz/1¼ cups freshly grated Gruyère cheese

6 eggs, separated

pinch of freshly grated nutmeg

salt and freshly ground black pepper

Preheat the oven to 220°C (425°F), gas mark 7.

Melt the butter over a low heat, add the flour and stir to obtain a smooth paste.

Gradually add the milk, stirring briskly with a balloon whisk, and allow to thicken stirring constantly, as for Béchamel sauce (see recipe p. 112).

Remove from the heat, add the grated cheese and then the egg yolks, one at a time, and beat until everything is smoothly combined. Season to taste.

Whisk the egg whites, taking care not to over-beat, until they form soft peaks, then gently and carefully fold into the soufflé mixture. Pour into a well-buttered soufflé dish. Bake in the preheated oven for 20-25 minutes without opening the door and serve absolutely immediately. Soufflé will not wait!

menu idea | beef sirloin or rump steaks with red wine sauce | chestnut delicieux

serve with | aligoté, white mâcon, any strong dry white

GRILLED GOAT'S CHEESES
(CROTTINS DE CHAVIGNOL RÔTIS)

Serves 6

½ curly-leaf endive,
or frisée

1 garlic clove, peeled

4 tablespoons olive oil

1 tablespoon white wine
vinegar

6 teaspoons olive oil

6 slices baguette or
crusty bread

6 small, round goat's
cheeses (Crottins)

6 thyme sprigs

salt and freshly ground
black pepper

Remove any damaged or marked outer leaves of the endive, rinse and dry in a salad spinner. Rub the garlic clove around the inside of a salad bowl.

Make a vinaigrette with the 4 tablespoons of olive oil and tablespoon of vinegar, season to taste with salt and pepper.

Preheat the grill/broiler.

Drizzle 1 teaspoon olive oil over each slice of bread, and top with a goat's cheese and thyme sprig. Season generously with pepper and place under the preheated grill for 3–4 minutes, until the top turns crisp and golden.

Toss the curly-leaf endive or frisée in the vinaigrette and divide between 6 individual plates, add a grilled goat's cheese and serve immediately.

menu idea | cabbage and bacon soup | crème brûlée
serve with | white sancerre, mâcon blanc

MEAT AND POULTRY

ALL CUTS OF MEAT CAN BE DIVIDED INTO TWO CATEGORIES. THE FIRST CONSISTS OF TOP-QUALITY CUTS – OFTEN REFERRED TO AS PRIME CUTS – WHICH ARE MORE TENDER AND THEREFORE IDEAL FOR RAPID COOKING (GRILLING, FRYING, ROASTING). THE SECOND, KNOWN AS GRADE TWO CUTS, INCLUDES BRAISING CUTS THAT NEED TO BE PREPARED IN A PARTICULAR WAY AND CUTS THAT HAVE TO BE COOKED SLOWLY FOR A LONG TIME.

MEAT CAN BE KEPT FOR 2-3 DAYS IN THE COLDEST PART OF THE REFRIGERATOR, IN ITS ORIGINAL PACKAGING. HOWEVER – AND THIS USUALLY APPLIES TO CUTS FROM OLDER ANIMALS – MEAT IS OFTEN SOLD TOO FRESH AND IT IS WELL WORTH ALLOWING IT TO MATURE A LITTLE BEFORE PREPARING IT. AN EXPERIENCED BUTCHER WILL KNOW HOW LONG MEAT SHOULD BE HUNG FOR THE BEST FLAVOUR AND TEXTURE.

BEEF

Buying beef

• Good quality beef can be recognized by its deep red colour, a good outer layer of yellow fat and the fine network of fat running through the meat.

• Cuts can be divided into several categories (for roasting, grilling, braising, slow cooking and boiling) and two qualities – prime cuts or top-quality meat and second grade meat.

Method and cooking times

• For top-quality beef, which is grouped under the term sirloin, use the first three cooking methods only, i.e. roasting, grilling, braising. Sirloin can be divided into four cuts – fillet or tenderloin, sirloin steak, rump steak and "on the bone", which not only provides the famous rib of beef but also joints for roasting and cuts for grilling and pan frying.

• Cooking times:

- to oven roast: 20 minutes at 245ºC (475ºF), gas mark 9, then lower heat to 190ºC (375ºF), gas mark 5 and cook for 15 minutes to the pound (500 g) for rare, plus 15 minutes extra at the end for medium-rare or 30 minutes extra for well-done. This is for a joint weighing 1.8-2.5 kg (4-5 lb); adjust length of initial cooking time if the joint is smaller. Test with a skewer in the thickest part of the joint.

- for pan-fried or grilled steaks (fillet, sirloin, rump): 2-4 minutes on each side depending on how thick the steaks are. Remove from the heat, cover and leave the steaks to "relax" for 5 minutes – this tip is also useful for roasts. Don't pan-fry a steak that is less than 1.5 cm/⅝ inch thick, unless it is the "minute steak" cut. However, some inferior cuts of beef will produce a very tasty meat that is ideal for pan-frying. Take the advice of your butcher.

- choose cuts from older animals for braising and stewing. Among others, the cuts that give the best results are chuck steak, shoulder and topside (bottom round). For boiling and stewing – French pot-au-feu (see p. 152) is the ultimate dish when it comes to beef stew – combine the above cuts with cuts such as middle ribs (short ribs) and/or brisket.

Cook the cheaper cuts in casseroles slowly with vegetables in a good stock. A few minutes careful preparation and the occasional check to ensure it does not overcook and lose its flavour will reward you with an economical, tasty and nourishing family meal.

VEAL

Buying veal

• Top-quality veal is nice and firm and has a pale pink colour – this means it has come from a calf that is no more than three months old, fed exclusively on its mother's milk enriched with cereal flours.

• Joints of veal are cut from the leg, shoulder, flank divided into the fillet and loin, the best end of neck, and ribs. Cheaper cuts are the breast and the scrag end of neck. A thick, round horizontal slice is known as veal fillet (this also applies to pork). The shoulder is used for stews and roasts, while the best end of neck can be cut into cutlets.

Method and cooking times

Since veal is a young and delicate meat that is liable to dry out (just like prime cuts of pork), it is best cooked in a covered cooking pot or flameproof casserole on top of the stove rather than in the oven. But first seal in the flavour and juices with an initial searing in a frying pan over a high heat.

• Cooking times:

- for veal cutlets: fry or grill for about 7 minutes on each side, cover, and leave to "relax" for 5 minutes.

- for escalopes: 4-8 minutes according to how thick they are.

- for a roast: follow the temperature and timing for each individual recipe. Cooking roast veal requires a certain attention to detail since it should not be cooked for too long or on too high a heat. The meat should always be left to "relax".

PORK

Buying pork

• Like veal, pork should be firm to the touch and have a pale pink colour. Red flesh is the sign of an older animal or meat of mediocre quality. These days, it is more important than ever to know where your meat comes from, so buy free-range pork if at all possible.

• When buying fresh pork, the most popular cuts are tenderloin and small end of tenderloin, leg, rolled shoulder, belly, chops and spare ribs.

The liver and kidneys, which have a stronger flavour than that of lamb, are very tasty and a good addition to many types of casseroles and pâtés.

Method and cooking times

• Like veal, lean cuts of pork are best cooked slowly in a high-sided, covered cooking pot or flameproof casserole. Fattier cuts and/or cuts and with elements of fat such as chops and spare ribs and pork products such as sausages are ideally suited to the dry heat of a grill or barbecue.

Leg, shoulder, tenderloin and hams are the best cuts for roasting.

• When roasting pork with the rind on always slash it in criss-cross fashion and rub in plenty of salt (but do not add any oil) to make a very crunchy and tasty "crackling".

• Never prick sausages with a fork as this will make them burst – use a large needle or the point of a sharp knife.

• Cooking times:

– for roast leg or loin of pork: 20 minutes at 240ºC (475ºF), gas mark 9, then lower heat to 190ºC (375ºF), gas mark 5 and continue roasting for 35 minutes to the pound (500 g).

– Test with a skewer in the thickest part of the joint. Pork should be cooked through and not served "rare".

– for pork chops: fry or grill for 4 minutes on each side over a high and then medium heat, and leave to "relax" for a few minutes.

– for a small end of tenderloin: fry or grill for 15 minutes over a high and then low heat.

LAMB

Buying lamb

• The generic term "lamb" can be very misleading since its flavour can either be extremely delicate or very strong, depending on the age of the animal. It is nevertheless the meat with the most distinctive flavour.

Depending on the region it comes from and its particular breeding season, lambs do not start to come to market until they are about 5-7 months. Sheep are truly a free-range animal, roaming the fields and hillsides grazing on the natural pasture. The earliest and most expensive British lamb is the traditional Easter lamb that has been raised on the sweet, new spring grass.

Salt-meadow lambs are raised and fattened on pastures close to the sea. The salt and iodine give the flesh its unique flavour.

For economic reasons, mutton has gone from the butcher's and supermarkets, which is a great pity as it was tasty meat for good, old-fashioned dishes.

• Whatever the age of the animal, choose meat with nice, white fat – you can remove any surplus if you want a lighter and more diet-friendly dish.

• Lamb is cut into prime cuts (leg, chops, saddle) and grade two cuts (shoulder, breast, neck).

Shoulder can be prepared like a more economic version of a leg, or boned and cut into cubes for making stews, curries, tajines.

Breast and neck are fattier cuts and are used in stews.

Saddle, best end of neck, crown, shoulder and leg are ideal for roasts.

Because lamb is rich in fat, it doesn't dry out when cooked. It is often prepared with herbs, especially rosemary.

Method and cooking times

• Cooking times:

– Roast lamb is best cooked on the bone. For a leg: 30 minutes at 230ºC (450ºF), gas mark 8, then lower the heat to 180ºC (350ºF), gas mark 4 and cook for 30 minutes to the pound (500 g). Test with a skewer in the thickest part of the joint. Some people prefer their cooked lamb "pink" rather than well-done.

– for chops: cooking times for chops are similar to those for grilled red meat and depend on whether you like them rare, medium rare or well-done. But first seal the flavour by grilling over a high heat. There's no need to oil the rack or griddle pan because the meat has its own layer of fat.

BÉARNAISE SAUCE

Béarnaise sauce makes an ideal accompaniment for beef and lamb.

Put 3 tablespoons vinegar, 1 sprig tarragon and 1 finely chopped shallot in a pan, and simmer over medium heat until the liquid is reduced by 2/3. Remove from the heat and strain. Put the liquid into the top of a double boiler or into a bowl that can be set over a pan. Off the heat, add 2 egg yolks to the strained liquid, beating with a balloon whisk or electric hand-held whisk until the mixture becomes light and frothy. Place the top of the double boiler, or the bowl, over barely simmering water (do not let the container touch the water or the eggs will scramble). Continue to whisk until the eggs thicken and then gradually add 100 g/3½ oz butter, knob by knob, whisking constantly. Season to taste.

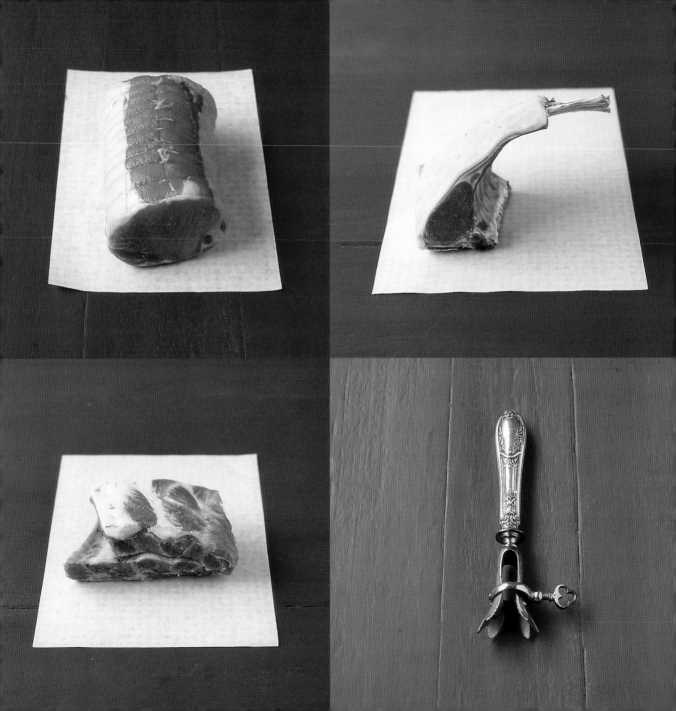

POULTRY

Buying poultry

• You can buy very different types of poultry to suit your purse. Commercially produced poultry may look good on the supermarket shelves but can be disappointing when cooked. It's better to go for quality rather than quantity.

• Although it may mean eating it less often, it's best to buy local free-range poultry from your local butcher, or free-range birds from the better supermarkets. Free-range corn-fed poultry has its own very distinctive flavour.

Your butcher will also be able to suggest the best poultry to meet your requirements and will have it dressed or jointed for you, even boned if you give him some notice.

• The meat of top-quality poultry should be pearly white or, if the bird has been fed on corn, yellow, with no dark patch, but beware cheap plump birds as they may well have had water added to enhance their shelf appearance. Always read the label closely.

• Poultry is best eaten as soon as possible (within 2 days) and should be kept in the coldest part of the refrigerator – but make sure you remove the giblets if they are tucked inside.

Method and cooking times

• All well-produced young poultry is ideal for oven-roasting as well as in numerous stove-top cooked dishes.

• Always remove any obvious fat on poultry.

• The white meat of chicken can often be rather dry and is better poached, grilled in its skin or roasted. The thighs are particularly tasty in stews and casseroles, and can also be marinated before being grilled. Wings and drumsticks are delicious grilled, and make excellent finger food.

• Cooking times:

– for roast chicken: 20 minutes to the pound (500 g) in a preheated oven at 190°C (375°F), gas mark 5 and 15–20 minutes over.

– to check that poultry is cooked, pierce the thickest part of the thigh with a sharp, thin skewer – the cooking juices should run golden and clear, not pink .

Jointing a chicken

Pull the leg away from the breast and cut through the joint, then separate the thigh from the drumstick. Separate the back from the breast and then remove both sides of the breast and cut them in two, leaving some of the breast around the wings.

RABBIT

Buying rabbit

• Rabbit is often ignored which is a pity since, not only is it delicious, it is also lean, extremely digestible and relatively inexpensive. Butchers in country areas will often have wild rabbits, which they will skin for you.

Young rabbits are best, as their meat is pale and tender. Buy them whole with their kidneys, which are a sign of freshness.

A young rabbit weighs around 1.5 kg/3lb and is enough for 4-6 people.

Look out for pink flesh, no marks on the liver, white fat around the kidneys and short, plump legs.

Method and cooking times

• Rabbit and hare are ideal for slow cooking as their meat tends to dry out.

• If you decide to roast a rabbit or hare in the oven, prevent it from drying out by covering it with some form of protective coating, i.e. butter, Dijon mustard, or slices of smoked streaky bacon (or Canadian strips). You will need to baste the joint regularly.

• Cooking times:

– for a whole rabbit: about 45-50 minutes at 220°C (425°F), gas mark 7, basting at 10 minute intervals with the pan juices or any cooking sauce the recipe specifies.

– for a leg: 40 minutes.

– for a saddle: 25 minutes.

ROLLED BEEF (BOEUF À LA FICELLE)

Serves 6

3 carrots

½ celeriac (celery root)

2 leeks

6 baby turnips

1 onion, peeled and stuck with a clove

1 tablespoon coarse salt

peppercorns

1.5 kg/3 lb fillet of beef, rolled and tied with string

1 bowl tomato coulis (see recipe p. 320)

fresh mixed herbs (parsley, thyme, tarragon, chives), chopped

Peel the vegetables, cut the carrots and celeriac into large sticks, and roughly chop the white part of the leeks (keep the green part for your stockpot). Place in a deep saucepan with the onion, salt and a few peppercorns. Add the beef, just cover with lightly salted water, and bring slowly to the boil.

When the water is boiling, plunge the piece of beef into the cooking pot — attaching one end of the string to one of the handles makes it easier to retrieve the meat when it is cooked. Simmer gently for 30–40 minutes (depending on whether you like your beef rare or slightly more cooked), removing any scum at regular intervals. Unlike pot-au-feu (see recipe p. 152), the beef should remain pink and juicy.

Reheat the tomato coulis and season with fresh herbs to taste.

Remove the beef from the pot, cut off the string and place the meat on a serving dish surrounded by the vegetables. Serve the tomato sauce separately.

Note The quality of the meat makes rolled beef a deluxe version of pot-au-feu, although a less expensive version can be prepared with topside or brisket. These cuts of beef will have to be cooked for longer, so the vegetables should be added later than given in this recipe. It can also be served with steamed vegetables — small courgettes (zucchini), baby potatoes, French beans, fresh peas — as well as those cooked in the broth. The broth doesn't need to have the fat removed and can be served as an entrée. Or, if you prefer, refrigerate overnight, lift off the solidified fat, and use as the stock for soup.

menu idea | kouign-aman

serve with | nuits-saint-georges, côtes du rhône

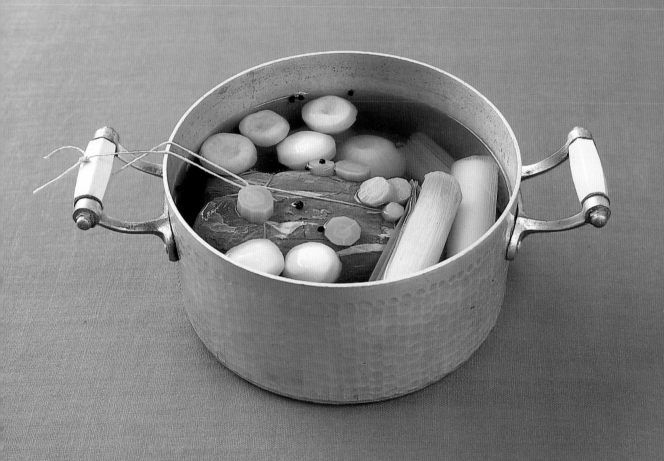

BŒUF BOURGUIGNON

Serves 6

3 carrots

3 large onions or 1 onion,
plus 2 dozen button onions

1.5 kg/3 lb topside, cut into
cubes

1 bottle red Burgundy

1 bay leaf

10 sprigs flat-leaf parsley

150 g/5 oz bacon, diced

1 tablespoon plain
(all-purpose) flour

salt and freshly ground
black pepper

To serve: a few sprigs
freshly chopped parsley

Twenty-four hours before cooking this dish, peel the carrots and onions; cut the carrots into thickish rounds and thinly slice the onions, leaving the button onions whole, if using, Then marinate the beef, carrots and onions in the wine, seasoned with salt, pepper, bay leaf and parsley sprigs.

The following day remove the beef from the marinade and drain on absorbent kitchen paper. Drain the onions and carrots but keep the marinade.

Release the fat from the diced bacon by frying in a cooking pot or flameproof casserole, over a medium heat. Add the cubed meat and brown lightly on all sides, then remove from the pot and replace with the onions and carrots.

When the onions are well cooked, return the meat to the pot and stir in the flour. Continue to cook for a few minutes, stirring continuously. Add the marinade and season with salt and pepper. Cover and leave to simmer for 3 hours over a very low heat. Check after 2 hours so that the meat does not overcook. Add the mushrooms (if using) about an hour before the end.

Remove the bay leaf and parsley sprigs, sprinkle with freshly chopped parsley and serve with steamed potatoes.

menu idea | peaches in red wine

serve with | rully, côte de beaune, any full-bodied red

TRADITIONAL BEEF STEW (POT-AU-FEU)

Serves 6

625 g/1¼ lb silverside or top leg

625 g/1¼ lb lean shoulder or blade-bone

1 knuckle of veal

1 onion, peeled

1 bouquet garni

6 carrots

6 small leeks

6 turnips

1 small celeriac (celery root)

1 small green cabbage

salt

To serve: coarse salt, olive oil (or herb vinaigrette), various sorts of mustard

Put the three cuts of meat into a deep pan with the onion and bouquet garni and cover with lightly salted water. Cover with a lid and bring gently to the boil, removing any scum that forms. Lower the heat and continue to cook, partially covered, for 2 hours turning the meat at intervals.

While the meat is cooking, peel and roughly chop the carrots, leeks, turnips and celeriac. Discard the outer leaves of the cabbage, cut it into quarters, and blanch in boiling water for 10 minutes. Drain and keep to one side.

When the meat has been cooking for 1 hour, add the vegetables (except the cabbage) to the cooking pot and continue cooking for a further 45 minutes. Then add the cabbage and cook for another 15 minutes.

Lift the meat from the pot and cut into pieces. Remove the bouquet garni, strain the vegetables and arrange with the meat on a warm serving dish.

Serve with coarse salt, olive oil or herb vinaigrette, and various sorts of mustard.

Note When draining the vegetables, you can keep the stock for use in other recipes.

menu idea | dandelion leaf and bacon salad | fig tart

serve with | côtes du rhône, beaujolais

BEEF COOKED IN RED WINE
(DAUBE PROVENÇALE)

Serves 6

3 carrots

3 onions

1.3 kg/3 lb silverside or top leg, cut into 75 g/3 oz pieces

1 bottle good red wine

200 ml/7 fl oz/¾ cup wine vinegar

2 cloves

1 sprig fresh thyme

1 bay leaf

few sprigs fresh parsley

6 tablespoons olive oil

4 garlic cloves

6 anchovies in brine (optional)

handful of pitted black olives (optional)

salt and freshly ground black pepper

To serve: pasta and grated Gruyère cheese

Twenty-four hours before cooking this dish, peel and slice the carrots and one of the onions. Leave to marinate with the meat in the wine seasoned with vinegar, cloves, fresh herbs, salt and pepper.

The following day remove the meat from the marinade and drain on absorbent kitchen paper. Peel and thinly slice the 2 remaining onions and fry in 3 tablespoons of the olive oil, in a pan or flameproof casserole, over a medium heat. While the onions are cooking, pan-fry the pieces of beef in the rest of the oil over a high heat. When they are nicely browned on all sides, add to the casserole with the marinade, including the sliced onion and carrots.

Leave to simmer, without a lid, for 20 minutes. Peel and crush the garlic and rinse and crush the anchovies (if using). Add to the cooking pot, cover and leave to simmer over a *very* low heat (this is essential) for at least 4 hours and check that the meat is not over-cooking. If using the olives, add 30 minutes before the end. The meat should have a melting texture and the sauce should be thick and creamy. Remove the herbs and check the seasoning. Serve immediately with buttered pasta shells or macaroni and grated Gruyère cheese.

Note If you want the daube to taste even better, cook it in the oven, in a covered earthenware or cast-iron casserole, at 120°C (250°F), gas mark ½, for 5 hrs or more.

menu idea | crunchy vegetable salad | apricots in ginger
serve with | côtes du rhône

BEEF AND ONION STEW (CARBONADE FLAMANDE)

Serves 6

1.5 kg/3 lb silverside or top leg, cut into cubes

75 g/3 oz butter

4 onions

1 tablespoons plain (all-purpose) flour

1 litre/1¾ pints/4 cups beer

2 tablespoons vinegar

1 sprig fresh thyme

1 bay leaf

few sprigs fresh parsley

3 sugar lumps

2 slices gingerbread (optional)

1 tablespoon mustard (optional)

6 slightly sharp apples [Granny Smith, Braeburn, Cox's Orange Pippin]

2 dozen prunes, pitted

salt and freshly ground black pepper

Lightly brown the pieces of meat in half the butter, over a low heat, in a pan or flameproof casserole. Remove from the pot and keep to one side. Peel and slice the onions and brown lightly in the pan used for the meat. Sprinkle with the flour, mix well and add the beer. Return the meat to the pan and add the vinegar, herbs, sugar, salt and pepper. (When you add the herbs and seasoning to the carbonade, you can also add 2 slices gingerbread and 1 tablespoon mustard for extra flavour.) Cover and leave to simmer for 1½ hours over a low heat.

After about an hour, peel and core the apples, cut into thick slices and fry in the rest of the butter. Add to the cooking pot with the prunes and continue cooking for another 15 minutes, until the cooking time is up. Remove the herbs and serve piping hot.

Note Prunes don't need to be cooked but if they are a bit on the dry side, add them to the cooking pot ½ hour before the end of the cooking time (i.e. after 1 hour) to give them time to soften.

menu idea | sugar tart
serve with | côtes du rhône, merlot

SHEPHERD'S PIE (HACHIS PARMENTIER)

Serves 6

For the mashed potato:

1.5 kg/3 lb floury potatoes (Maris Piper, King Edward, Bintje...)

50 g/2 oz butter

300 ml/½ pint/1¼ cups warm milk

nutmeg

salt

For the meat filling:

3 shallots

2 tablespoons olive oil

800 g/1¾ lb leftover cooked lamb, or minced (ground) raw lamb

2 tablespoons clear meat juices (with the fat removed), stock or water

75 g/3 oz/¾ cup freshly grated Parmesan (optional)

salt and freshly ground black pepper

Peel the potatoes, cut into evenly sized pieces and cook in boiling salted water for about 20 minutes until tender (i.e. when you can insert the blade of a knife easily). Drain well and mash with a potato masher or press through a fine-mesh sieve – don't use an electric blender as this will make them too soft and sticky. Return to a low heat and, stirring briskly, gradually incorporate the butter, a knob at a time, and just enough of the warm milk to obtain a slightly thicker consistency than usual (the potato will tend to soften in the oven). Season with salt and add a pinch of freshly grated nutmeg. Keep to one side.

Peel and finely chop the shallots and fry in the oil over a low heat. Meanwhile, grind up the leftover cooked meat in a food processor When the shallots are transparent, add the meat and leave to brown for 6 minutes, stirring at regular intervals. Add the meat juices (stock or water), bring to the boil and remove from the heat. Season with salt and pepper.

Preheat the oven to 200°C (400°F), gas mark 6.

Spread half the potato over the base of a well-greased ovenproof dish, cover with the meat and top with the remaining potato. Sprinkle with grated Parmesan (if using) and cook in the oven until the top is crusty and golden, about 30 minutes.

Note Instead of leftover meat or minced lamb, you can use sausage meat or cooked ham hock with the fat removed. While some like a grated-cheese topping, others prefer bread-crumbs. Parmesan makes a good compromise as it is very tasty and also enables you to cut cleanly through the crusty topping.

menu idea | spinach salad with goat's cheese | chocolate refrigerator cake

serve with | beaujolais

STEAK WITH GREEN PEPPERCORNS
(TOURNEDOS AU POIVRE VERT)

Serves 6

6 tournedos

20 g/¾ oz butter

100 g/3½ oz green peppercorns (fresh, freeze-dried or pickled in vinegar or brine)

250 ml/9 fl oz crème fraîche, or thick, creamy yogurt (do not use non-fat varieties as these will separate in the cooking)

salt

Seize the flavour of the steaks by frying in the butter over a medium heat for 1-2 minutes on each side, depending on how rare or well done you like them. Season with salt, place them on a serving dish, cover, and leave to "relax" but keep them warm.

Deglaze the meat pan over a medium heat with 2 tablespoons boiling water, scraping the cooking residue from the sides. Finely grind two teaspoons of the green peppercorns in a spice grinder or with a mortar and pestle. Add the ground and whole peppercorns and the crème fraîche or yogurt to the pan and simmer gently, stirring constantly, until the sauce has a smooth, creamy consistency. Season to taste with salt, pour over the tournedos and serve immediately.

Note Tournedos are small, round thick slices of steak from the small end of fillet or tenderloin. In France, they are barded (i.e. larded or covered with fat bacon) and tied with string. This quality of meat should be cooked rare or very rare and the slices should always be about at least 2 cm/¾ inch thick.

menu idea | macaroni gratin | lemon tartlets
serve with | a good bordeaux or burgundy

BEEF SIRLOIN OR RUMP STEAKS WITH RED-WINE SAUCE (ENTRECÔTES À LA BORDELAISE)

Serves 6

6 large shallots

500 ml/18 fl oz/2¼ cups red Bordeaux

100 g/3½ oz butter

2-3 steaks, about 500-625 g/1¼ lb each

1 tablespoon light vegetable oil

salt and freshly ground black pepper

Peel and finely chop the shallots, and put them in a small pan with the red wine. Leave to simmer over a medium heat until the liquid has reduced by half. Season with salt and stir in the butter, a knob at a time. Season with pepper and keep warm.

Heat a frying pan, brush the steaks with the vegetable oil and fry over a medium heat for 2-3 minutes on each side, depending on how thick they are and whether you prefer them rare or medium rare. When the meat is cooked, cut into thick slices and serve with sautéed potatoes or French beans. Serve the sauce separately.

Note If you leave the meat to "relax" for a few minutes, it will more tender and succulent.

menu idea | spinach salad with goat's cheese | cannelés
serve with | any good bordeaux

BLANQUETTE DE VEAU

Serves 6

1.5 kg/3 lb veal (a mix
from the breast and
shoulder, or shoulder only)
cut into 5-cm/2-inch cubes

3 large carrots

4 leeks

1 onion, peeled and stuck
with a clove

1 bouquet garni (3 sprigs
parsley, 1 celery stalk, 1 bay
leaf and 1 thyme sprig)

peppercorns and coarse
salt

30 g/1 oz butter

30 g/1 oz plain
(all-purpose) flour

250 ml/9 fl oz thick crème
fraîche or thick creamy
yogurt

2 egg yolks

juice of 1 lemon

salt and freshly ground
black pepper

To serve: Basmati rice

Rinse the meat under running water and place in a large
covered cooking pot or flameproof casserole. Peel and roughly
chop the carrots and leeks, and add to the pot with the onion,
bouquet garni, a few peppercorns and a pinch or two of salt.

Cover with water and bring to the boil, removing any scum.
Leave to simmer over a low heat for about 2$\frac{1}{2}$ hours or until
tender, removing any additional scum as it rises.

Just before serving, melt the butter in a small pan, add the flour
and mix to a smooth paste. Add 3 ladles of the cooking stock
and simmer for a few minutes, stirring constantly until
thickened and smooth.

Beat the crème fraîche with the egg yolks, gradually adding the
lemon juice, in a bowl. Add gradually to the sauce base in the
small pan, stirring constantly, and allow to thicken over gentle
heat. Season with salt and pepper.

Drain the veal and vegetables – keeping the stock for use in
other recipes (see below) – and arrange on a serving dish.
Cover with the sauce (or serve separately) and serve with rice.

Note If possible, cook the veal 24 hours in advance so that you
can remove the solidified fat from the surface of the stock the
next day.

menu idea | fruity duck salad | apple rabotes

serve with | bergerac

LAMB CHOPS
(CÔTELETTES D'AGNEAU)

Serves 6

1.5 kg/3 lb white mushrooms

75 g/3 oz butter

2 tablespoons plain (all-purpose) flour

200 ml/7 fl oz/³/₄ cup milk

nutmeg

12 lamb chops

1 tablespoon light vegetable oil

100 ml/3¹/₂ fl oz/¹/₂ cup thick crème fraîche, or thick, creamy yogurt

salt and freshly ground black pepper

Wipe the mushrooms with absorbent kitchen paper or a damp cloth (don't rinse) and slice thinly. Heat half the butter in a pan and cook the mushrooms over low heat. When they have released all their juices, drain – but keep the liquid – and process in an electric blender to obtain as fine a purée as possible.

Melt the rest of the butter in a pan, stir in the flour and leave to cook for 2 minutes over a medium heat, without letting it brown. Gradually add the milk and cooking juices from the mushrooms, stirring continuously, until the sauce thickens. Season with salt and pepper, and a little freshly grated nutmeg. When the sauce has a smooth, creamy consistency, add the mushroom purée and leave to simmer over a very low heat.

Meanwhile, coat the chops with a little oil, and season with salt and pepper on both sides. Heat a frying pan or a griddle pan and cook the chops over moderate heat, for about 1¹/₂ minutes on each side, depending on how thick they are and your preference for "pink" or well-done lamb. Cook the chops in two batches and serve straight from the pan so that they're not left standing – lamb chops are quite fatty and the fat congeals rapidly as they cool.

Just before serving, add the crème fraîche to the mushroom sauce and serve with the lamb chops.

menu idea | fruity duck salad | floating islands
serve with | any good red bordeaux

LAMB CURRY
(CURRY D'AGNEAU)

Serves 6

1 tablespoon fresh ginger, grated

pinch powdered saffron

2 garlic cloves, crushed

500 g/17 fl oz/2 cups plain yogurt

1.5 kg/3 lb neck of lamb, cut into cubes

4 tomatoes

4 onions

1 large apple (Bramley, Granny Smith, Braeburn...)

2 tablespoons olive oil

1 tablespoon curry powder

250 ml/9 fl oz/1 cup, plus extra, coconut milk

salt and freshly ground black pepper

To serve: desiccated coconut (optional)

Mix the ginger, saffron and crushed garlic with the yogurt and marinate the lamb in the mixture for 1 hour.

Peel the tomatoes by plunging into boiling water for 2 minutes to loosen the skins, remove the seeds and mash the flesh. Peel and thinly slice the onions; peel and cut the apple into small sections.

Remove the meat from the marinade and brown in the olive oil over medium heat for about 10 minutes, and then add the onions. When the onions are transparent, add the curry powder and, after a few minutes, the tomatoes, apple and coconut milk. Stir to mix, cover, and leave to simmer for 40 minutes, adding a little more coconut milk if necessary. Season to taste with salt before serving.

Sprinkle the curry with desiccated coconut (optional) and serve with Basmati rice, raita (yogurt with cucumber and mint), thin slices of mango, pineapple or banana, and various chutneys.

menu idea | chilled tomato soup | lemon mousse
serve with | red rioja or chianti

LAMB CASSEROLE À LA NORMANDE
(DAUBE D'AGNEAU À LA NORMANDE)

Serves 6

500 g/1 lb onions

3 carrots

3 leeks

1 litre/1¾ pints/4 cups cider

1.5 kg/3lb shoulder of lamb, cut into cubes

2 cloves

3 apples

6 potatoes

50 g/2 oz butter

nutmeg

salt and freshly ground black pepper

Peel and thinly slice the onions, carrots and leeks and marinate in the cider with the lamb and cloves for 24 hours.

The next day, peel and slice the apples and potatoes. Drain the lamb and marinated vegetables – keeping the marinade. Melt the butter in a frying pan and brown the meat.

Preheat the oven to 150°C (300°F), gas mark 2.

Put a layer of marinated vegetables, a layer of meat, a layer of apples and a layer of potatoes in an earthenware or cast-iron casserole. Season with salt and pepper, and a little freshly grated nutmeg. Repeat the layers until you have used up all the ingredients, finishing with a layer of potatoes. Pour on the cider used for the marinade, cover and cook in the preheated oven for 2½ hours. Check the seasoning and reduce for a few minutes over moderate heat if there is too much liquid.

Note For an even better result, you can seal the lid of the earthenware casserole with a paste made from 2 parts flour, 1 part coarse salt and a little water.

menu idea | watercress soup | chestnut delicieux
serve with | merlot, cabernet sauvignon

BRAISED LEG OF LAMB WITH MUSHROOMS
(GIGOT D'AGNEAU BRAISÉ AUX CÈPES)

Serves 6

1 leg of lamb, weighing
about 1.5 kg/3 lb

2 tablespoons goose fat,
or oil

300 ml/½ pint/1¼ cups
vegetable stock

1 thyme sprig

1 bay leaf

600 g/1 lb fresh ceps
(porcini mushrooms)

3 tablespoons oil

1 garlic clove, peeled

few parsley sprigs

salt and freshly ground
black pepper

Brown the leg of lamb in the goose fat or oil, in a deep cooking pot or flameproof casserole, turning to make sure it is well browned on all sides. Add the stock, thyme and bay leaf, cover and leave to simmer over a low heat for 40 minutes.

While the lamb is simmering, wipe the ceps with absorbent kitchen paper or a damp cloth – don't rinse. Remove the base of the stalk and any damaged or discoloured pieces, and slice thinly. Heat the oil in a large frying pan and fry the mushrooms for 3 minutes or until they have released all their juices. Drain and keep to one side.

Finely chop the garlic clove and parsley. When the lamb has been simmering for 40 minutes, add the ceps, garlic and parsley. Leave uncovered and increase the heat to reduce the sauce.

Cook for a further 10 minutes, to allow the flavour to develop, check the meat is done with a sharp skewer and serve straight from the cooking pot.

Note Sautéed potatoes or potatoes mashed or puréed with garlic and goat's cheese, Cheddar or Edam make an ideal accompaniment.

menu idea | watercress soup | raspberry delight
serve with | any good red bordeaux, merlot

ROAST LEG OF LAMB
(GIGOT RÔTI DES ALPILLES)

Serves 6

1 leg of lamb, about
1.5 kg/3 lb

2 tablespoons olive oil

20 garlic cloves

a few sprigs fresh thyme,
rosemary, oregano and
savory, chopped

1 tablespoon coarse salt

Rub the leg of lamb with the oil. Peel 3 of the garlic cloves and cut in half lengthways. Make six small cuts in the leg of lamb with a sharp knife and insert ½ garlic clove into each cut. Sprinkle the lamb with the chopped herbs and marinate in the refrigerator for 12 hours.

Remove the lamb from the refrigerator for an hour or two before cooking and place in a roasting pan.

Preheat the oven to 240°C (475°F), gas mark 9.

Peel the remaining garlic cloves and arrange around the leg of lamb. Drizzle with olive oil, season with salt and pepper, and cook in the preheated oven for 30 minutes. Turn off the heat, and leave the meat to "relax" for 10 minutes with the door open. The meat will be beautifully pink and tender. Cut into slices and serve with the cooking juices.

Unless you (and your guests) like a lot of garlic, put most of the cloves around the leg of lamb.

Serve the lamb with French beans and baked tomato halves sprinkled with the cooked garlic, parsley and breadcrumbs, or with a potato gratin.

menu idea | pissaladière | quick ice-cream
serve with | beaujolais, chianti, red rioja

LAMB STEW GARNISHED WITH SPRING VEGETABLES (NAVARIN PRINTANIER)

Serves 6

350 g/12 oz baby carrots

350 g/12 oz baby turnips

1 bunch small spring onions (scallions)

250 g/9 oz fresh French beans

150 g/5 oz/1 cup shelled fresh broad (fava) beans

75 g/3 oz butter, chilled

1 tablespoon olive oil

1.5 kg/3 lb neck of lamb, cut into cubes

150 ml/¹/₄ pint/²/₃ cup stock or water

200 g/7 oz/1¹/₂ cups shelled fresh peas

2 sprigs fresh tarragon or ¹/₂ bunch fresh chervil, chopped

1 teaspoon sugar

salt and freshly ground black pepper

Peel or scrub the carrots and turnips, and leave whole; peel the onions, leaving 2 cm/³/₄ inch green stem; top and tail the French beans and cut into small sections. Unless the broad beans are young, remove the tough outer skin by bringing the beans to the boil in a pan of cold water, draining and removing skins.

Melt 25 g/1 oz of the butter with the olive oil in a deep pan or flameproof casserole and brown the lamb pieces on all sides. When they are nicely browned, add the carrots, turnips and onions. Season with salt and pepper, cover and cook over a very low heat for 45 minutes, checking that the ingredients don't stick to the pan and adding stock or water if necessary.

While the meat is cooking, cook the French beans in boiling salted water for 7 minutes, drain and keep to one side. After 35 minutes, add the peas, half the tarragon or chervil, and sugar to the cooking pot or casserole. Leave to cook for 5 minutes and then add the broad beans and, 5 minutes later, the French beans. Leave to cook for a further 5 minutes and then remove from the heat and add the rest of the herbs and butter.

Serve with new potatoes.

Note Most of the vegetables can be replaced with other seasonal vegetables, for example artichoke hearts or asparagus tips.

The flavour of this dish, once cooked, like most made by stewing meat, improves by letting stand overnight and gently reheating.

menu idea | omelette with goat's cheese and fresh mint | poached pears with blackcurrants
serve with | any good red bordeaux, merlot

TAJINE OF LAMB WITH AUBERGINES (EGGPLANTS)
(TAGINE D'AGNEAU AUX AUBERGINES)

Serves 6

1.2 kg/2½ lb neck or shoulder of lamb, cut into cubes

4 tablespoons olive oil

2 kg/4lb aubergines (eggplants)

500 g/1 lb onions

1 garlic clove, crushed

1 preserved lemon (or 1 fresh lemon), cut into small pieces

1 teaspoon ground cumin

1 teaspoon ground turmeric

salt and freshly ground black pepper

To serve: black olives, fresh coriander (cilantro), flat-leaf parsley (optional)

Fry the meat in 2 tablespoons of the olive oil over a moderate heat for 10 minutes, until browned on all sides.

Rinse and roughly chop the aubergines (eggplants) and peel and slice the onions, and then fry in the remaining oil in a deep pan or flameproof casserole. Add the lamb, garlic, lemon, spices, salt and pepper. Cover and leave to cook for about 1 hour.

The tajine is cooked when the meat is soft and starts to break up.

Note Preserved lemons are preserved in brine and can be bought from a delicatessen or specialist greengrocer. If you can't find any, use a fresh lemon instead.

If you prefer a more intense flavour, you can increase the amount of turmeric, cumin and lemon used, and serve the tajine garnished with black olives and sprinkled with fresh coriander and flat-leaf parsley.

menu idea | carrot and cumin salad | quetsch plums in syrup
serve with | red rioja or good beaujolais

PORK AND VEGETABLE STEW
(POTÉE LORRAINE)

6 small carrots

6 small French turnips

3 leeks

3 celery stalks

6 potatoes

1 green cabbage

1 upper shoulder slightly salted pork

250 g/9 oz fresh, lean breast of pork

1 smoked sausage, for cooking

peppercorns

To serve: mustard and gherkins

Peel and/or rinse the vegetables (except the cabbage) and leave whole. Discard the outer leaves of the cabbage, cut into quarters and rinse under cold running water.

Put the shoulder and breast of pork and the vegetables (except the potatoes) in a large cooking pan with a few peppercorns. Cover with cold water and bring to the boil. Partially cover and leave to simmer over low heat for 2 hours, removing any scum that rises.

After 1½ hours, add the potatoes and smoked sausage pricked with a needle.

Drain the meat and vegetables (keeping the stock for use in other recipes) and arrange on a serving dish. Serve with mustard and gherkins.

Note Italian mostarda (spicy, aromatic candied fruits preserved in a mustard syrup) is particularly good with this dish and can be found, in jars, in delicatessens and good supermarkets.

menu idea | Nancy macaroons
serve with | pinot noir

GAMMON STEAKS WITH WHITE BEANS
(JAMBON DE VENDÉE AUX MOGETTES)

Serves 6

4 x 400 g/14 oz cans
white beans (haricot,
Great Northern, navy)

3 onions

3 garlic cloves

3 tomatoes

2 tablespoons olive oil

1 sprig fresh thyme

1 bay leaf

50 g/5 oz butter

6 thick gammon steaks

salt and freshly ground
black pepper

Rinse the canned beans and leave to drain in a sieve or colander.

Peel and thinly slice the onions and garlic. Peel the tomatoes by plunging into boiling water for 2 minutes to loosen the skins, and remove the seeds. Put the oil in a deep pan or flameproof casserole and gently fry the onions, garlic and tomatoes over a very low heat for 10 minutes.

Add the beans and herbs and add sufficient water to allow the ingredients to simmer gently together for about 20 minutes, without sticking, to create a substantial sauce. Season to taste with salt and pepper. Check regularly to see that the liquid level is not drying out. If there is too much liquid in the cooking pot, remove the lid and increase the heat. The beans should still hold their shape when cooked – soft but not mushy.

Melt the butter in a frying pan and cook the gammon steaks for 2 minutes on each side. Remove the herbs from the beans before serving with the pan-fried ham.

menu idea | English shrimps in cider | lemon mousse
serve with | merlot

CHICKEN À LA BASQUAISE
(POULET BASQUAISE)

Serves 6

2 tomatoes

1 kg/2 lb red or green
(bell) peppers

3 small, mild green chilli
peppers

3 onions

1 garlic clove

4 tablespoons olive oil

1 large chicken, cut into
pieces

mild chilli pepper

salt

Peel the tomatoes by plunging into boiling water for 2 minutes to loosen the skins, remove the seeds and chop roughly. Rinse the (bell) peppers, remove the seeds and membrane and cut into thin strips. Rinse the chilli peppers and cut into thin strips, discarding the seeds, or reserving some to taste, if you don't want the dish to have too hot a flavour.

Peel the onions and garlic and fry lightly in the oil in a deep pan or flameproof casserole. Add the chicken pieces and brown on all sides over a fairly high heat. Then add the peppers and tomatoes, and season with salt and a pinch or two of chilli pepper, to taste. Cover and leave to simmer for 45-50 minutes, depending on the size of the chicken pieces, checking at regular intervals to make sure they don't stick to the bottom of the pan. Adjust the seasoning and serve immediately with rice.

Note The peppers will have more flavour and be more digestible if you cook them in a preheated oven at 200°C (400°F), gas mark 6, for 20 minutes, then seal into a plastic bag to cool for a short while. This will also allow you to peel the skins easily.

Instead of using olive oil to brown the chicken, you can melt 200 g/7 oz fatty country bacon or cured Bayonne ham, cut into diced pieces.

menu idea | eggs mimosa | clafoutis with black cherries
serve with | côtes du rhône

186

CHICKEN WITH TARRAGON
(POULET À L'ESTRAGON)

Serves 6

1 chicken, about 2.2 kg/5lb

65 g/2½ oz butter

1 bay leaf

200 g/7 oz small salad
onions, peeled

200 ml/7 fl oz/¾ cup
white wine

3 sprigs fresh tarragon,
chopped

2 tablespoons plain
(all-purpose) flour

salt and freshly ground
black pepper

Brown the chicken in 30 g/1 oz of the butter, in a deep cooking pot or flameproof casserole, turning so that it is browned on all sides. Season with salt and pepper, add the bay leaf, salad onions and white wine. Cover and leave to cook over moderate heat for 1 hour. Check the cooking progress regularly.

Blend the rest of the butter with the chopped tarragon and flour. When the chicken is cooked − check by piercing the thickest part of the thigh with a thin skewer (the cooking juices should be golden and clear, not pink) − remove from the pot and set aside to keep warm. Remove the bay leaf, stir the tarragon butter mixture into the liquid contents in the cooking pot to thicken the sauce and then bring to the boil twice. Serve immediately with fresh peas and oven-baked potatoes.

Note To reduce the cooking time to 20−30 minutes, joint the chicken before you cook it.

menu idea | cheese puffs | dark chocolate mousse
serve with | sauvignon blanc

NORMANDY CHICKEN
(POULET VALLÉE D'AUGE)

Serves 6

1 chicken, about 2.2 kg/5lb cut into 8 pieces

2 tablespoons plain (all-purpose) flour

75 g/3 oz butter

100 ml/3½ fl oz/½ cup Calvados

10 small salad onions, peeled

2–3 crisp, slightly sharp apples (Granny Smith, Braeburn, Cox's Orange Pippin)

250 ml/9 fl oz/1 cup thick double (heavy) cream

1 egg yolk

salt and freshly ground black pepper

Coat the chicken pieces in seasoned flour. Melt 25 g/1 oz of the butter in a deep pan or flameproof casserole and brown the chicken pieces on all sides, over medium heat. When the chicken is nicely browned, pour over the Calvados and set alight. Reduce the heat, cover the pan and leave the chicken to "sweat". After 15 minutes, add the salad onions.

Peel and thickly slice the apples. Melt the remaining butter in a frying pan and sauté the apples until brown.

When the chicken pieces are cooked (after about 40 minutes), arrange them on a serving dish, surrounded by the sautéed apples, and keep warm. Pour the cream into the pan used for the chicken, stir in the egg yolk, and allow to thicken, taking care not to let the mixture boil. Check the seasoning and pour the sauce over the chicken. Serve immediately.

Note To make coating the chicken easier, put the seasoned flour in a large freezer bag with 2–3 chicken pieces, hold the bag closed and shake well so that the pieces are evenly coated with flour.

menu idea | apple crumble
serve with | mâcon blanc, oaked chardonnay

CHICKEN À LA FORESTIÈRE (POULET SAUTÉ À LA FORESTIÈRE)

Serves 6

75 g/3 oz butter

150 g/5 oz smoked bacon, diced

1 chicken, about 2.5 kg/ 5½ lb, cut into pieces

200 g/7 oz chanterelle mushrooms

3 shallots

100 ml/3½ fl oz/½ cup dry white wine

6 large potatoes

salt and freshly ground black pepper

To serve: a few sprigs flat-leaf parsley, chopped

Melt 25 g/1 oz of the butter in a deep pan or flameproof casserole and fry the diced bacon over a medium heat for a few minutes. Remove the bacon, and brown the chicken pieces on all sides. Wipe the mushrooms with absorbent kitchen paper or a damp cloth (don't rinse) and cut into two or three, depending on their size. Peel and finely chop the shallots.

Add the mushrooms, shallots and fried bacon to the chicken pieces in the pan and season with salt and pepper. Cover, and cook over a medium heat for about 20 minutes, checking to ensure that nothing is sticking, then remove the lid, add the white wine and continue cooking without the lid for a further 20 minutes.

While the chicken is cooking, peel and roughly chop the potatoes, and bring to the boil in a pan of salted water, remove from the heat and drain well. Melt the remaining butter in a deep frying pan and sauté the chopped potatoes.

Put the chicken with the bacon and vegetable garnish in a serving dish with the sautéed potatoes and serve sprinkled with chopped parsley.

Note Instead of chanterelle mushrooms, you can use any wild or exotic mushrooms that you prefer. Good quality button mushrooms are a good alternative.

menu idea | autumn salad | orange savarin
serve with | any good dry red

OVEN-BAKED CHICKEN WITH GARLIC (POULET AUX 40 GOUSSES D'AIL)

Serves 6

1 chicken, about 2.2 kg/5lb

1 sprig each fresh parsley, sage, thyme, rosemary, chopped

1 bay leaf

150 ml/¼ pint olive oil

40 garlic cloves (don't be frightened!)

salt and freshly ground black pepper

To serve: slices of toasted crusty bread, green salad

Preheat the oven to 190°C (375°F), gas mark 5.

Season the inside of the chicken with salt and pepper. Place in an ovenproof dish, sprinkle with the chopped herbs and bayleaf and pour over the olive oil.

Arrange the unpeeled garlic cloves around the chicken. Season with salt and pepper.

Cover the dish with baking foil and roast in the oven for 1½ hours. When cooked – check by piercing the thickest part of the thigh with a knife or skewer (the cooking juices should be golden and clear, not pink) – the chicken should be soft, like the garlic.

Serve immediately with slices of toasted crusty bread (for spreading with crushed garlic cloves) and a green salad seasoned with olive oil and thyme.

Note The chicken will have a more concentrated flavour if cooked in a covered cast-iron or earthenware casserole.

menu idea | mussel salad with curry sauce | quick ice-cream
serve with | strong white

GUINEA FOWL WITH VANILLA
(PINTADE À LA VANILLE)

Serves 6

2 vanilla pods (beans)

60 g/2 oz butter

2 small guinea fowl, about 1.2 kg/2½ lb each

1 kg/2 lb large purple figs

salt and freshly ground black pepper

To serve: polenta or Thai rice

Preheat the oven to 200°C (400°F), gas mark 6.

Split open the vanilla pods with the point of a sharp knife and remove the black seeds. Use a fork to soften the butter and mix in the vanilla seeds and a little salt.

Place the guinea fowl on an ovenproof dish, coat with vanilla butter and roast in the oven for 20 minutes.

Rinse and quarter the figs and, after 20 minutes, arrange around the guinea fowl and baste with the cooking juices. Continue cooking for another 20 minutes.

Cut up the guinea fowl and arrange on a serving dish.

Serve with polenta or Thai rice with pistachios.

Note When figs are out of season, you can use fresh pears and add 200 ml/7 fl oz/¾ cup sweet white wine to the cooking juices.

menu idea | cream of carrot soup | apple upside-down tart
serve with | cabernet sauvignon, merlot

QUAILS ROASTED IN MUSCAT
(CAILLES RÔTIES AU MUSCAT)

Serves 6

12 quails (bobwhites in
the US), prepared by your
butcher

150 g/5 oz fat bacon slices

1 tablespoon olive oil

150 ml/¼ pint/⅔ cup
Muscat de Rivesaltes (or
any other "naturally sweet
white wine" made from the
Muscat grape)

50 g/2 oz butter

salt and freshly ground
black pepper

To serve: grapes,
preferably Muscat
(optional)

Season the quails with salt and pepper, wrap each one in a strip
of fat bacon and tie with string.

Heat the oil in a deep pan or flameproof casserole and brown
the quails on all sides over a medium heat. Reduce the heat,
and continue cooking for 15 minutes. Turning the quails from
time to time.

Remove the quails from the pan and keep warm. Pour the wine
into the pan, scraping any cooking residue from the bottom, add
grapes (if using) halved if large, and bring to the boil. Add the
butter, a knob at a time, and season with a little salt and pepper.

Arrange the quails on a serving dish, cover with the sauce, and
serve immediately.

menu idea | artichokes à la grecque | crêpes Suzette
serve with | merlot, shiraz

DUCK À L'ORANGE
(CANARD À L'ORANGE)

Serves 6

1 onion

1 carrot

25 g/1 oz butter

1 young duck, about
2.5 kg/5 lb

200 ml/7 fl oz/¾ cup
dry white wine

200 ml/7 fl oz/¾ cup
vegetable or chicken
stock, or 1 stock cube
dissolved in 200 ml/7 fl oz/
¾ cup warm water

3 oranges

salt and freshly ground
black pepper

Peel and thinly slice the onion and carrot, and lightly fry in the butter in a deep cooking pot or flameproof casserole. Add the duck and brown on all sides over a fairly high heat. Season with salt and pepper.

When the duck is nicely browned on all sides, add the white wine, reduce the heat and continue cooking for 10 minutes. Then add the stock, cover and leave to simmer over a low heat for 1 hour.

In the meantime remove the rind from one of the oranges with a zester or vegetable peeler, cut into fine strips and blanch in boiling water for 1 minute. Squeeze the juice from the peeled orange and then thinly slice the other two oranges and remove the pips. When the duck has been simmering for 1 hour, add the orange juice, rind and orange slices to the pot and mix carefully.

Continue cooking (uncovered) for 15 minutes over a high heat to reduce the liquid and caramelize the oranges and the skin of the duck. Check that the duck is cooked through by piercing the thickest part of the bird with a fine skewer; the juices should run clear. Serve immediately with puréed celery.

Note Try to find untreated oranges – buy organic if possible.
You can use port or a young Banyuls instead of white wine.

menu idea | crunchy vegetable salad | lemon mousse
serve with | any good red bordeaux

DUCK WITH BABY TURNIPS
(CANARD AUX NAVETS)

Serves 6

1 young duck, about 2.5 kg/
5½ lb

50 g/2 oz butter

15 small salad onions

500 g/1 lb baby turnips

1 teaspoon sugar

salt and freshly ground
black pepper

Gently brown the duck in 20 g/³⁄₄ oz of the butter, over medium heat, in a flameproof casserole. When it is nicely browned, lower the heat, cover and continue cooking for 1 hour.

While it is cooking, peel the onions and turnips and put them in a deep frying pan with the rest of the butter, sugar and a little salt and pepper. Cover and leave to sweat over a very low heat for 15 minutes, checking at regular intervals to make sure the vegetables don't stick to the pan and adding a little water if necessary. Remove the lid after 15 minutes and, when the vegetables are tender, increase the heat so that they caramelize.

Pour off all the duck fat from the casserole and add the caramelized turnips and onions. Turn off the heat, cover and leave to stand for 5 minutes to allow the meat to "relax" and the vegetables to take on the flavour of the duck.

Serve immediately.

menu idea | mushroom salad with yogurt | sugar tart
serve with | any good red burgundy

FILLETS OF DUCK BREAST WITH CEPS
(MAGRETS DE CANARD AUX CÈPES)

Serves 6

1.2 kg/2½ lb fresh ceps
(porcini mushrooms)

4 tablespoons light
vegetable oil, for cooking

2 garlic cloves

1 bunch parsley

3 large duck breasts, with
the skin attached

salt and freshly ground
black pepper

Wipe the mushrooms with absorbent kitchen paper or a damp cloth (don't rinse) and chop roughly. Heat 2 tablespoons of the oil in a large frying pan and, when it's nice and hot, throw in the mushrooms. Cook until they have released all their natural juices, then drain well.

Peel and finely chop the garlic and chop the parsley. Make 3-4 slits in the skin of the duck breasts and cook (skinside down) in a separate frying pan, over a medium heat, for 7 minutes. Discard the fat released during cooking, turn the breasts and continue cooking for 5 minutes. Turn off the heat and cover.

Heat the rest of the oil in the pan used for the mushrooms and add the drained ceps. Add the chopped garlic and parsley, season with salt and pepper, and fry for a few minutes.

Slice the duck fillets and arrange on a serving dish, surrounded by mushrooms.

Note The cooking times given are for medium fillets. When ceps (porcini mushrooms) are out of season, use frozen or preserved mushrooms – the ones preserved in oil are best.

menu idea | Landes-style smoked duck salad | autumn-fruit compote
serve with | merlot, shiraz

ROAST GOOSE WITH PEARS
(OIE RÔTIE AUX POIRES)

Serves 6

8 large, firm pears

1 small goose, about 3 kg/
6½ lb

30 g/1 oz sugar

salt and freshly ground
black pepper

Peel and core 2 of the pears, cut into diced pieces and use to stuff the goose. Prick the skin all over with a skewer, especially below the legs, so the fat can be released during cooking.

Rub the outside of the goose with salt, place on a rack in a roasting pan and put straight into a cold oven set at 150°C (300°F), gas mark 2. Leave to cook for 3 hours. While it is cooking, baste the goose at frequent intervals with the fat released, pouring any surplus into a container (it will come in handy for other recipes and makes wonderful roast potatoes) when there is too much in the pan.

After 2½ hours, pour off the remaining fat and arrange the other 6 pears – peeled but left whole – around the goose. Sprinkle with sugar, salt and pepper, and drizzle with a little of the goose fat. Increase the oven temperature to 180°C (350°F), gas mark 4 (a little higher if the goose has not browned enough), and leave to cook until the pears are tender and caramelized.

Place the goose and pears on a serving dish.

Pour off any fat remaining in the roasting pan and deglaze with 100 ml/3½ fl oz/½ cup hot water. Leave to boil on the hob, add the juices released when the goose is carved and serve separately in a sauceboat.

Note You can use a large free-range duck for this recipe instead of a goose.

menu idea | watercress soup | Yule log
serve with | côte de beaune, shiraz

ESCALOPES OF FOIE GRAS WITH APPLES
(ESCALOPES DE FOIE GRAS AUX POMMES)

Serves 6

1 kg/2 lb crisp, slightly
sharp apples (Granny
Smith, Braeburn, Cox's
Orange Pippin…)

50 g/2 oz butter

1 whole duck foie gras,
cut into 6 slices

3 teaspoons plain
(all-purpose) flour

150 ml/¼ pint/⅔ cup
grape juice

salt and freshly ground
black pepper

To serve: A few fresh
chives, chopped

Peel and core the apples and cut into fairly thick sections.
Melt the butter in a frying pan and brown the apples for about
15 minutes and keep warm.

Season the slices of foie gras with salt and pepper, and carefully
coat with flour. Dry-fry them for 1 minute on each side in a very
hot, non-stick frying pan and then remove from the heat.

Arrange the apple sections on the individual plates and top
with an escalope. Deglaze the pan with the grape juice, making
sure any cooking residue is dissolved, and then reduce slightly.
Pour the sauce over the escalopes and serve immediately,
sprinkled with chopped chives.

Note To make sure the escalopes are nice and firm, and don't
break up during cooking, put them in the freezer for 10 minutes
before you start preparing this dish.

To strengthen the sauce, you can add a dash of sherry vinegar
to the grape juice, or deglaze the pan with Sauternes or Banyuls.

menu idea | warm chestnut salad | Yule log
serve with | gewurztraminer

208

RABBIT WITH MUSTARD
(LAPIN À LA MOUTARDE)

Serves 6

1 rabbit, cut into 6 pieces

3 tablespoons mustard

6 sage leaves

6 thin slices smoked bacon

200 ml/7 fl oz/³⁄₄ cup single (light) cream

1 tablespoon olive oil

To serve: small baked potatoes or brown rice, green salad

Preheat the oven to 190°C (375°F), gas mark 5.

Coat the rabbit pieces with the mustard, place a sage leaf on each piece, and wrap in a slice of smoked bacon. Place the rabbit pieces in a greased ovenproof dish, sprinkle with 3 tablespoons water and cook in the oven for 35 minutes.

Remove the rabbit from the oven and arrange on a serving dish. Deglaze the cooking dish with the cream and pour over the rabbit pieces.

Serve with small potatoes cooked in their skins and a green salad, or brown rice.

menu idea | spinach tart | rhubarb and orange compote

serve with | shiraz, or any fruity red

RABBIT WITH GARLIC AND ROSEMARY
(LAPIN À L'AIL ET AU ROMARIN)

Serves 6

1 kg/2¼ lb tomatoes

1 rabbit, cut into 6 pieces

10 garlic cloves, peeled

3 sprigs rosemary

4 tablespoons olive oil

salt and freshly ground
black pepper

To serve: **Tagliatelle or
courgettes (zucchini)
au gratin**

Preheat the oven to 200°C (400°F), gas mark 6.

Peel the tomatoes by plunging into boiling water for 2 minutes
to loosen the skins, remove the seeds and crush the flesh.
Spread the tomatoes over the base of an ovenproof dish and
top with the rabbit pieces, whole garlic cloves and rosemary
leaves. Drizzle with olive oil, and season with salt and pepper.

Cook in oven for 30 minutes. When the rabbit is cooked, it
should be crisp and golden on the outside and tender on the
inside. Serve immediately with fresh tagliatelle or courgettes
(zucchini) au gratin.

Note You can use canned tomatoes if preferred. You can also
cover each piece of rabbit with tapenade before arranging it on
the bed of tomatoes.

menu idea | Provençal tomato soup | French doughnuts

serve with | beaujolais, red rioja

NOT ONLY DO FRESHWATER AND SALTWATER FISH COME FROM DIFFERENT ENVIRONMENTS, BUT THEY ALSO TASTE DIFFERENT. WE ARE SO ACCUSTOMED TO THE IODIZED FLAVOUR OF SEA FISH THAT FRESHWATER FISH MAY SEEM RATHER BLAND WITH A STRONG MUDDY AFTERTASTE. IN ADDITION, ALTHOUGH THERE IS A WIDE VARIETY OF SALTWATER FISH TO CHOOSE FROM, THERE ARE FEW REALLY FLAVOURSOME FRESHWATER FISH AND THESE ARE RARELY STOCKED BY FISHMONGERS: LAKE AND RIVER FISHING IS HIGHLY LOCALIZED AND MAY BE RESTRICTED TO THE REGION'S RESTAURATEURS.

FRESHWATER FISH

• Pike, carp, char, perch, pikeperch and trout are all delicious freshwater fish that make an enjoyable meal.

• Mixed "estuary" fish, like eels and shad, deserve special mention. The eggs of these fish hatch in the sea, then the young adults swim upstream or remain in stagnant water.

SALTWATER FISH

There is a wide choice of saltwater fish. The most important thing to remember when buying fish is that freshness counts for more than any preconceived recipe.

BUYING FISH

• Choose your fish supplier carefully and become a regular. Make a point of thanking them if they fillet an inexpensive fish.

• Check out the fish counters in large supermarkets. Some deal direct with wholesale fish merchants and guarantee a high turnover due to their large customer base.

• Look for certain give-away signs: fresh fish should smell of the sea (not chlorine), their skin should be shiny from head to tail, their eyes should be clear, and they should be firm to the touch.

• If you can, it is better to have the fish freshly filleted for you or, steaks cut from a whole body. Avoid buying fillets or pre-cut chunks or steaks if there are blood spots around the backbone.

Approximate amount per person

• Fillet: 175 g/6 oz

• Steak or chunk: 200 g/7 oz

• Smoked fish (salmon, halibut, trout: 125 g/4 oz)

• Whole individual fish: 250 g/8 oz

• Large fish (serving 6 people: 2 kg/4 lb)

COOKING METHODS

In court-bouillon

• This classic cooking method was used in traditional recipes for cooking whole hake or salmon in a fish-kettle. If your hob or oven is not large enough to use one of these, it's easy enough to poach fillets, chunks, or small individual fish in a large pan instead. Fillets do not take much cooking: simply immerse them in the simmering court-bouillon, turn off the heat, cover, and they'll be ready in a few minutes.

Steaming

• Steaming is best suited to fish chunks and firm-fleshed fish because softer, more delicate fish can become waterlogged. Choose monkfish (anglerfish), cod, paupiettes of sole or salmon. Season the stock or the fish itself with spices or herbs for added flavour.

In foil

• Cooking fish in foil is probably one of the quickest and easiest methods. It also has the advantage of being clean and virtually fail-safe: all you need are a few herbs in the cavity of the fish, a little seasoning and lemon or lime zest. This a good way to cook individual fish, like trout, mackerel, or salmon steaks, because their cooking times can be estimated.

Braising in the oven

• Braising is a method of baking fish in the oven on a bed of vegetables. The fish is cooked in white wine, stock or another liquid and basted frequently. Use a fairly hot oven, protecting the fish with foil if necessary when you begin cooking. This method is more labour intensive than previous methods and is more "cost-effective" when cooking a large fish for sharing – such as bass, sea bream, or John Dory.

Grilling

• Grilled fish can be cooked quickly on a greased rack. This cooking method is best suited to so-called "fatty" fish: sardines, tuna, salmon, mackerel. The thicker the fish, such as a tuna steak, for example, the lower the heat should be.

In a preheated oven

• A delicious way of cooking thick steaks of tuna or salmon is to preheat the oven to 220°C (425°F), gas mark 7, then turn it off and slowly cook the fish steaks on a greased baking sheet for 10-15 minutes. If the steaks are not too thick or if you like fish cooked medium rare, you can open the oven door slightly after 5 minutes.

À la meunière

• Wipe the fish or fillets and coat them with flour so that they are completely dry. Then shallow-fry, preferably in clarified butter.

Frying

• Prepare the fish in the same way, then plunge into sizzling hot oil. Don't forget to drain it afterwards on absorbent kitchen paper.

ANCHOVY PASTE

(ANCHOÏADE)

Serves 6

about 60 salted anchovies
(fresh or canned)

4 garlic cloves

300 ml/10 fl oz/1¼ cups olive oil

To serve: savoury bread, toast or crudités

Bone the fresh anchovies and cut off the tails. Rinse under cold water to remove any excess salt and dry carefully. Peel the garlic and remove any green sprout. Crush the anchovies and garlic into a smooth paste with a pestle and mortar, then blend in the olive oil. Serve on slices of savoury bread, toast or with crudités.

SORREL SAUCE

15 g/½ oz butter

2 shallots, peeled and chopped

1 bunch of sorrel

200 ml/7 fl oz/¾ cup crème fraîche
or thick, creamy yogurt

salt and freshly ground black pepper

Melt the butter over a low heat and gently fry the shallots. Remove the stalks from the sorrel and add to the pan. When it has "melted" to a purée, cover, and cook over a low heat for 7–8 minutes. Fold in the crème fraîche and warm through. Season to taste and serve immediately.

HOLLANDAISE SAUCE

2 tablespoons water

1 teaspoon lemon juice

3 egg yolks

150 g/5 oz butter, at room temperature

salt and freshly ground black pepper

A double boiler is a useful aid in cooking this sauce. Heat the measured water and lemon juice. Remove from the heat, add the egg yolks and beat in a figure 8 motion. Put the pan back over a very low heat and let the mixture thicken while stirring constantly. Remove from the heat again and gradually add the butter in small knobs, one at a time, making sure that it blends smoothly with the sauce after each addition. The sauce should have the same consistency as mayonnaise. Season the sauce to taste, transfer to a bowl and place it in a basin of hot water to keep warm. This sauce will curdle if overheated, so take your time while preparing it.

TARTARE SAUCE

Make some mayonnaise (see recipe p. 102) and add 2 tablespoons of capers, 4 chopped gherkins, some finely chopped parsley, tarragon and chives, and 2 teaspoons of mustard.

WHITE BUTTER SAUCE

(BEURRE BLANC)

125 g/4 oz shallots,

125 ml/4 fl oz/½ cup dry white wine

200 ml/7 fl oz/1 cup white wine vinegar

200 g/7 oz butter, chilled

salt and freshly ground black pepper

Peel and finely chop the shallots. Place in a small pan with the white wine and vinegar and reduce almost completely over a low heat. Remove the pan from the heat and place over a larger one filled with simmering water. Do not let the smaller pan touch the water. Gradually mix in small knobs of the well-chilled butter, beating continuously to obtain a light, creamy sauce. Season to taste with salt and pepper and keep standing over the boiling water after the larger pan has been taken from the heat.

ROUILLE

1 slice of bread, crusts removed

6 garlic cloves

few strands saffron

1 pinch of chilli powder

1 egg yolk

250 ml/8 fl oz olive oil

Soak the bread in a little fish stock or water and process with the garlic, spices and egg yolk in an electric blender. Gradually stir in the olive oil as if making mayonnaise.

MARINATED HERRINGS
(HARENGS MARINÉS)

Serves 6

1 kg/2 lb fresh herring fillets

2 onions

1 bunch of flat-leaf parsley

1 thyme sprig, chopped

2 bay leaves

500 ml/17 fl oz/2 cups white wine

200 ml/7 fl oz/³/₄ cup white wine vinegar

salt and freshly ground black pepper

To serve: crème fraîche or sour cream, potatoes

Rinse the herring fillets in cold water and dry carefully. Lay them in a dish, sprinkling a little salt between each layer, and refrigerate for 2 hours.

Wipe the fish to remove the salt. Peel and thinly slice the onions and spread in an even layer over the bottom of a terrine with some of the chopped parsley, thyme, the bay leaves and a little coarsely ground pepper. Add a layer of herring fillets and continue alternating layers of fish and herbs.

Boil the white wine and the vinegar together for a few minutes and pour into the terrine. Leave to cool, then cover. Marinate for 48 hours in the refrigerator before serving with crème fraîche, together with a salad or boiled new potatoes.

menu idea | leek flamiche | mont-blanc
serve with | well chilled muscadet

SALMON MILLE-FEUILLE
(MILLE-FEUILLE DE SAUMON)

Serves 6

9 large slices of Scottish
smoked salmon

400 ml/14 fl oz/1¾ cups
whipping cream

2-3 teaspoons creamed
horseradish

a few dill sprigs, chopped

50 g/2 oz salmon or
trout roe

a few corn salad leaves
(lambs' tongue or mache)

Cut the salmon into 24 even rectangles or small circles (with a sharp pastry cutter). Lightly whip the cream and stir in the horseradish and half the chopped dill.

Arrange the salmon on the serving plates, alternating 4 layers of salmon with horseradish cream to make a little stack.
Top with a spoonful of roe and garnish with the salad leaves and remaining chopped dill.

Note Choose a good quality Scottish smoked salmon which is not too salty.

menu idea | roast monkfish (anglerfish) | dark chocolate mousse
serve with | riesling, pinot grigio, any dry white

SALMON TARTARE
(TARTARE DE SAUMON)

Serves 6

1 onion

½ bunch flat-leaf parsley

½ bunch of chives

1 kg/2 lb fresh salmon fillet

1 tablespoon Tabasco

4 tablespoons ketchup

2 tablespoons cognac

200 g/7 oz/¾ cup crème fraîche, sour cream, or yogurt

salt and freshly ground black pepper

To serve: lemon or lime quarters and toasted rye bread

Peel and chop the onion, then chop the parsley and chives.

With a sharp knife, finely dice the salmon on a chopping board. Mix with the onion, parsley and chives, then add the Tabasco, ketchup, cognac and crème fraîche. Mix the tartare thoroughly. Season with salt and pepper to taste, and mix again.

Arrange a portion on each plate and serve with lemon or lime quarters and slices of toasted rye bread.

menu idea | courgettes (zucchini) au gratin | tiramisu
serve with | pouilly-fuissé, white rioja

FRESH TUNA CASSEROLE
(THON FRAIS EN COCOTTE)

Serves 6

1 thick fresh tuna steak, about 1.25–1.5 kg/2½–3 lb (or several steaks)

plain (all-purpose) flour

4 tablespoons olive oil

200 ml/7 fl oz/¾ cup dry white wine

1 kg/2 lb tomatoes

3 garlic cloves, peeled and crushed

1 or 2 sprigs thyme

2 bay leaves

2 tablespoons tomato purée (paste)

salt and freshly ground black pepper

To serve: courgettes (zucchini) or fresh tagliatelle and fresh basil

Rinse the tuna, dry with kitchen paper and coat both sides with flour.

Heat the oil in a flameproof casserole and lightly brown the tuna on both sides. When the fish has turned golden brown, cover with the white wine and cook for several minutes. Peel the tomatoes by plunging them in boiling water for 1–2 minutes to loosen the skins. Remove the seeds and chop the flesh. Add the tomatoes to the tuna along with the crushed garlic, thyme sprigs and bay leaves. Season with salt and pepper, cover the casserole and simmer for 30 minutes over a low heat.

Thin the tomato purée with some of the cooking liquid and pour back into the casserole. Cook without covering for several minutes to thicken the sauce. Remove the thyme and bay leaves and serve immediately.

Serve with courgettes (zucchini) or fresh tagliatelle and add some fresh, torn basil leaves at the last minute.

Note When fresh tomatoes are not in season, use canned, peeled plum tomatoes in tomato juice, which have more flavour.

menu idea | crunchy vegetable salad | chocolate refrigerator cake

serve with | any light dry red

ST-JEAN-DE-LUZ TUNA WITH ONIONS
(THON AUX OIGNONS DE SAINT-JEAN-DE-LUZ)

Serves 6

1 kg/2 lb white onions

3 tablespoons olive oil

pinch of sugar

2 tablespoons vinegar

about 1.25 kg/2½ lb tuna

1 garlic clove

salt and freshly ground
black pepper

To serve: long-grain
or Basmati rice

Peel and finely slice the onions. Heat half the olive oil in a flameproof casserole and fry the onions for 30 minutes over a very low heat, until they are transparent. Add the sugar and vinegar and season with salt and pepper.

Scrape the tuna but don't remove the skin. Cut the garlic clove into several slices, make a few small cuts in the tuna with the point of a sharp knife, insert a garlic sliver in each and fry in a separate pan.

When the tuna is golden brown, add to the casserole with the onions. Cook for about 30 minutes over a very low heat, turning after 15 minutes. Serve the tuna surrounded by the onions and white rice.

Note You can also use bonito tuna, which is not as large in diameter but has a more delicate flesh.

menu idea | green pea soup | lemon tartlets
serve with | any crisp dry white

ORIENTAL TUNA STEAK
(STEAK DE THON À L'ORIENTALE)

Serves 6

1 kg/2 lb fresh tuna, one or several steaks

1 thyme sprig

1 tablespoon coriander seeds

1 teaspoon dried oregano

1 small chilli, diced

6–8 tablespoons lemon juice

125 ml/4 fl oz/½ cup white wine

4 tablespoons olive oil

salt and freshly ground black pepper

To serve: tabbouleh

Rinse and dry the tuna.

To make the marinade: shred the thyme and crush the coriander seeds with a pestle and mortar or with the back of a spoon. Mix these flavourings in a deep dish, large enough to take the tuna, with the oregano and diced chilli. Season to taste with salt and pepper. Mix in the lemon juice, white wine and olive oil.

Add the tuna, turn in the marinade, cover and place in the refrigerator for about 1 hour, turning again after 30 minutes.

Drain the tuna and cook for 2 minutes on each side in a preheated non-stick frying pan. Remove from the heat, cover, and leave to stand for 5 minutes before serving.

The cooking time will vary depending on the thickness of the steaks. The skin should be crisp and the flesh rare and very soft. Serve hot or cold, with tabbouleh.

menu idea | Provençal tomato soup | French doughnuts
serve with | pinot grigio, white rioja, mâcon blanc

SALT COD À LA BRESTOISE
(MORUE AUX POIREAUX À LA BRESTOISE)

Serves 6

1 kg/2 lb salt cod

1 kg/2 lb leeks

3 onions

50 g/2oz butter

1 kg/2 lb potatoes, unpeeled

plain (all-purpose) flour

½ bunch of chervil

salt and freshly ground black pepper

Soak the cod for 24 hours, changing the water as often as possible.

Wash and shred the leeks, peel and slice the onions and sweat them together in half the butter for 30 minutes over low heat, without letting them colour. At the same time, boil the potatoes in a pan of salted water. Cook the cod in unsalted water for 5 minutes. Strain, put the cooking liquid to one side and flake the cod, carefully removing all bones.

Sprinkle the mixed leeks and onions with flour and add 200 ml/7 fl oz/¾ cup of fish stock. Mix well, simmer briskly for 5 minutes and add the chervil. Add a little salt – not too much because of the salted cod – and pepper.

Preheat the oven to 180ºC (350ºF), gas mark 4.

Drain, peel and slice the potatoes. Butter a baking dish and spread a layer of potatoes over the bottom. Cover with the flaked cod and top with the leek sauce. Bake for 20 minutes in the preheated oven. Serve immediately.

menu idea | cream of carrot soup | orange savarin
serve with | sylvaner, or any medium dry white

SALT COD BRANDADE
(BRANDADE DE MORUE)

Serves 6

1 kg/2 lb salted cod

250 ml/8 fl oz/1 cup milk

250 ml/8 fl oz/1 cup water

2 bay leaves

150 ml/5 fl oz/²/₃ cup olive oil

250 ml/8 fl oz/1 cup whipping cream

12 thin slices of French bread

freshly ground black pepper

To serve: black olives

Soak the cod for 24 hours, changing the water several times.

Cut into chunks and poach in the milk and measured water, seasoned with bay leaves, over a low heat for 10 minutes. Strain, remove the skin and bones and flake the cod.

Heat half the olive oil very gently over low heat and add the cod, stirring vigorously to obtain a smooth paste.

Warm the cream and blend into the fish paste to form a purée. Season to taste with pepper.

Fry the bread slices in the remaining olive oil. Serve the brandade in a deep dish, garnished with the fried bread and black olives.

menu idea | spinach salad with goat's cheese | gâteau battu
serve with | rosé, pink zinfandel

COD OR SALT COD IN GARLIC MAYONNAISE
(AÏOLI À LA PROVENÇALE)

Serves 6

1.25 kg/2½ lb cod (salt cod,
if available or preferred)

6 garlic cloves, peeled

2 egg yolks

500 ml/17 fl oz/2 cups
olive oil

6 artichokes

6 carrots

3 fennel bulbs

500 g/1 lb runner
(pole) beans

1 cauliflower

500 g/1 lb green beans

6 cherry tomatoes

2 bay leaves

6 hardboiled eggs,
quartered

salt and freshly ground
black pepper

If using salt cod, soak it for 24 hours, changing the water as
often as possible.

To prepare the garlic mayonnaise: crush the peeled garlic with
a pestle and mortar preferably made of marble or porcelain.
Add the egg yolks and around 1 teaspoon of salt. Mix together
then add the olive oil drop by drop to make the mayonnaise.
If it becomes too thick, add 2-3 tablespoons of warm water,
stirring continuously. Season with pepper to taste.

Prepare the vegetables as appropriate and boil in salted water:

- the artichokes for 30 to 40 minutes, depending on size;

- the whole carrots for 20 to 30 minutes, depending on size;

- the whole fennel for 20 minutes, then cut it into quarters;

- the runner (pole) beans for 15 minutes.

- the cauliflower cut into florets for 10 minutes;

- the green beans for 6 minutes;

Leave the raw tomatoes whole.

Simmer the cod for 20 minutes in water seasoned with 2 bay
leaves. Strain and keep warm.

Arrange the warm vegetables in a large dish with the cod at
the centre surrounded by the hardboiled eggs. Serve the garlic
mayonnaise separately.

menu idea | quick ice cream
serve with | rosé, any light dry red

BRAISED COD IN GINGER
(COCOTTE DE CABILLAUD AU GINGEMBRE)

Serves 6

1 large green cabbage

175 ml/6 fl oz/³/₄ cup water

2 garlic cloves, peeled

1 piece of fresh ginger

200 ml/7 fl oz/³/₄ cup single (light) cream

6 cod fillets, about 175 g/ 6 oz each

salt and freshly ground black pepper

Shred the cabbage and blanch for 5 minutes in boiling salted water. Drain and place in a high-sided flameproof casserole dish with the measured water and peeled garlic cloves. Add salt and pepper to taste, cover and simmer for 10-15 minutes.

Peel and finely grate the ginger and infuse it in the cream in a small pan over a low heat, adding a little salt to taste. Remove the garlic from the cabbage, crush the cloves with a fork, and mix into the ginger cream.

Arrange the cod fillets on top of the cabbage, cover, and return to the heat for about 10 minutes or until cooked through.

Make a bed of the cabbage in a serving dish and lay the fish on top. Serve the ginger cream separately in a sauceboat.

Note This recipe can also be made with ground ginger, although the sauce won't have such a subtle flavour.
As an alternative use paprika or curry powder.

menu idea | vichyssoise | lemon tartlets
serve with | well chilled mâcon, aligoté, white burgundy

BLUE TROUT
(TRUITES AU BLEU)

Serves 6

3 litres/5¼ pints/12 cups water

350 ml/12 fl oz/1½ cups wine vinegar

1 bouquet garni

1 onion, sliced

1 carrot, sliced

1 tablespoon peppercorns

2 tablespoons cooking salt

6 trout, preferably freshly caught, but otherwise fresh fish-farmed

To serve: melted lemon butter and steamed vegetables

Prepare a court-bouilllon with the measured water, 200 ml/7 fl oz/¾ cup of the vinegar, bouquet garni, onion, carrot, peppercorns and salt to taste. Bring up to simmering point and simmer for 20 minutes. Turn off the heat and leave to infuse until completely cold.

Gut and clean the fish and put in a fish kettle or large pan. Bring the remaining vinegar up to boiling point and pour over the fish. Allow to stand for a few minutes, then add the cold court-bouillon. Bring back to a simmer and cook for 10 minutes.

Strain the trout and serve on a hot dish with melted lemon butter and steamed vegetables.

menu idea | purple salad | mocha biscuit cake
serve with | chinon blanc, sancerre, oaked chardonnay

SALMON TROUT FILLETS WITH MUSHROOMS (FILETS DE TRUITE SAUMONÉE AUX CHAMPIGNONS)

Serves 6

625 g/1¼ lb chanterelle mushrooms

3 tablespoons olive oil

1 garlic clove

4 parsley sprigs

1 kg/2 lb salmon trout fillets

coarse salt and freshly ground black pepper

Carefully clean the mushrooms. Sauté in 2 tablespoons of the olive oil. Peel and finely chop the garlic and parsley and add to the mushrooms. As soon as the mushrooms begin to lose their water, strain them and put them back in the frying pan to simmer.

In a large frying pan, fry the salmon trout fillets on both sides for 30 seconds in the remaining oil.

Sprinkle with salt and pepper. Serve piping hot on a dish surrounded by the mushrooms.

Note Although the cooking time may seem very short, it ensures the fish remains soft. If you use thicker fillets, cook for a few more seconds.

menu idea | warm chestnut salad | egg custard
serve with | any crisp dry white

SALMON TROUT FILLETS WITH LENTILS
(PETIT SALÉ DE TRUITE SAUMONÉE AUX LENTILLES)

Serves 6

500 g/1 lb green Puy lentils

1 onion, halved

1 bay leaf

6 fairly thick slices of smoked bacon

6 salmon trout fillets

1 tablespoon olive oil

flat-leaf parsley, chopped

salt and freshly ground black pepper

Put the lentils in a pan of cold water and bring to the boil for 2 minutes, then strain. Cover the lentils with hot water, add the onion, bay leaf and salt to taste and cook for 30 minutes.

Dice the smoked bacon and gently dry-fry. When cooked, strain the lentils. Remove the onion and bay leaf, mix the lentils with the diced bacon and keep warm.

Just before serving, shallow-fry the trout fillets in the olive oil for 2 minutes on each side. Season with salt and pepper, cover the pan and leave to stand for 3 minutes. Arrange the fillets on a bed of lentils and sprinkle with chopped parsley.

Note Salmon can be used instead of trout. Alter the cooking time accordingly.

menu idea | cabbage and bacon soup | chocolate fondant
serve with | mâcon blanc, sauvignon blanc

SEARED SALMON STEAKS
(SAUMON À L'UNILATÉRALE)

Serves 6

**6 salmon steaks, about
175 g/6 oz each**

4 tablespoons olive oil

½ lemon

**coarse salt and freshly
ground black pepper**

To serve: **steamed green
vegetables and mashed
or puréed potatoes**

Buy salmon steaks with skin on one side only.

Salt the skinless side. Heat the oil in a large non-stick frying
pan and sear the salmon steaks skin side down for 2 minutes
over a high heat. Lower the heat and continue cooking for a
further 5 minutes, until the steaks are cooked halfway
through. Cover and stand for 1 minute. Drain on kitchen paper
and serve immediately, sprinkled with salt and pepper and a
squeeze of lemon juice.

The salmon can be served with assorted steamed green
vegetables and potatoes mashed or puréed with olive oil.

Note Cooked in this way, the salmon is crispy and soft. Using
a non-stick frying pan is essential to prevent the salmon skin
from sticking to the surface and peeling off.

menu idea | spinach salad with goat's cheese | peaches in red wine

serve with | white bordeaux, sancerre, oaked chardonnay

SALMON ESCALOPE PARCELS
(ESCALOPES DE SAUMON EN PAPILLOTES)

Serves 6

3 tomatoes

3 courgettes (zucchini)

1 aubergine (eggplant)

6 salmon escalopes, about
125 g/4 oz each

a few sprigs of thyme and
rosemary

sea salt and freshly ground
black pepper

Peel the tomatoes by first plunging into boiling water for
1-2 minutes to loosen the skins. Remove the seeds and dice
the flesh. Cut the courgettes (zucchini) and unpeeled
aubergine (eggplant) into wafer-thin slices.

Preheat the oven to 200°C (400°F), gas mark 6.

Cut 6 rectangles of foil and place a salmon escalope on each
with some vegetables, herbs and a little salt and pepper on
top. Seal the foil well and cook in the preheated oven for
10-15 minutes. Open a foil parcel to check that the fish and
vegetables are ready and serve immediately.

Note Use large rectangles of foil so that the ingredients are
not too tightly packed and can cook evenly. You don't need to
add any extra fat when cooking salmon, which is a so-called
"fatty" fish, although you can put a spoonful of olive oil or
tomato purée in each parcel.

menu idea | melon surprise | mocha biscuit cake
serve with | pouilly-fumé, white rioja

ROAST MONKFISH (ANGLERFISH)
(GIGOT DE LOTTE)

Serves 6

3 tablespoons olive oil

3 shallots, peeled and thinly sliced

3 garlic cloves

1 monkfish (anglerfish) tail, about 1 kg/2 lb

250 ml/8 fl oz/1 cup white wine

1 bouquet garni made with thyme, rosemary, bay

salt and freshly ground black pepper

To serve: ratatouille or aubergine (eggplant) purée

Preheat the oven to 220°C (425°F), gas mark 7.

Oil a dish with some of the olive oil and line the bottom with a layer of sliced shallots. Peel the garlic and insert in the flesh of the monkfish with the tip of a knife.

Put the fish in the dish, drizzle with the rest of the oil and the white wine. Add the bouquet garni and season with salt and pepper. Cook for 10 minutes in the, preheated oven. Turn the monkfish, baste with the cooking juices and cook for a further 10 minutes.

Serve the monkfish whole on a dish with ratatouille or aubergine (eggplant) purée.

Note Baste more often if necessary to ensure that the fish doesn't become too dry during cooking.

menu idea | salmon mille-feuille | dark chocolate mousse
serve with | chablis, sancerre, aligoté

MONKFISH (ANGLERFISH) À L'ARMORICAINE
(LOTTE À L'ARMORICAINE)

Serves 6

10 raw langoustines
(Dublin Bay prawns)

500 g/1 lb tomatoes

4 shallots

1 garlic clove

4 flat-leaf parsley sprigs

6 tarragon sprigs

1.25 kg/2½ lb small
monkfish tails

3 tablespoons olive oil

3½ tablespoons cognac

1 bouquet garni

1 sugar lump

500 ml/17 fl oz/2 cups
dry white wine

Cayenne pepper

3 tablespoons double
(heavy) cream

salt and freshly ground
black pepper

To serve: long-grain
or Basmati rice

Peel the raw langoustines, saving only the heads and shells for this recipe.

Peel the tomatoes by plunging into boiling water for 1–2 minutes to loosen the skins. Remove the seeds and chop the flesh into large chunks. Peel and finely dice the shallots, garlic, parsley and tarragon.

Rinse the monkfish tails in cold water, wipe and cut into thick slices. Heat the oil in a high-sided pan and brown the heads and shells of the langoustines with the monkfish. Fry for several minutes until golden brown, then add the shallots. Pour in the cognac and flambé the contents of the pan. Add the garlic, herbs, tomatoes, bouquet garni, sugar and white wine, and season to taste with salt, Cayenne and black pepper. Cover and simmer for 15 minutes.

Strain the fish with a skimmer and keep warm. Put the sauce through a fine-meshed sieve, pressing firmly to extract all the juices. Put into a small pan, add the cream and heat gently. Reheat the fish in the sauce.

Serve immediately with rice.

menu idea | crab soup | gâteau breton
serve with | mâcon, aligoté, white rioja

RED MULLET À LA NIÇOISE
(ROUGETS À LA NIÇOISE)

Serves 6

12 red mullets, about
125 g/4 oz each

125 g/4oz tapenade

3 parsley sprigs, chopped

3 fresh basil sprigs,
chopped

6 sage leaves

freshly ground black
pepper

If possible, try to get the liver from the mullets when they are
gutted for you. Wash out and dry the fish. Dice the fish livers,
mix with the tapenade and chopped herbs, and season with
pepper to taste.

Stuff the mullets with this mixture, close and flatten them
with the palm of your hand to make sure that the stuffing
sticks to the flesh.

Wrap each mullet in foil, seal well and grill for 5 minutes on
each side. Remove the foil before serving either hot or cold.

Note As the mullets are protected by foil, they can be cooked
on the barbecue or in the embers. You can also add a few
anchovies in oil to the stuffing.

menu idea | oven-baked tomatoes | fiadone
serve with | any dry white

GRILLED MULLET WITH THREE (BELL) PEPPER PURÉE (ROUGETS GRILLÉS AUX TROIS POIVRONS)

Serves 6

2 red (bell) peppers

2 yellow (bell) peppers

2 green (bell) peppers

3 tablespoons olive oil

1 teaspoon coriander seeds, crushed

juice of 1 lemon

9 mullets, about 200 g/7 oz each, scaled and filleted

1 bunch of fresh coriander (cilantro)

salt and freshly ground black pepper

Remove the seeds and pithy membrane from all the peppers. Cut into small dice. Heat 2 tablespoons of the oil in a high-sided frying pan and soften the diced peppers over a low heat. Add salt, pepper, the crushed coriander seeds and the lemon juice. Cover and simmer for 30 minutes, stirring occasionally and adding a little water if necessary.

Brush each mullet with olive oil. Sprinkle salt and pepper on the flesh side.

When the peppers are cooked, heat a non-stick frying pan and fry the mullets for just 1 minute per side, or they can be grilled. Put the cooked peppers onto a serving platter, arrange the mullet fillets on top and sprinkle with finely shredded fresh coriander.

Note Turn the mullets over carefully when cooking because their flesh is very delicate. Bass fillets can be used instead of mullet. This dish is also excellent served cold.

menu idea | vichyssoise | almond blancmange
serve with | aligoté, mâcon blanc

BASS IN A SALT CRUST
(BAR EN CROÛTE DE SEL)

Serves 6

1 bass, about 1.5 kg/3 lb

2 egg whites

2 kg/4 lb coarse sea salt

2 fennel or dill sprigs

To serve: light cream sauce with pastis, boiled potatoes and braised fennel

The bass should be gutted and cleaned but not scaled. The skin prevents the flesh becoming too dry during cooking and protects it from direct contact with the salt. It will also be easier to peel off.

Preheat the oven to 220°C (425°F), gas mark 7.

Mix the egg whites with the salt. Stuff the fennel or dill sprigs into the cavity of the bass. Make a bed of salt in a large dish, lay the fish on top and cover it carefully with the rest of the salt. Cook for 45 minutes in the preheated oven.

It is obviously difficult to check whether the fish is fully cooked, but if you don't like your fish rare then extend the cooking time a little. A sharp metal skewer passed into the fish will give a good indication.

Break the salt crust around the fish at the table in front of your guests. Serve with a sauce made from single (light) cream and 1 tablespoon of pastis, boiled potatoes and braised fennel.

menu idea | mouclade | fig tart
serve with | white graves, aligoté, mâcon blanc

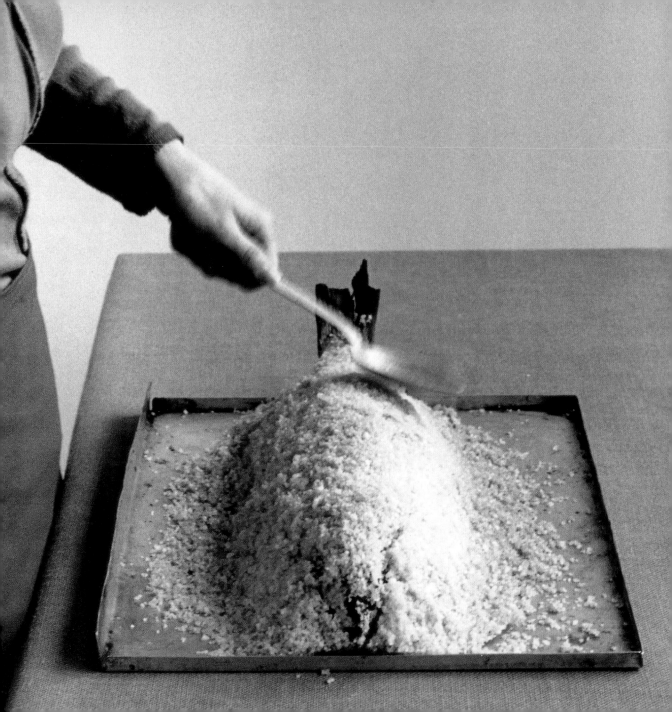

PIKE IN WHITE BUTTER SAUCE
(BROCHET AU BEURRE BLANC)

Serves 6

1 carrot

1 onion

2.5 litres/4½ pints/10 cups water

1 bouquet garni

1 bottle dry white wine

1 pike, about 1.25 kg/2½ lb

For the white butter sauce:

125 g/4 oz shallots

125 ml/4 fl oz/½ cup dry white wine

250 ml/8 fl oz/1 cup white wine vinegar

200 g/7 oz unsalted butter, cut into small pieces

salt and freshly ground black pepper

To serve: boiled potatoes

Peel and slice the carrot and onion. Bring the measured water to the boil and add the sliced carrot and onion, the bouquet garni, white wine, salt and pepper. Simmer for 25 minutes. Leave to cool and strain.

Put the washed, gutted pike in a fish kettle, add the strained, cold court-bouillon, bring to the boil, cover, and simmer gently for 15 minutes over a medium heat.

In the meantime, prepare the white butter sauce: Peel and finely chop the shallots. Put them in a small pan with the white wine and vinegar and simmer over a low heat until almost completely reduced. Remove from the heat and stand the pan in the top of larger pan filled with simmering water (or use a double boiler). Gradually blend in the well-chilled butter, beating continuously after each addition to obtain a light, creamy sauce. Season with salt and pepper and keep standing over the boiling water after the larger pan has been taken from the heat.

Carefully remove the pike from the court-bouillon, peel off its skin and place on a dish. Serve the white butter sauce separately in a sauceboat, accompanied by boiled potatoes.

Note It's better to make this classic recipe from the Loire region with river pike as the flesh of the pond variety is not so delicate. Bass can be used instead of pike.

menu idea | courgettes (zucchini) stuffed with mushrooms | orange savarin
serve with | chardonnay

SEA BREAM À LA BERCY
(DAURADE BERCY)

Serves 6

1 sea bream, about 1.5 kg/
3 lb

125 g/4 oz butter

2 shallots, sliced

parsley, chopped

500 ml/17 fl oz/2 cups
dry white wine

1 teaspoon plain
(all-purpose) flour

salt and freshly ground
black pepper

Buy the sea bream already gutted and scaled. Wash and score the fish on both sides and season with salt and pepper.

Preheat the oven to 190°C (375°F), gas mark 5.

Butter a baking dish and make a bed of the shallots and chopped parsley. Place the sea bream on top. Melt 50 g/2 oz of the butter and pour over the fish, then cover the sea bream to a third of its height with the white wine. Cook in the preheated oven for 30 minutes, basting frequently.

Preheat the grill (broiler).

Take the dish from the oven, lift out the bream and keep it warm. Place the cooking juices in a small pan and reduce on the hob. Mix the flour with the rest of the butter and pour this mixture into the pan stirring briskly until it thickens. Return the sea bream to the dish, pour over the sauce, and grill the surface until it turns golden brown. Serve immediately.

menu idea | rice and cockle salad | chilled pears with redcurrant syrup

serve with | muscadet, or any light dry white

SKATE WITH CAPERS
(RAIE AUX CÂPRES)

Serves 6

2 kg/4 lb skate wings

1 onion stuck with a clove

10 peppercorns

1 tablespoon cooking salt

1 bouquet garni

125 ml/4 fl oz/½ cup vinegar

125 g/4 oz butter

1 shallot, thinly sliced

4 tablespoons salted capers, rinsed and dried

salt and freshly ground black pepper

To serve: boiled potatoes

Wash the skate wings in cold water and cut into 6 pieces. Put in a high-sided cooking pot with the onion, peppercorns, salt, bouquet garni and vinegar. Cover with water, bring to the boil and then remove from the heat.

Allow the pieces of skate to cool in the cooking pot, then peel off the skin.

Melt the butter, cook the thinly sliced shallot until transparent, add the skate and the capers. Gently reheat and serve immediately with boiled potatoes.

Note It's better to use salted capers whose flavour is not affected by the vinegar or salted water.

menu idea | cream of mussel soup with saffron | caramel pear cake
serve with | aligoté, white rioja

SOLE WITH HERBS
(FILLETS DE SOLE AUX HERBES)

Serves 6

12 sole fillets, about 125 g/
4 oz each

40 g/1½ oz butter

2 shallots, finely chopped

200 ml/7 fl oz/¾ cup
crème fraîche, or thick,
creamy yogurt

a few chive sprigs,
chopped

a few chervil sprigs,
chopped

a few flat-leaf parsley
sprigs, chopped

salt and freshly ground
black pepper

To serve: tagliatelle or rice

Preheat the oven to 180°C (350°F), gas mark 4.

Roll the fillets and arrange in a buttered ovenproof dish.
Dot with knobs of butter and surround with the chopped
shallots. Bake for 10 minutes in the preheated oven.

Remove the dish from the oven and add the crème fraîche
or yogurt and the chopped herbs. Season to taste. Put back
in the oven for 2 minutes. Arrange the sole fillets on a dish
and serve immediately with tagliatelle or rice.

menu idea | marinated fish salad | crème brûlée
serve with | white sancerre, or chablis

PAUPIETTES OF SOLE IN DILL SAUCE
(PAUPIETTES DE SOLE À L'ANETH)

Serves 6

14 sole fillets

1 egg white

1 bunch of fresh dill

2 tablespoons thick crème fraîche, or thick, creamy yogurt

30 g/1 oz butter

200 ml/7 fl oz dry/¾ cup white wine

salt and freshly ground black pepper

To serve: braised fennel or cucumber

Process 2 of the sole fillets in an electric blender to obtain a smooth paste. Season with salt and pepper and fold in the egg white. Chill for 1 hour.

Chop the dill, mix with the fish and egg white paste, then blend in the crème fraîche or yogurt. Check the seasoning and chill for a further 15 minutes.

Preheat the oven to 180ºC (350ºF), gas mark 4.

Rinse the remaining sole fillets and dry with kitchen paper. Spread each with a thin layer of the dill mousseline and roll them up. Arrange the paupiettes in a liberally buttered baking dish, pour over the white wine, add season with salt and pepper to taste. Cook for 15 minutes in the preheated oven, basting halfway through cooking.

Serve immediately with fennel or cucumber braised in butter or cream.

Note If the mousseline is not thick enough, hold the paupiettes in shape with a wooden cocktail stick.

menu idea | peas à la française | apple upside-down tart
serve with | muscadet, or chardonnay

FISH AND PRAWN (SHRIMP) KEBABS
(BROCHETTES DE POISSON ET DE GAMBAS)

Serves 6

1 tablespoon curry powder

125 ml/4 fl oz/½ cup white wine

4 unwaxed lemons

2 salad onions

3 tablespoons olive oil

1 teaspoon fennel seeds

400 g/14 oz large raw prawns (shrimp)

400 g/14 oz John Dory fillets

400 g/14 oz turbot fillets

salt and freshly ground black pepper

To serve: fresh shredded coriander (cilantro) and Thaï or Basmati rice

6 wooden skewers, presoaked

To prepare the marinade: mix the curry powder with the white wine, add the juice of 1 of the lemons, the onions (white bulbs and green stalks finely chopped), olive oil, fennel seeds, salt and a little pepper. Mix well.

Peel the prawns (shrimp), removing the head, and deveining the body with a small pointed knife. Slice the fish into large chunks. Wash the remaining 3 lemons and cut into cubes.

Thread the pieces of fish, prawns and lemon alternately onto the wooden skewers. Place in a dish and pour over the marinade. Let the kebabs marinate for 1 hour in the refrigerator. Grill (broil) the kebabs for 3 minutes each side under a preheated grill (broiler), basting with the marinade once or twice during cooking.

Serve immediately, sprinkled with fresh shredded coriander and Thaï or Basmati rice flavoured with the rest of the warm marinade.

Note Other types of market-fresh fish and shellfish can be used for these kebabs: monkfish (anglerfish), langoustines (Dublin Bay prawns), cod, sea bream, scallops, etc.

menu idea | crab soup | prune quiche

serve with | sauvignon blanc, mâcon

LEMON SOLE FILLETS WITH CREAMED BROCCOLI
(FILLETS DE LIMANDE À LA CRÈME DE BROCOLIS)

Serves 6

1.5 kg/3 lb broccoli

2 litres/3½ pints/8 cups water

1 cup white wine vinegar

1 onion, peeled and sliced

1 lemon, sliced

1 bay leaf

½ bunch of parsley

1 kg/2 lb lemon sole fillets

200 ml/7 fl oz/¾ cup single (light) cream

salt and freshly ground black pepper

Wash the broccoli, divide into florets and steam for 10 minutes. It is cooked when the stalks are tender enough to be pierced by a knife.

Meanwhile prepare a court-bouillon with the measured water, white wine vinegar, sliced onion, sliced lemon, bay leaf and half the parsley. Simmer for 10 minutes, then turn off the heat. Add the lemon sole fillets, cover, and leave to stand for 10 minutes.

Put the broccoli and remaining parsley sprigs in an electric blender. Season with salt and pepper and process to a purée. Warm the purée over a low heat and fold in the cream. Check the seasoning.

Strain the lemon sole fillets and arrange them on a serving dish surrounded by the broccoli purée.

Note This recipe can be used for all types of filleted fish such as cod or perch, which can also be steamed.

menu idea | sorrel soup | rice pudding – French style
serve with | riesling

274

JOHN DORY FILLETS WITH MUSHROOMS
(FILLETS DE SAINT-PIERRE AUX GIROLLES)

Serves 6

3 John Dory fillets, about 500 g/1 lb each

olive oil

1 kg/2 lb tomatoes

pinch of sugar

500 g/1 lb chanterelle mushrooms

1 garlic clove, peeled and chopped

salt and freshly ground black pepper

To serve: tagliatelle

Preheat the oven to 180°C (350°F), gas mark 4.

Brush the fillets with olive oil and season with salt and pepper.

Peel the tomatoes by plunging them in boiling water for 1-2 minutes to loosen the skins, remove the seeds and crush the flesh. Add sugar and 2-3 tablespoons olive oil. Season with salt and pepper and pour into a baking dish. Cook for 10 minutes in a preheated oven.

In the meantime, clean the mushrooms and sauté in a tablespoon of olive oil. Cover with a lid and cook for 5 minutes until they lose their water, strain and heat without browning in a little oil with the chopped garlic to seize their flavour.

After cooking the tomatoes for 10 minutes, lay the fillets on top, and leave to brown for a further 5 minutes in the oven.

Just before serving, arrange the fish on its bed of tomatoes in a deep dish surrounded with the mushrooms. Serve immediately with tagliatelle.

Note Some freshly chopped parsley adds a fragrant touch to the crushed tomatoes.

menu idea | French onion soup | autumn-fruit compote
serve with | oaked chardonnay, white rioja

POACHED SMOKED HADDOCK
(HADDOCK POCHÉ)

Serves 6

1 kg/2 lb smoked haddock
fillets

1 shallot

125 g/4 oz butter, melted

1 litre/1¾ pints/4 cups milk

1 bay leaf

1 large lemon

To serve: boiled or baked
potatoes or crispy grilled
bacon

Rinse the haddock and soak for 5 minutes in cold water.

Peel and finely chop the shallot and fry over a very gentle
heat in the butter until transparent.

Simmer the haddock fillets for 5 minutes in the milk with the
bay leaf. Strain well and use kitchen paper to remove any
residue of milk froth.

Squeeze the lemon and add the juice to the melted butter
and shallots. Arrange the haddock on a dish and drizzle with
melted butter mixture.

Serve immediately with classic boiled or baked potatoes,
or with crispy grilled bacon, as in Scotland.

menu idea | cream of cauliflower soup | sugar tart
serve with | sauvignon blanc

SARDINES STUFFED WITH SWISS CHARD AND BOURSIN CHEESE (SARDINES FARCIES AUX BLETTES ET AU BOURSIN)

Serves 6

30 large fresh sardines

200 g/7 oz Swiss chard leaves

6 parsley sprigs

2 x 175 g/6 oz portions Boursin cheese (use Brousse or Brocciu, if available)

2 eggs, lightly beaten

1 garlic clove

3 tablespoons olive oil

salt and freshly ground black pepper

30 wooden cocktail sticks

Scale the sardines and remove their heads by pulling gently from the dorsal side. Take out the innards and slit open the ventral cavity with a pair of scissors, using your finger to free the flesh to the backbone. Gently take hold of the backbone and cut it off at the tail. Wash the sardines and dry them with kitchen paper, then flatten them.

Blanch the Swiss chard, drain and carefully wring out the leaves. Chop the parsley and Swiss chard, put into a terrine and mix thoroughly with the cheese, eggs and very thinly sliced garlic. Season with salt and pepper.

Preheat oven to 210°C (425°F), gas mark 7.

Oil a baking dish. Open and lay the sardines flat, skin side down. Put a little stuffing in the middle of each one and roll it up, starting at the head end. Hold it in place with a wooden cocktail stick. Lay the sardines side by side in the dish and brush with the remaining olive oil. Cook for 20 minutes in the preheated oven. Serve warm or cold.

menu idea | braised artichoke hearts | fiadone

serve with | chilled rosé, or pink zinfandel

MACKEREL FILLETS IN LEMON MARINADE
(FILLETS DE MAQUEREAU MARINÉS AU CITRON)

Serves 6

6 mackerels, filleted

3 lemons

2 tablespoons olive oil

2 teaspoons coriander seeds

3 rosemary sprigs

salt and coarsely ground black pepper

To serve: baked potatoes

Rinse and dry the mackerel fillets with kitchen paper.

Squeeze the lemons and pour the juice into a deep dish along with the olive oil, crushed coriander seeds and rosemary sprigs. Marinate the fish in this mixture for at least 1 hour in the refrigerator.

Strain the fillets, retaining the liquid, and wipe the fish with kitchen paper. Heat a non-stick frying pan and dry-fry the fish for 2-3 minutes on each side. The leftover marinade can be reduced, strained and served as a sauce with potatoes baked in the oven or in barbecue embers.

Note This recipe is an easily digestible way to eat mackerel – an inexpensive fish that is very good for the health.

menu idea | mushroom salad with yogurt | fig tart
serve with | muscadet, or any dry white

STUFFED SQUID
(CHIPIRONS FARCIS)

Serves 6

6 large or 12 medium squid

2 onions

2 garlic cloves

1 bunch flat-leaf parsley,
chopped

2 thick slices of lightly
smoked, cured ham

4 tablespoons olive oil

150 g/5 oz/2½ cups stale
breadcrumbs

mild chilli powder

5 large tomatoes

1 thyme sprig, chopped

salt and freshly ground
black pepper

Remove the squid heads, saving the tentacles, then gut, rinse and dry them.

Prepare the stuffing by peeling and chopping the onions, garlic, half the parsley, ham and the tentacles.

Heat the olive oil, add the stuffing ingredients and mix thoroughly, cooking for 5 minutes. Add salt and pepper to taste. Soak the breadcrumbs in a little water, squeeze out and add to the stuffing. Remove from the heat and mix in the rest of the chopped parsley and a pinch of chilli powder. Fill the squid with this stuffing and fasten with 2 crossed wooden cocktail sticks.

Peel the tomatoes by plunging them into boiling water for 1-2 minutes to loosen the skins. Remove the seeds and cut the flesh into large pieces. Heat the remaining olive oil in a high-sided cooking pot and lightly fry the squid. Add the tomatoes and thyme. Cover and simmer for 30 minutes.

menu idea | piperade | clafoutis with black cherries

serve with | chilled rosé, or pink zinfandel

SQUID À LA MODE DE L'ESTAQUE
(CALAMARS À LA MODE DE L'ESTAQUE)

Serves 6

3 onions, peeled and thinly sliced

2 tablespoons olive oil

1 kg/2 lb cleaned squid, ink sacs removed

1 kg/2 lb tomatoes

1 bunch flat-leaf parsley, finely chopped

few thyme and rosemary sprigs, leaves removed

bay leaf

salt and freshly ground black pepper

To serve: Basmati or long-grained rice

Fry the onions for 5 minutes in the oil. Slice the squid into rings and brown for 3 minutes over a high heat.

Peel the tomatoes by plunging them into boiling water for 1-2 minutes to loosen the skins. Remove the seeds and crush the flesh. Add the tomatoes, the finely chopped parsley, thyme, rosemary and bay leaf. Season with salt and pepper. Cover and simmer over a low heat for 30 minutes. Serve immediately with plain boiled rice.

Note You can liven up the sauce by adding some small pitted black olives.

menu idea | anchovy paste | apricots in ginger
serve with | red rioja or any chilled dry rosé

GRILLED KING PRAWNS (SHRIMP) (GAMBAS À LA PLANCHA)

Serves 6

24 large raw king prawns (shrimp), unshelled

5 tablespoons olive oil

2 garlic cloves, peeled and finely chopped

1 small red chilli, finely chopped

few saffron threads

salt, freshly ground black pepper

To serve: chopped parsley, lemon quarters and thick-cut chips

Devein the prawns (shrimp) by slitting the back with the tip of a sharp pointed knife.

Mix the olive oil with the finely chopped garlic, chilli and the saffron threads in a large bowl. Add the prawns, cover, and marinate for 2–3 hours in the refrigerator.

Preheat a cast iron griddle pan over a high heat and cook the prawns for 2 minutes on each side. Season with salt and pepper, sprinkle with chopped parsley and serve with lemon quarters and thick-cut chips (fries).

Note You can also cook the prawns under the grill (broiler) or, even better, on the barbecue or a real *plancha*.

menu idea | gazpacho | crème catalane

serve with | well chilled rosé

BASQUE TORO (TORO BASQUE)

Serves 6

2 carrots, peeled and sliced into rounds

4 tablespoons olive oil

150 ml/5 fl oz/²/₃ cup white wine

3.5 litres/6¼ pints water

1 bouquet garni

2 onions, peeled and thinly sliced

1 kg/2 lb tomatoes

2 small green (bell) peppers

2 garlic cloves

625 g/1¼ lb potatoes

1 litre/1¾ pints mussels

10 langoustines (Dublin Bay prawns)

½ teaspoon mild chilli powder

pinch of saffron

1.5 kg/3 lb mixed sliced fish (keep heads and trimmings for the fumet)

salt and freshly ground black pepper

Prepare a fumet (stock) with the peeled, sliced carrots and the fish trimmings that have been browned for 10 minutes over a low heat in 2 tablespoons of oil. Pour in the white wine and 2.5 litres/4½ pints of the measured water and add the bouquet garni. Cover and simmer for 1½ hours.

In a separate pan, brown the onions in the remaining oil. Peel the tomatoes by plunging them into boiling water for 1-2 minutes to loosen the skins. Remove the seeds and chop the flesh. Remove the seeds and pithy membrane from the green peppers. Slice the peppers and crush the garlic. Add the tomatoes, peppers and garlic to the onions and cook for about 10 minutes. Cover with the remaining measured water and simmer over a low heat for a further hour.

Cook the potatoes separately in salted water until tender.

Thoroughly scrub the mussels. Place in a large pan with a little water and cook over brisk heat, shaking regularly, until all have opened. Discard any that remain shut. Devein the langoustines (Dublin Bay prawns) with the tip of a sharp pointed knife, then grill (broil) for about 2 minutes each side.

Put the fumet through a fine-meshed strainer, pressing hard to extract all the stock. Process the tomato broth in an electric blender and pour both liquids into a large pan. Add the chilli powder and saffron. Reheat, and poach the sliced fish in the liquid when it begins to simmer. After 7 minutes, add the potatoes and the langoustines, followed by the mussels a few minutes later. When all is heated through, serve immediately.

menu idea | crème catalane

serve with | well chilled rosé

BOUILLABAISSE

Serves 6

3 kg/6 lb Mediterranean fish (scorpionfish, sea bream, conger eel, angler fish, bass, mullet, crabs, Dublin Bay prawns, etc.)

2 onions

2 garlic cloves

3 tomatoes

1 celery stalk

2 potatoes

4 tablespoons olive oil

grated rind of 1 orange

few saffron threads

1 bay leaf

thyme sprigs

2 fennel sprigs

3 litres/5¼ pints/12 cups fish fumet (stock) (see recipe p. 290)

salt and freshly ground black pepper

To serve: crusty bread and Rouille (see recipe p. 220)

Prepare and clean the fish, cutting into even pieces so that they'll fit in a large pan.

Peel and slice: the onions, garlic, tomatoes, celery and potatoes. Heat 2 tablespoons of the olive oil in a large pan and brown the vegetables. Add the grated orange rind, saffron, bay leaf, thyme and fennel. Pour in the fish fumet, add salt and pepper and simmer over moderate heat for 20 minutes. Add the firmer-fleshed fish followed 5 minutes later by the other fish and shellfish. Simmer briskly for a further 3 minutes or until all the different fish types are cooked through.

While cooking, prepare the Rouille as described on page 220.

Remove the fish and keep warm in the serving dish. Discard the herbs, add the rest of the oil and check the seasoning. Boil for a further 2 minutes and pour over the fish.

Serve with chunks of crusty bread and Rouille. Eat the broth separately or everything together, according to taste.

Note It is better to use local fish for Bouillabaisse, because the success of this recipe depends on the choice of fish.

menu idea | peaches in red wine

serve with | white rioja

PAELLA

Serves 6

2 garlic cloves

1 onion

250 g/8 oz risotto rice
(arborio, carnarolli)

6 tablespoons olive oil

12 slices of spicy chorizo

1 pinch of mild chilli powder
or Cayenne pepper

300 g/10 oz sauté of pork
or pancetta, cut into large
cubes

1 small rabbit, cut into
6 pieces (or 6 chicken thighs)

125 g/4 oz fresh garden peas

1 green (bell) pepper

1 red (bell) pepper

1 litre/1³/₄ pints/4 cups
chicken stock

125 ml/4 fl oz/¹/₂ cup dry
white wine

few saffron threads

12 large mussels

12 large prawns (shrimp),
unshelled

salt and freshly ground
black pepper

Peel and finely chop the garlic and onion. Rinse the rice in cold water and leave to soak.

Heat the oil in a large high-sided frying pan or a paella pan and fry the chorizo. After 2 minutes, add the garlic, chilli powder and onion. When the onion is transparent, add the pieces of pork and rabbit (or chicken) and fry gently for 12-15 minutes, turning continuously to ensure they are browned on all sides. Shell the garden peas and cut the peppers into thin strips. Drain the rice, add to the pan, and mix thoroughly with the other ingredients. Season with salt and pepper. Heat the chicken stock and add the wine. Flavour with saffron diluted in a little stock. Pour ¹/₃ of the stock over the contents of the pan, without stirring. Lower the heat and simmer.

In the meantime, wash and scrape the mussels. Place in a pan with a little water and cook over brisk heat, shaking regularly, until they have all opened. Discard any that remain shut. Devein the prawns (shrimp) by inserting the tip of a very sharp pointed knife along the back. When the stock is absorbed, pour the remainder into the pan, adding the peppers and peas. When the rice is al dente, add the mussels and prawns and cover. Cook until the prawns are cooked through.

Note The paella can be covered in foil and left to stand in a warm oven, 110°C (225°F), gas mark ¹/₄. A wide choice of ingredients can be used in this paella: ham, chicken, fish, Dublin Bay prawns, shrimp, squid, cockles, broad (fava) beans and other vegetables.

menu idea | crème catalane

serve with | white rioja

SHELLFISH

SHELLFISH FALL INTO TWO CATEGORIES: THOSE EATEN COOKED AND THOSE SAFE FOR RAW CONSUMPTION. SHELLFISH IN THE SECOND CATEGORY SHOULD BE ULTRA FRESH AND EATEN SOON AFTER PURCHASE. THE BEST INDICATION OF FRESHNESS IS IF THE SHELLFISH REMAIN TIGHTLY CLOSED OR SHUT SPONTANEOUSLY WHEN TOUCHED. COOKED SHELLFISH SHOULD ALSO BE EATEN QUICKLY. THEY CAN SOMETIMES BE COOKED A LITTLE IN ADVANCE, BUT NOT MORE THAN 24 HOURS BEFORE CONSUMPTION.

BUYING AND COOKING

Amount per person and cooking times

• Winkles: 150 g/5 oz
Bring to the boil in a pan of cold water, then strain immediately.

• Whelks: 150-200 g/5-7 oz
Place in a pan of cold water and simmer for 40 minutes.

• Scallops: 2-5 depending on size and your menu (appetiser or main course)

• Queen scallops: 200 g/7 oz

• Cockles: 200 g/7 oz

• English shrimps: 100-150 g/3½ oz-5 oz
Cook for just a few seconds. They're tastier served dry.

• Prawns/US shrimp: 150 g/5½ oz
Don't use tropical or frozen pink prawns. Cook for 1 minute.

• Mediterranean prawns: 4-7 depending on the size
Cook for 2-3 minutes, according to the recipe.

• Langoustines/Dublin Bay prawns: depending on size or whether as an appetiser or main course
Cook for no more than 2 minutes.

• Crab: ½
Cook for 10-15 minutes depending on size and leave to cool in the court-bouillon.

• Lobster: ½ as a main dish, less as a garnish for a seafood platter.

• Oysters: 6-12, depending on what they're served with.

• Large mussels: 4-6 on a seafood platter.

• Small mussels: about 400 g/14 oz
Cook until fully opened.

• Dog cockles: 250 g/9 oz
Cook until fully opened.

• Clams: 250 g/9 oz
Cook until fully opened.

GENERAL PURPOSE COURT-BOUILLON

2 litres/3½ pints/8 cups water

2 carrots, peeled and sliced

2 bay leaves

1 large sprig of thyme

1 sprig of parsley

1 handful of cooking salt

1 tablespoon freshly ground black pepper

Put all the ingredients in a pan and bring to the boil.

"SEAWATER" COURT-BOUILLON

1 handful of unrefined iodized sea salt

2 litres/3½ pints/8 cups water

Simply add the salt to the water and bring to the boil. This court-bouillon comes into its own when you don't want to adulterate the flavour of a crab or lobster, for example, or when you have nothing else to hand.

SPICY COURT-BOUILLON

2 litres/3½ pints/8 cups water

1 onion stuck with a clove

3 lemon slices

2 fennel sprigs (or a dash of pastis)

1 piece of ginger

1 teaspoon coriander seeds

1 handful of cooking salt

1 tablespoon freshly ground black pepper

Place all the ingredients in a pan and bring to the boil.

PRESENTATION AND GARNISH

Serve seafood platters with rye bread and slices of toasted crusty bread, creamy lightly-salted butter, mayonnaise (see recipe p. 102), Rouille (optional, see recipe p. 220), chilled white wine or very dry cider.

ENGLISH SHRIMPS IN CIDER (CREVETTES AU CIDRE)

Serves 6

1 litre/1³/₄ pints/4 cups
extra dry cider

1 thyme sprig

1 bay leaf

1 tablespoon cooking salt

a few black peppercorns

1 kg/2 lb raw shrimps

salt and freshly ground
black pepper

To serve: bread and butter

Prepare a court-bouillon with all the ingredients except the shrimps and leave to reduce for 10 minutes. Add the raw shrimps and bring the stock back to the boil. Cook for just 30 seconds, then strain carefully in a small-meshed sieve.

Dry the shrimps by rolling and blotting in a clean dish-towel. Season with salt and pepper to taste and serve with bread and slightly-salted butter.

menu idea | mouclade | kouign-aman
serve with | dry cider, or pinot grigio

MOUCLADE

Serves 6

1.5 kg/3 lb small mussels

2 egg yolks

150 ml/5 fl oz/²/₃ cup crème fraîche or single (light) cream

2 shallots

50 g/2 oz butter

1 teaspoon curry powder

200 ml/7 fl oz/³/₄ cup dry white wine

salt and freshly ground pepper

Wash and scrape the mussels then toss them in a pan over a high heat until fully opened. Discard any that have not opened.

When cooked, remove the top half of the shell from each mussel, leaving it in the bottom half of the shell.

Preheat the oven to 220°C (425°F), Gas Mark 7.

Arrange the mussels side by side in an ovenproof dish as shown in the picture. Strain the mussel juice through a piece of fine muslin or cheesecloth. Mix the egg yolks in a bowl with 1 tablespoon of the crème fraîche or cream.

Peel and finely chop the shallots. Melt the butter in a pan and lightly fry the shallots until transparent, then add the mussel juice, curry powder, wine and the remaining crème fraîche or cream. Add salt and pepper to taste and cook for 20–30 minutes until the sauce is creamy. Remove from the heat, stir the egg yolk mixture into the sauce and pour over the mussels. Bake for 5 minutes in the preheated oven.

menu idea | English shrimps in cider | gâteau breton
serve with | muscadet

MOULES MARINIÈRES

Serves 6

3 litres/5 pints mussels

200 ml/7 fl oz/³/₄ cup dry white wine

4 shallots, peeled and sliced

2 thyme sprigs

200 ml/7 fl oz/³/₄ cup crème fraîche or single (light) cream

6 parsley sprigs, finely chopped

freshly ground black pepper

Wash and scrape the mussels. Put them in a high-sided cooking pot with the white wine, shallots, thyme and pepper. Heat over a fairly brisk heat, then cover and cook for about 5 minutes until all the mussels have opened. Scoop out the mussels with a skimmer and put them in a dish, discarding any that have not opened.

Filter the cooking juice through fine muslin or cheesecloth, to remove any sand and shell fragments. Pour into the cooking pot and reduce over a high heat for 5 minutes. Add the crème fraîche or cream followed by the mussels and finally the chopped parsley. Serve immediately.

menu idea | risotto milanaise | tiramisu

serve with | muscadet, chinon blanc, or any crisp dry white

LANGOUSTINES IN COURT-BOUILLON
(LANGOUSTINES AU COURT-BOUILLON)

Serves 6

2 litres/3½ pints/8 cups water

1 bottle dry white wine

1 piece of lemon rind

1 bay leaf

4 parsley sprigs

2 thyme sprigs

1 tablespoon cooking salt

1 teaspoon freshly ground black pepper

2 kg/4 lb langoustines/ Dublin Bay prawns

To serve: bread and butter or mayonnaise (see recipe p. 102)

Prepare a court-bouillon with all the ingredients, except the langoustines. Bring to the boil and cook for 10 minutes, then add the shellfish.

As soon as the court-bouillon has come back to the boil, strain. Leave to cool, then place in the refrigerator until nicely chilled.

Eat immediately with bread and butter or mayonnaise.

menu idea | crabs with herb mayonnaise | apple crumble
serve with | chablis, sancerre

CRABS WITH HERB MAYONNAISE
(TOURTEAUX À LA MALOUINE)

Serves 6

4 eggs

½ bunch of chervil

½ bunch of chives

10 flat-leaf parsley sprigs

1 bowl of mayonnaise
(see recipe p. 102)

cooked meat from 3 large
crabs

salt and freshly ground
black pepper

Hard-boil the eggs for 8-10 minutes. Rinse them in cold water, peel off their shells and chop roughly.

Shred the herbs. Gently mix the chopped eggs and herbs with the mayonnaise.

Serve the crabmeat cold with the herb mayonnaise.

menu idea | English shrimps in cider | crêpes Suzette

serve with | gewurztraminer, white zinfandel

ROAST LOBSTER WITH TARRAGON BUTTER
(HOMARD RÔTI AU BEURRE D'ESTRAGON)

Serves 6

3 live lobsters, about
600–700 g/1¼ lb–1½ lb
each

125 g/4 oz butter, melted

4 tarragon sprigs

salt and freshly ground
black pepper

To serve: Basmati rice

To kill the lobsters, insert a sharp knife behind the head, where it meets the body.

Bring a large pot of salted water to the boil, add the lobsters, bring back to the boil and cook for 4 minutes. Remove the lobsters, cut off the claws, return the claws to the pot and cook them for a further 4 minutes.

Preheat the oven to 180°C (350°F) gas mark 4.

Take the pot from the heat, leaving the claws in the boiling water. Split the lobsters in half. Arrange them in a dish, flesh side up. Brush with melted butter and season with salt and pepper to taste. Gently roast the lobster halves in the preheated oven for 5 minutes, brushing them once or twice with melted butter.

In the meantime, crack open the claws and arrange them on the serving dish. Sprinkle the lobster halves with shredded tarragon and brush with any remaining melted butter. Place them next to the claws and serve with Basmati rice.

Note Crayfish can be used instead of lobsters.

menu idea | langoustines in court-bouillon | strawberry charlotte
serve with | pouilly-fuissé, sauvignon blanc

COCKLES IN CREAM SAUCE
(COQUES À LA CRÈME)

Serves 6

6 litres/10½ pints cockles

3 shallots

30 g/1 oz butter

1 thyme sprig

1 bottle dry cider

200 ml/7 fl oz/¾ cup crème fraîche or single (light) cream

½ bunch of chervil

Rinse the cockles in running water. Leave them to soak in a basin of cold water for 1 hour to remove all traces of sand and strain carefully, to ensure that any grit is left behind in the basin.

Peel and finely dice the shallots. Melt the butter and gently fry the diced shallots for 10 minutes in a large stockpot. Add the cockles, thyme and cider. Cover the pot and increase the heat. Cook for 5 minutes until the cockles are half-opened. Remove them individually as they open and strain the juice through fine muslin or cheesecloth to filter out any sand. Discard any that have not opened.

Reduce the stock to obtain 300 ml/10 fl oz/1¼ cups of liquid. Add the crème fraîche or cream and the cockles, with or without their shells, bring to the boil, then pour into the serving dish. Garnish with chervil and serve immediately.

menu idea | Scandinavian salad | almond blancmange
serve with | chablis, dry cider

SCALLOPS WITH FENNEL
(NOIX DE SAINT-JACQUES AU FENOUIL)

Serves 6

1.5 kg/3 lb fennel

5 tablespoons olive oil

24 scallops (edible white part)

juice of 2 limes

1 bunch of chervil, shredded

salt and freshly ground black pepper

Finely slice the fennel and brown in 3 tablespoons of the olive oil over a low heat. Add salt and pepper to taste, cover and cook in a little water until tender.

Heat the remaining oil in a frying pan. Season the scallops with salt and pepper and fry for 1 minute on each side over brisk heat.

Arrange the fennel slices and scallops on a serving dish. Deglaze the pan with the lime juice., pour over the scallops and sprinkle with the shredded chervil.

Note If the scallops are very large, halve them before frying. You can also use the corals for this recipe or save them for something else. This dish is delicious served with chicory (Belgian endive).

menu idea | Swiss chard au gratin | cheesecake
serve with | crisp dry white

SCALLOPS WITH SAFFRON
(COQUILLES SAINT-JACQUES AU SAFRAN)

Serves 6

1 kg/2 lb small asparagus spears

1 shallot

50 g/2 oz butter

24 scallops

2 pinches of powdered saffron

1 tablespoon Noilly Prat, or dry vermouth

200 ml/7 fl oz/¾ cup crème fraîche or whipping cream

salt and freshly ground black pepper

Clean and trim the asparagus keeping only the tips (about 10 cm/4 inches). Cook for about 8 minutes in a large pan of boiling salted water. Strain and keep them warm.

Peel and finely chop the shallot. Melt the butter in a frying pan and soften the shallot over a low heat. Add the edible white part of the scallops as well as the corals and the powdered saffron. Season with salt, turn the scallops over and sweat for 2 minutes.

Add the Noilly Prat and crème fraîche or cream and simmer for a further 4 minutes. Season with pepper then add the asparagus tips and heat them through. Serve immediately.

Note The cooking time for asparagus varies, depending on thickness. It is ready to eat when the stalks are tender enough to be pierced by a knife. You can use dry white wine instead of Noilly Prat.

menu idea | aubergine (eggplant) purée | strawberry charlotte
serve with | white graves, white rioja

PASTA, RICE AND POTATOES

PASTA

Owing to the immense popularity of Italian products, there's now a host of different types of pasta in the shops. Pasta falls into two main categories: fresh and dried.

• Fresh pasta is made at home, by small businesses or on an industrial scale using fresh eggs. The best type is made in Italian delicatessens, but it also comes vacuum-packed and can be found in the "fresh food" sections of supermarkets. Most of these products, particularly those made by very small companies, are perfectly acceptable in quality.

• Dried pasta is made from durum-wheat semolina. Fresh eggs are also sometimes added, although they do nothing to improve the flavour of this type of pasta. On the other hand, manufacturers tend to use powdered or reconstituted eggs, which have an adverse effect on flavour. This is why it is best to use pasta, preferably Italian pasta, made exclusively from durum-wheat semolina. Dried pasta is sometimes flavoured with other ingredients such as spinach, tomato, cuttlefish ink, saffron or mushrooms. There is a wide variety of choice when it comes to shape, flavour and composition: wholemeal pasta, semi-wholemeal pasta and pasta made with spelt or other cereals.

• Follow the cooking instructions on the packet, although the recommended cooking time usually represents a minimum.

• Make sure you strain the pasta well, especially if you're using a runny sauce and particularly if the pasta is tube- or shell-shaped, as these will hold water.

Handy hint

If you place the serving dish under the colander when straining the pasta, it will be warmed by the cooking water.

RICE

There are hundreds of rice varieties in the world. This widely cultivated cereal is popular because it is easily digestible and has energy-giving properties. The appearance of rice depends on its place of origin and its method of processing – a factor which obviously affects flavour. There are two main types of rice:

– long-grain "indica" rice, whose grains remain separate when cooked. The most famous varieties are Basmati rice, Surinam rice with very long, thin grains, perfumed rice from Vietnam or Thailand, and American rice, which retains its shape well during cooking;

– short-grain "japonica" rice, which is rich in starch. This category includes sticky rice made in Thailand and China and used in the preparation of sushi, Carnaroli or Arborio rice used to make risotto, Spanish Bomba or Calasparra rice, the main ingredient of paella, and Camargue rice, ideal for rice desserts. These varieties all come in the form of brown rice or semi-brown rice, which retain essential vitamins and minerals.

Cooking methods

• **Steamed:** wash the rice in cold water and put in a pan with 4 times its volume of salted water. Cook for 15 minutes over a low heat with the lid tightly on. Turn off the heat and leave until all the water is absorbed and you're ready to serve, or reheat in a microwave or warm oven. Alternatively, soak the rice for 1 hour. Bring a large pan of water to the boil. Line a sieve with a clean cloth, strain the rice and pour it into the sieve. Place over boiling water, cover and cook until the grains are separate and still firm to the bite.

• **À la Créole (in water):** bring a large pan of salted water to the boil, add the rice and boil for about 15 minutes. The drawback of this very simple method is that the rice loses its nutritional qualities.

• **Risotto:** gently fry some short-grain rice in fat with some onions. Gradually add the stock in small quantities until the rice is cooked *al dente*. Risotto can be flavoured with all kinds of ingredients, which should be combined with the right type of stock – vegetable, chicken, beef or fish fumet.

POTATOES

Like rice, there are numerous varieties of potato that should be selected with your chosen cooking method in mind. The two main types of potato – main-crop potatoes and new potatoes – can be divided into two categories: those with floury flesh and those with firm, waxy flesh.

• The best way to recognise the potatoes you need is by their shape: round ones such as, Maris Piper, Pentland varieties, and King Edward are good, all-purpose potatoes. These can be used for making soups, stews and mashed or puréed potato, baking in their jackets, and frying. The others, which are more oval, such as, Charlotte, Nicola, Ratte, or even fingerlings, Pink Fir Apple, have a firmer, waxy flesh when boiled and work well in salads, sautéed, or in gratin dishes.

Handy hints

• Buy potatoes at the market whenever possible as there are more varieties to choose from.

• Scrub with a small brush when washing and don't peel before cooking: this prevents the loss of vitamins.

• Begin cooking in cold salted water.

• Store potatoes in a dark, well-ventilated place, which is neither too hot nor too cold.

BOLOGNAISE SAUCE

Serves 6

150 g/5 oz streaky bacon, or pancetta

2 carrots

1 celery stalk

1 onion

4 tablespoons olive oil

150 g/5 oz/²/₃ cup minced (ground) stewing veal

250 g/8 oz/1 cup minced (ground) beef

3 tomatoes

150 ml/5 fl oz/²/₃ cup red wine

2 tablespoons tomato purée (paste)

300 ml/10 fl oz/1¼ cups hot water

salt and freshly ground black pepper

Finely chop the bacon, carrots, celery and onion, keeping each ingredient separate. Heat the oil in a pan and soften the onion, then the bacon, carrots and celery. Add the veal followed by the beef, mixing well. Cook until all the meat has browned. Peel the tomatoes by plunging into boiling water for 2 minutes to loosen the skins, remove the seeds and chop roughly, retaining as much of the juice as possible. Add to the pan together with the wine. Dilute the tomato purée in the measured water and pour into the cooking pot. Add salt and pepper to taste. Cover and simmer for 1½ hours.

SPAGHETTI CARBONARA

Serves 6

500 g/1 lb spaghetti

200 g/7 oz smoked bacon or pancetta

1 teaspoon oil

3 eggs

175 g/6 oz/1½ cups freshly grated Parmesan cheese

salt and freshly ground black pepper

Bring a large pan of salted water to the boil and cook the spaghetti for 10–15 minutes, depending on whether you like your pasta *al dente* or not so firm. In the meantime, dice the bacon and fry in the oil. Dry on kitchen paper. Strain the spaghetti, place in an oven-proof dish that has been heated in the oven and add the bacon. Break the eggs and add them one by one, stirring vigorously. Season liberally with salt and pepper and mix in half of the cheese. Serve immediately with the rest of the Parmesan as a side dish.

Note Don't oversalt this dish as the bacon and Parmesan are already salty.

PISTOU

Adds flavour to soups, fillings or a dish of steamed vegetables.

Serves 6

1 garlic clove

1 bunch of fresh basil

100 g/3½ oz/¾ cup freshly grated dampened Parmesan cheese or a mixture of Parmesan and pecorino

6 tablespoons olive oil

salt and freshly ground black pepper

Peel the garlic. Wash and dry the basil, remove and discard the stalks. Crush the leaves with a pestle and mortar or put through a small mincer (grinder) with the garlic and a pinch of salt. Gradually add the grated cheese, followed by the olive oil in a thin trickle.

Note If you are serving the pistou with pasta, dilute it with a little cooking liquid.

TOMATO COULIS

(COULIS DE TOMATES)

Can be served hot or cold.

Serves 6

2 garlic cloves

2 onions

3 tablespoons olive oil

1 kg/2 lb tomatoes

1 bouquet garni or 1 basil sprig

salt and freshly ground black pepper

Peel and finely slice the garlic and onions. Heat the oil in a high-sided frying pan and sweat the garlic and onions until lightly browned. Peel the tomatoes by plunging into boiling water for 2 minutes to loosen the skins, remove the seeds and crush the flesh. Add to the pan with the bouquet garni. (If using basil, don't add until a few minutes before the end of the cooking time.) Season with salt and pepper and simmer for 30 minutes. Remove the bouquet garni or basil.

Note Process in an electric blender or vegetable mill with the basil if you want a smoother sauce. In winter, opt for peeled canned tomatoes, which have more flavour, or use tomato concentrate to improve the flavour.

SPÄTZLE

Serves 6

300 g/10 oz /2½ cups
plain (all-purpose) flour

3 eggs

65 g/2½ oz butter

salt

Mix the flour, eggs, a little salt and enough water to obtain a soft dough which isn't too dense.

Bring a large pan of salted water to the boil. Place some of the dough on a pastry board, roll out thinly and cut into strips as in the picture opposite and drop into the boiling water. As soon as they float to the surface, scoop them out with a slotted spoon and rinse under cold water. Repeat until you've used all the dough. Reheat the spätzle over a low heat in a pan with the butter.

Note A delicious type of pasta popular across Eastern Europe from Alsace to Hungary, spätzle are the ideal garnish for dishes cooked in a sauce, game, stews and goulash.

menu idea | bœuf bourguignon | quetsch plums in syrup
serve with | pinot or muscat d'alsace, white zinfandel

FARFALLE IN MUSHROOM SAUCE

Serves 6

300 g/10 oz chanterelle mushrooms

500 g/1 lb farfalle (butterfly pasta)

1 garlic clove, chopped

3 flat-leaf parsley sprigs

2 tablespoons oil

200 ml/7 fl oz/³⁄₄ cup crème fraîche or whipping cream

salt and freshly ground black pepper

Prepare the chanterelle mushrooms without rinsing: trim the stalk to remove any dirt, wipe with kitchen paper and clean the gills with a soft brush. Cut them into pieces if too large.

Bring a large pan of salted water to the boil and add the farfalle. Cook for 10–15 minutes, depending on whether you like your pasta *al dente* or not so firm.

Peel and finely chop the garlic. Wash, dry and chop the parsley.

Heat 1 tablespoon of the oil to sizzling and add the mushrooms. Fry for 2 minutes until the mushrooms lose their water, then strain in a sieve. Heat the remaining tablespoon of oil and lightly fry the mushrooms for 5 minutes. Halfway through cooking, add the garlic and finely chopped parsley. Season with salt and pepper.

Remove from the heat and blend in the crème fraîche or cream. Keep the mushroom sauce warm. When the farfalle are cooked, strain and pour them into the serving dish. Add the sauce, mix lightly together and serve immediately.

Note You can use ceps (porcini) instead of chanterelles.

menu idea | chicken with tarragon | raspberry delight
serve with | rosé, or pinot grigio

PENNE WITH OLIVES AND ANCHOVIES

Serves 6

25 g/1 oz canned anchovy fillets

50 g/2oz/½ cup chopped green olives

50 g/2 oz/½ cup dried breadcrumbs

4 tablespoons extra-virgin olive oil

500 g/1 lb ripe tomatoes

2 garlic cloves

1 onion

1 teaspoon dried marjoram

500 g/1 lb penne (pasta quills)

125 g/4oz/1 cup freshly grated Parmesan cheese

salt and freshly ground black pepper

Chop the anchovies and mix with the olives in a bowl. Stir in the breadcrumbs, moisten with 2 tablespoons of the olive oil and put to one side.

Peel the tomatoes by plunging into boiling water for 2 minutes to loosen the skins, remove the seeds and crush the flesh.

Peel and finely chop the garlic and onion. Heat the rest of the oil in a pan and brown the chopped onion and garlic. Add the tomato pulp, marjoram, salt and pepper and simmer for 10 minutes.

In the meantime, cook the penne in a large pan of salted water. Mix the olive, anchovy and breadcrumb mixture with the tomato sauce. Strain the pasta and top with the sauce.

Serve piping hot with the grated Parmesan.

Note To save time, you can use a small pot of anchovy paste instead of the olive/anchovy mixture.

menu idea | anchovy paste | lemon tartlets
serve with | any light dry rosé or red

MACARONI GRATIN

Serves 6

400 g/14 oz/3½ cups macaroni

65 g/2½ oz butter

250 ml/9 fl oz/1 cup crème fraîche or whipping cream

nutmeg

125 g/4 oz Emmental cheese, thinly sliced

75 g/3 oz/¾ cup freshly grated Parmesan cheese

salt and freshly ground black black pepper

Bring a large pan of salted water to the boil. Cook the macaroni until *al dente* then strain.

Preheat the oven to 200°C (400°F), gas mark 6.

Butter an ovenproof dish with a little of the butter. Put the macaroni in a pan with the crème fraîche or cream, grated nutmeg and a little salt and pepper over a low heat and cook gently until all is combined and heated through.

Pour half the macaroni into the baking dish, sprinkle with half the cheese, cover with the rest of the macaroni and top with the remaining cheese. Dot with small knobs of the remaining butter and bake for 25-30 minutes in the oven until nicely browned.

menu idea | fruity duck salad | quick ice cream

serve with | beaujolais, cabernet sauvignon

BAKED LASAGNE

Serves 6

Double quantity of
Bolognaise sauce
(see recipe p. 320)

50 g/2 oz butter

400 g/14 oz oven-ready
lasagne sheets

125 g/4 oz/1 cup freshly
grated Parmesan cheese

For the Béchamel sauce:
(see recipe p. 112 for
method)

500 ml/18 fl oz/2 cups
milk

50 g/2 oz butter

50 g/2 oz/scant ½ cup
plain (all-purpose) flour

Preheat the oven to 200°C (400°F), gas mark 6.

Spread a thin layer of Bolognaise sauce over the bottom of a buttered ovenproof dish, cover with a layer of pasta sheets, top with a little more Bolognaise sauce followed by a layer of Béchamel sauce, a fresh layer of pasta and so on until all the ingredients have been used up. Finish with a layer of Béchamel sauce and top with the grated Parmesan.

Dot with knobs of butter and bake for 20-25 minutes in the oven until golden brown. Serve piping hot.

Note You don't need to be precise when layering the lasagne in the dish. However, the Bolognaise sauce must be runny enough to moisten the pasta, otherwise the cheese topping will be dry. You can use creamed spinach instead of Bolognaise sauce with layers of pasta and slices of cooked ham. If you need a thicker sauce, (to cover fresh lasagne), continue cooking for a little longer after removing the lid.

menu idea | crunchy vegetable salad | chilled pears with redcurrant syrup
serve with | valpolicella, cabernet sauvignon

TAGLIATELLE WITH MUSSELS

Serves 6

2 litres/3½ pints small mussels

2 small red chilli peppers

3 garlic cloves

2 shallots

5 tablespoons olive oil

1 tablespoon finely ground mixed peppercorns

150 ml/5 fl oz/⅔ cup dry white wine

3 tomatoes

300 g/10 oz fresh tagliatelle

1 bunch of basil

salt and freshly ground black pepper

Wash and scrape the mussels. Rinse and finely chop the chilli peppers, discarding the seeds if you don't want too hot a sauce. Peel and chop the garlic and shallots and lightly fry in 2 tablespoons of hot oil in a high-sided cooking pot. Add the mussels, peppercorns and chilli peppers and mix thoroughly. Add the white wine, cover and cook for 5 minutes over a medium heat until all the mussels have opened. Discard any that have not.

Shell the mussels and put to one side. Strain the cooking juice through fine muslin or cheesecloth and reduce to about 100 ml/ 3½ fl oz/½ cup of liquid. Peel the tomatoes by plunging into boiling water for 2 minutes to loosen the skins, remove the seeds and chop the flesh roughly.

Cook the pasta for 5 minutes in boiling salted water. Remove the leaves from the basil (saving a few for garnish) and finely chop the rest. Strain the pasta and place in a large bowl with the basil, mussels, reduced stock and tomatoes. Gently stir everything together, garnish with basil leaves and serve immediately

menu idea | onion soup with garlic | soft cheese tart

serve with | muscadet

RISOTTO MILANESE

Serves 6

50 g/2 oz beef marrow,
if available

75 g/3 oz butter

2 small onions, peeled
and sliced

400 g/14 oz/2 cups
Arborio or Carnaroli
risotto rice

few saffron strands or a
pinch of saffron powder

250 ml/9 fl oz/1 cup dry
white wine

1.5 litres/2³/4 pints/6 cups
chicken stock or skimmed
veal stock

125 g/4oz/1 cup freshly
grated Parmesan cheese

Soften the diced beef marrow in 30 g/1 oz of the butter in a pan. Peel and finely slice the onions. Melt the remaining butter in a high-sided frying pan and sweat the onions without allowing them to brown. Add the rice and stir until all the grains are coated with the butter. When translucent, add the saffron, followed by the white wine and continue cooking over a low heat.

Once the white wine has been absorbed, add the hot stock a ladleful at a time, ensuring each addition is fully absorbed before adding the next. Stir gently only to incorporate each addition, then leave the risotto to cook on its own. When the rice is still firm to the bite, add the rest of the butter and half the Parmesan. Without stirring, move the frying pan in a circular motion to mix the different ingredients together. Take the risotto to the table in a preheated dish and serve with the rest of the cheese.

Note Choose your ingredients carefully, beginning with the type of stock and the rice. Freeze cooking stock from boiled chicken or stewed veal in advance. This basic recipe allows you to make all types of risotto, using asparagus tips, courgettes (zucchini), mushrooms, small vegetables, tomatoes, etc.

menu idea | salade Niçoise | almond blancmange
serve with | valpolicella, cabernet sauvignon

ALIGOT DE L'AUBRAC

Serves 6

1.5 kg/3 lb floury potatoes

500 g/1 lb fresh Tomme cheese for Aligot

500 ml/18 fl oz/2 cups crème fraîche

1 garlic clove

salt

Peel the potatoes, cut into even pieces and cook in salted water for about 30 minutes. They are cooked when they can be easily pierced by a knife.

In the meantime, cut the cheese into thin strips and place on a plate near heat. Put the crème fraîche in a small pan and warm gently over low heat.

Peel and finely chop the garlic.

Strain the potatoes carefully. Mash them with a handheld masher. Put the mashed potato in a pan over a low heat and add the finely chopped garlic and warmed cream, stirring vigorously. Quickly mix in the fresh cheese, beating until it has melted. The Aligot should be smooth and runny. Serve immediately, as it won't keep.

menu idea | stuffed cabbage | egg custard
serve with | fitou, beaujolais

GRATIN DAUPHINOIS

Serves 6

1.5 kg/3 lb Charlotte or
other waxy potatoes

1 garlic clove

65 g/2½ oz butter

300 ml/10 fl oz/1¼ cups
single (light) cream

salt and freshly ground
black pepper

Peel the potatoes and slice them as thinly as possible, ideally with a vegetable slicer or mandolin. Blot the slices dry on kitchen paper or a clean towel.

Preheat the oven to 150°C (300F), gas mark 2

Rub an earthenware ovenproof dish with the split garlic clove and butter generously. Spread a layer of potatoes over the bottom, season with salt and pepper and cover with a small amount of cream. Repeat this action and continue until you've used all the ingredients and the potatoes are completely submerged by the cream. Dot with small knobs of butter and bake in the hot preheated oven for a good hour, then increase the temperature to 180°C (350°F), gas mark 4 for the last 20 minutes.

Serve in the cooking dish straight from the oven as soon as the top has turned a nice golden colour.

Note Make sure your baking dish is large enough to allow the cream to cover the potatoes completely. You should never use grated cheese in this classic recipe.

menu idea | steak with green peppercorns | peaches in red wine
serve with | beaujolais

POMMES SARLADAISES

Serves 6

1.5 kg/3 lb new potatoes

3 tablespoons goose fat

2 garlic cloves, peeled

6 flat-leaf parsley sprigs

salt and freshly ground black pepper

Peel the potatoes and cut into slices about $1/2$ cm/$1/4$ inch thick. Melt the fat in a large high-sided frying pan, heat to sizzling point then add the potatoes. Brown for 20 minutes over a medium heat, stirring occasionally.

Finely chop the garlic and parsley. Sprinkle over the potatoes, mix thoroughly and continue cooking for 20 minutes, partially covered. Remove the lid and increase the heat so that the potatoes are nice and crispy. Transfer to a warm dish and serve immediately.

Note You can use fat from duck conserve as well as fat from foie gras.

menu idea | steak with green peppercorns | tiramisu

serve with | bergerac, cabernet sauvignon, shiraz, any full-bodied red

VEGETABLES

VERY FEW VEGETABLES ARE EATEN EXCLUSIVELY RAW OR COOKED AND THERE ARE ANY NUMBER OF HANDY HINTS AND TIPS TO HELP YOU PRODUCE DELICIOUS VEGETABLE DISHES AND ACCOMPANIMENTS. FOR EXAMPLE, SOME COOKING METHODS ARE BETTER SUITED TO A PARTICULAR TYPE OF VEGETABLE THAN OTHERS BUT, AS A GENERAL RULE, STEAMING IS PREFERABLE TO PRESSURE COOKING – THE HEAT IS MUCH GENTLER AND IT WILL PRESERVE ALL THE VITAMINS AND GOODESS IN THE VEGETABLES.

COOKING FRESH VEGETABLES

• **Artichokes:** usually steamed. Small artichokes can be braised in the oven or a deep cooking pot.

• **Asparagus:** usually steamed, but small asparagus spears are delicious cooked in butter. Green asparagus doesn't need peeling unless it is late in the season.

• **Aubergines (eggplants):** before cooking, cut into slices, sprinkle both sides with cooking salt, place in a colander and allow to drain for about 30 minutes – 1 hour. Rinse under running water and blot dry with kitchen paper. This simple trick stops the aubergines from soaking up too much oil during cooking, and removes any bitterness. They can be cooked in stews, au gratin, braised, sautéed, grilled or fried.

• **Beetroot (beets):** ideal in soups, cooked in butter or oil, oven baked or steamed.

• **Broad (fava) beans:** slow cooked in a covered casserole with very little liquid, butter or oil.

• **Broccoli:** steamed, au gratin or slow cooked in a covered casserole with very little liquid.

• **Cabbage (red or white):** remove the stalk before braising.

• **Carrots:** steamed, in stews, puréed or slow cooked in a covered casserole with very little liquid.

• **Cauliflower:** blanch for 2-3 minutes (especially if large) before cooking in a gratin, a sauce, or steaming. Only cook the florets as the stalks can be quite bitter.

• **Celeriac:** steamed, puréed, or slow cooked in a covered casserole with very little liquid.

• **Celery stalks:** braised in the oven.

• **Chicory (Belgian endive):** remove the bitter stalk before braising, cooking in a gratin or steaming.

• **Courgettes (zucchini):** steamed, braised, au gratin, stuffed, grilled, fried or slow cooked in a covered casserole with very little liquid. Peel larger courgettes by removing alternate strips of skin

• **Cucumber:** peel and slow cook in a covered casserole with butter or cream.

• **Fennel:** braised in the oven in a little water, au gratin.

• **French beans:** steamed or occasionally boiled. To preserve their crunchy texture, plunge into a bowl of iced water.

• **Kale or borecole:** remove the stalk and blanch before braising with meat or steaming and serving with butter.

• **Leeks:** steamed, blanched and cooked in a gratin, cooked in butter.

• **Lettuce:** braised in stock or slow cooked in a covered casserole with very little liquid, butter or oil.

• **Mushrooms:** sautéed or fried in butter or oil, in meat and vegetable stews and casseroles. They are tastier if lightly browned before being added to a stew or casserole.

• **Peas:** steamed, slow cooked in a covered casserole in a little butter.

• **Pumpkin and marrow:** steamed, au gratin, puréed, sautéed in thin strips.

• **Radishes:** slow cooked in a covered casserole with a little butter.

• **Spinach:** should not be boiled. Cook gently over a low heat in just the water clinging to the leaves after washing, or in a little butter or oil. If desired, add cream or Béchamel sauce (see recipe p. 112) when cooked.

• **Sweet (bell) peppers:** steamed, fried, braised, grilled.

• **Swiss chard:** should not be boiled. Cook the leaves like spinach and the stalks like asparagus – see above. If desired, add cream or Béchamel sauce (see p. 112) when cooked.

• **Tomatoes:** oven baked, grilled, in stews, stuffed or pan fried.

• **Turnips:** steamed, braised, puréed or slow cooked in a covered casserole with very little liquid, butter or oil (preserve their crunchy texture as for French beans).

COOKING DRIED VEGETABLES (PULSES)

The harder and drier they are, the longer pulses have to be soaked. They also require more careful rinsing.

• **Chickpeas:** 48-72 hours, changing the water several times + 1½-2 hrs cooking. If time is at a premium, chickpeas are available in cans – just rinse and heat through.

• **Haricot beans:** soak for 24 hours, changing the water several times + 1 hr cooking.

• **Lentils:** soak for about 2 hours if desired but they don't usually need soaking and they cook very quickly (about 10 minutes). However, they should be well rinsed before cooking as they can be "dusty".

• **Split peas:** as for haricot beans.

BRAISED ARTICHOKE HEARTS
(FONDS D'ARTICHAUTS BRAISÉS)

Serves 6

20 small artichokes

juice of 2 lemons

2 carrots

4 onions

4 shallots

4 tablespoons olive oil

300 ml/½ pint/1¼ cups dry white wine

300 ml/½ pint/1¼ cups water

coriander seeds

salt and freshly ground black pepper

To prepare the artichokes, break off the stalk by bending until it comes away from the base — the stringy fibres will come away with the stalk. Cut the base flat with a sharp knife and remove the tough outer leaves. Trim the top off the artichoke, to a height of 3 cm/1¼ inches, and remove the small leaves and choke from the centre. To prevent them discolouring, put the prepared artichokes into a bowl of cold water with added lemon juice.

Preheat the oven to 150°C (300°F), gas mark 2.

Peel and thinly slice the remaining vegetables. Drizzle the base of an ovenproof dish or casserole with 2 tablespoons of the olive oil and line with the vegetables. Drain the artichokes, arrange on the bed of vegetables, and pour over the white wine, measured water and the rest of the olive oil. Season with a few crushed coriander seeds, salt and pepper. Cover and cook in a preheated oven for 2 hours. Serve the artichokes with the vegetable garnish but not the cooking juices.

Note This accompaniment can be served hot or cold.

menu idea | chicken with tarragon | apple upside-down tart
serve with | rosé, shiraz, cabernet sauvignon

STUFFED ARTICHOKE HEARTS
(FONDS D'ARTICHAUTS FARCIS)

Serves 6

6 fairly large, young artichokes

juice of 2 lemons

300 g/10 oz goat's cheese

2 eggs, beaten

225 ml/8 fl oz/1 cup tomato coulis (see recipe p. 320)

4 tablespoons breadcrumbs

a few sprigs fresh mint

salt and freshly ground black pepper

Prepare the artichoke hearts as for Braised artichoke hearts (see p. 348), but don't cut the tops back as far and hollow out the centres more as the choke will be larger.

Mix the goat's cheese and eggs together with a fork. Season with salt and a generous amount of pepper, and fill each artichoke heart with the mixture. Place the hearts in a deep but not overly large cooking dish so that they are comfortably wedged together, pour over the tomato coulis and sprinkle with breadcrumbs. Cover and cook over a low heat for 1 hour.

Serve chilled, sprinkled with chopped mint.

Note You can replace the goat's cheese with fresh Normandy demi-sel cheese, ricotta, fromage frais, or fresh curd, cottage or cream cheese.

menu idea | eggs à l'andalouse | lemon mousse
serve with | rosé, or red or pink zinfandel

STUFFED AUBERGINES (EGGPLANTS) À L'ORIENTALE (AUBERGINES FARCIES À L'ORIENTALE)

Serves 6

6 aubergines (eggplants)

100 g/3½ oz/½ cup long-grain rice

2 onions

3 tablespoons olive oil

3 tomatoes

200 ml/7 fl oz/¾ cup white wine

50 g/2 oz/½ cup raisins

1 teaspoon ground cumin

few sprigs fresh parsley, chopped

salt and freshly ground black pepper

Preheat the oven to at 200°C (400°F), gas mark 6.

Rinse and dry the aubergines (eggplants), place on a baking sheet and bake for 20 minutes. Remove from the oven and leave to cool.

Reduce the oven temperature to 160°C (325°F), gas mark 3.

In the meantime, cook the rice in boiling salted water for 15 minutes. Strain, rinse in cold water and strain again. Peel and thinly slice the onions, and soften in a deep frying pan, in half the olive oil, over medium heat. While the onions are cooking, peel the tomatoes by plunging into boiling water for 2 minutes to loosen the skins, remove the seeds and chop the flesh. Add to the onions along with the white wine, raisins and cumin. Season with salt and pepper and leave to simmer for 15 minutes. Then add the rice and chopped parsley, mix well and check the seasoning. Increase the heat towards the end to reduce the liquid, if necessary.

Cut each aubergine in half, season with salt and score the flesh down the middle. Pull the flesh apart and fill the cavity with the rice mixture. Drizzle with the remaining olive oil and bake in the cooler oven for 20 minutes. Serve hot, warm or cold.

Note A little chopped mint, 50 g/2 oz/½ cup pine nuts and a pinch of cinnamon will give added flavour to the filling. You can use tomatoes or (bell) peppers instead of aubergines.

menu idea | pissaladière | quick ice cream
serve with | any light dry red

VICHY CARROTS
(CAROTTES VICHY)

Serves 6

1 kg/2 lb carrots

50 g/2 oz butter

juice of 1 lemon

1 lump brown sugar or
1 teaspoon Demerara sugar

100 ml/3½ fl oz/½ cup
water

3 sprigs flat-leaf parsley,
chopped

salt

Peel and slice the carrots. Then put half the butter, the carrots, lemon juice and sugar into a pan (in that order) and season with a little salt. Cover – making sure the lid fits tightly – and leave the carrots to sweat over a very low heat, shaking the pan at regular intervals to prevent them sticking.

After 15 minutes, add the measured water and continue cooking for 25–30 minutes or until the carrots are just tender but not overcooked. Before serving, add the remaining butter and sprinkle with chopped parsley.

Note You can also use this method – omitting the sugar and lemon juice – to braise chicory (Belgian endive).

menu idea | beef cooked in red wine | gâteau basque
serve with | any light dry red

SWISS CHARD AU GRATIN
(GRATIN DE BLETTES)

Serves 6

1.2 5kg/2½ lb Swiss chard

1 tablespoon flour

150 g/5 oz/1¼ cups grated
Gruyère or Emmenthal
cheese

40 g/1½ oz butter

For the Béchamel sauce:

60 g/2¼ oz/½ cup plain
(all-purpose) flour

60 g/2¼ oz butter

750 ml/1¼ pints/3 cups
milk

nutmeg

salt and freshly ground
black pepper

Wash the chard in plenty of cold water and drain thoroughly. Separate the stalks from the leaves – but keep the leaves as they can be cooked like spinach – and cut into small chunks. Bring a pan of lightly salted water (chard absorbs salt) to the boil and blend in the flour. Add the chard to the boiling water and leave to cook for 5-10 minutes until the chunks are transparent. Drain thoroughly, shaking the sieve to remove any excess water.

Preheat the oven to 200°C (400°F), gas mark 6.

While the chard is cooking, make a thickish Béchamel sauce (see recipe p. 112) with the flour, butter and milk. Season with salt, pepper and a pinch or two of freshly grated nutmeg.

Add the chard and half the grated cheese to the Béchamel sauce, mix well and turn into a greased ovenproof dish. Sprinkle with the rest of the cheese and top with small knobs of butter. Stand the dish on a baking sheet and bake for 25 minutes until the top is crisp and golden.

Note You can adapt this recipe by replacing the chard with steamed (as opposed to boiled) cauliflower, broccoli, chicory (Belgian endive), or leeks and ham.

menu idea | chicken with tarragon | caramel pear cake

serve with | a good white alsace or muscat

AUBERGINE MOULD (EGGPLANT MOLD) (PAPETON D'AUBERGINES)

Serves 6

2 kg/4 lb aubergines (eggplants)

4 tablespoons flour

5 tablespoons olive oil

2 garlic cloves, peeled and chopped

6 eggs

100 ml/3½ fl oz/½ cup whipping cream

cooking salt

salt freshly ground black pepper

To serve: 1 large dish tomato coulis (see recipe p. 320)

Peel and dice the aubergines (eggplants), place in a colander, and sprinkle with cooking salt (see p. 346). After an hour, rinse under running water, blot dry with kitchen paper and roll the aubergine cubes in the flour. Heat the oil in a deep frying pan, add the aubergines and chopped garlic, and leave to soften over a very low heat for 30 minutes, stirring occasionally so that they don't stick to the pan. Season with salt and pepper and leave to cool.

Preheat the oven to 180°C (350°F), gas mark 4.

Process the aubergines with the eggs and cream to a purée in an electric blender and pour the mixture into a greased soufflé dish or charlotte mould. Stand in a roasting pan filled with boiling water to come half way up the soufflé dish and cook in the preheated oven for 1 hour.

Remove the mould from the oven and turn out immediately onto a serving dish. Serve with hot tomato coulis.

menu idea | roast leg of lamb | chilled pears in redcurrant syrup

serve with | rosé or pink zinfandel

STUFFED CABBAGE (CHOU FARCI)

Serves 6

150 g/5 oz Swiss chard (or spinach) leaves

2 onions

2 garlic cloves

2 tablespoons olive oil

200 g/7 oz sausage meat

250 g/9 oz cold roast meat, diced

1 thickish slice ham, diced

1 bunch parsley

150 g/5 oz/2½ cups breadcrumbs, soaked in 200 ml/7 fl oz/¾ cup milk

2 eggs, beaten

1 sprig fresh thyme

1 large savoy cabbage

3 carrots

2 thin slices bacon

salt and freshly ground black pepper

Plunge the chard (or spinach) leaves into boiling water for 30 seconds and drain. Peel and chop the onions and garlic and fry lightly in the oil, in a deep frying pan, over a medium heat. Add the sausage meat, cold meat and ham and brown over high heat for a few minutes.

Remove from the heat. Chop the parsley and chard leaves, squeeze the milk from the breadcrumbs and add them to the pan along with the eggs and crushed thyme leaves. Season with salt and pepper and mix well so that the stuffing has a smooth consistency.

Remove the outer leaves of the cabbage and plunge into a large pan of boiling salted water for 30 seconds. Remove with a slotted spoon, rinse under running water and drain. Bring the water back to the boil, plunge in the whole cabbage, and cook for 6 minutes. Drain, rinse under running water and drain again. Carefully pull away the outer leaves and cover the heart of the cabbage with a layer of stuffing, fold back several leaves and repeat the process, covering the centre of the cabbage with a layer of stuffing and folding back more leaves as you go. Finish by covering with the larger outer leaves and tying in place with kitchen string, like a very large stuffed vine leaf.

Preheat the oven to 160°C (325°F), gas mark 3.

Peel and roughly chop the carrots. Line the base of a deep ovenproof casserole with the bacon slices, add the stuffed cabbage and carrots. Cover, and bake for 2 hours. The cabbage should be nice and golden when cooked.

menu idea | watercress soup | crème brûlée

serve with | cahors, shiraz, cabernet sauvignon

SWEET-AND-SOUR RED CABBAGE
(CHOU ROUGE À L'AIGRE-DOUX)

Serves 6

1 large red cabbage

50 g/2 oz butter (or
4 tablespoons olive oil)

2 large cooking apples

1 tablespoon granulated
sugar

2 cloves

200 ml/7 fl oz/¾ cup
wine vinegar

salt and freshly ground
black pepper

Discard the outer leaves and stalk of the cabbage, and shred finely. Melt the butter or oil in a large high-sided cooking pot, add the cabbage and soften over a low heat for 10 minutes.

Peel and core the apples, cut into thin slices, and add to the cooking pot. Season with salt and pepper. Then add the sugar, cloves and wine vinegar. Cover and leave to simmer for at least 1 hour, stirring occasionally.

Remove the cloves before serving.

Serve with roast pork or goose, or even smoked sausage.

Note The flavour of this dish improves if served next day.

menu idea | pork and vegetable stew | rice pudding – French style
serve with | rosé, shiraz, or cabernet sauvignon

MUSHROOM FRICOT
(FRICOT DE CÈPES)

Serves 6

1 kg/2 lb ceps (porcini mushrooms)

6 tablespoons olive oil

2 garlic cloves, peeled

6 sprigs parsley

salt and freshly ground black pepper

Wipe the mushrooms with absorbent kitchen paper (don't rinse!), removing the base of the stalk and any damaged or discoloured pieces. Separate the heads from the stalks and slice thinly.

Heat half the oil in a deep frying pan and add the mushrooms. Cook for 3-4 minutes, stirring gently so as not to damage them. As they begin to release their juices, remove from the heat and drain.

Finely chop the garlic and parsley. Heat the remaining oil in the frying pan and, when it is nice and hot, return the mushrooms to the pan with the garlic and parsley. Season with salt and pepper.

Cook for a few minutes more and serve immediately.

menu idea | beef sirloin or rump steaks with red-wine sauce | peaches in red wine

serve with | a full-bodied red bordeaux

COURGETTES (ZUCCHINI) STUFFED WITH MUSHROOMS (COURGETTES FARCIES AUX CHAMPIGNONS)

Serves 6

6 firm young courgettes (zucchini)

250 g/8 oz white button mushrooms

1 garlic clove

1 teaspoon coarse-grain mustard

juice of 1 lemon

2 tablespoons olive oil

200 ml/7 fl oz/³/₄ cup crème fraîche or sour cream

chives, snipped with scissors

salt and pepper

Rinse the courgettes (zucchini), remove the ends, and cook whole for 10 minutes in a pan of boiling salted water. Drain and leave to cool.

Wipe the mushrooms with absorbent kitchen paper (don't rinse!), remove any damaged or discoloured pieces, and chop roughly. Peel and finely chop the garlic and mix in a bowl with the mustard, lemon juice, olive oil and crème fraîche or sour cream. Season with salt and pepper.

Cut the courgettes in half lengthways and scoop out some of the flesh with a teaspoon.

Just before serving, mix the cream filling with the mushrooms and snipped chives and use it to fill the courgettes. Serve immediately.

Note Don't add the mushrooms until the last minute as they will release their juices and make the filling runny.

menu idea | oven-baked chicken with garlic | crème brûlée
serve with | any crisp dry white

BROAD (FAVA) BEANS WITH BACON
(FÈVES AU LARD)

Serves 6

350 g/12 oz shelled fresh broad (fava) beans from about 2 kg/4 lb pods

200 g/7 oz slightly salted bacon

1 tablespoon olive oil

1 onion

2 sprigs fresh savory

salt and freshly ground black pepper

Place the beans in a pan of cold water. Bring to the boil, drain and remove the tough skins.

Put the bacon into a pan of cold water and bring to the boil. Drain and cut into "matchsticks". Heat the oil in a deep frying pan, over a very low heat, and fry the bacon for 5 minutes. Peel and thinly slice the onion and add to the pan. Stir so that the onion is well coated with oil, add a little cold water, cover, and leave to cook until the onion is transparent. Then add the broad (fava) beans and crushed savory leaves and mix well. Season with salt and pepper and cook for 4 minutes.

Note Shelling and skinning fresh broad beans takes time and patience, but the result is delicious. If beans are not in season, or time is at a premium, you can use frozen or canned broad beans.

menu idea | shepherd's pie | lemon mousse

serve with | a good red burgundy, or red rioja

GLAZED TURNIPS
(NAVETS GLACÉS)

Serves 6

1 kg/2 lb baby turnips

50 g/2 oz butter

2 tablespoons granulated
sugar or honey

salt and freshly ground
black pepper

Scrub the turnips under running water and trim the stems to about 2 cm/³/₄ inch. Heat the butter in a deep frying pan until it bubbles. Add the turnips, turning so that they are well coated in butter, and then the sugar or honey.

Season with salt and pepper and turn again. Cover, and cook over a low heat until the turnips have caramelized and are just tender.

Serve piping hot as an accompaniment for roast poultry, especially duck.

Note In winter, you can use swede (rutabaga) instead of turnips.

menu idea | bass in a salt crust | Yule log
serve with | white côtes du rhône, or sauvignon blanc

RATATOUILLE

Serves 6

2 aubergines (eggplants)

2 onions

1 garlic clove

4 tablespoons olive oil

1 red (bell) pepper

1 green (bell) pepper

sprig each fresh thyme
and rosemary

1 kg/2 lb tomatoes

4 firm courgettes
(zucchini)

cooking salt

salt and feshly ground
black pepper

Rinse and dice the aubergines (eggplants). Place in a colander, sprinkle with cooking salt (see p. 346). After 1 hour, rinse under running water and blot dry with absorbent kitchen paper.

Peel and thinly slice the onions and garlic (remove the growing tip from the garlic) and fry lightly in the olive oil, in a deep cooking pan, over a medium heat. After a few minutes, add the diced aubergines. Rinse the peppers, remove the seeds and membrane and cut into fine strips. Add to the pan when the onions and aubergines are nicely browned. Add the thyme and rosemary sprigs, and season with salt and pepper.

Peel the tomatoes by plunging into boiling water for 2 minutes to loosen the skins, remove the seeds and chop roughly. Rinse but do not peel the courgettes (zucchini) and cut into evenly sized pieces. Add the tomatoes and courgettes about 20 minutes after the seasoning, stir the contents of the pan and continue cooking until the vegetables have released their juices and begin to break down. Remove the herbs and adjust the seasoning before serving.

Note Ratatouille is delicious hot or cold, and can be used to garnish an omelette or tart (see also Ratatouille tart, p. 130).

menu idea | rabbit with garlic and rosemary | rum baba

serve with | rosé, or any light red

COURGETTES (ZUCCHINI) AU GRATIN (TIAN DE COURGETTES)

Serves 6

5 small courgettes (zucchini)

2 garlic cloves

3 tablespoons olive oil

200 g/7 oz/1 cup short-grain rice

4 sage leaves

500 ml/17 fl oz/2 cups vegetable stock

3 eggs

200 ml/7 fl oz/¾ cup whipping cream

125 g/4 oz/1 cup freshly grated Parmesan cheese

nutmeg

salt and freshly ground black pepper

Rinse but do not peel the courgettes (zucchini) and cut into evenly sized pieces. Peel the garlic, remove the growing tips, and crush with the flat of a knife. Heat the olive oil in a deep frying pan, over a low heat, and add the garlic and rice, stirring with a wooden spatula to ensure that the grains are well coated with oil. When they are translucent, add the courgettes and crushed sage leaves. Season with salt, cover and leave to cook so that the courgettes release their juices, stirring occasionally to prevent the contents sticking to the pan.

After about 15 minutes add the stock and cook for a further 20 minutes until all the liquid has been absorbed by the rice. Remove from the heat.

Preheat the oven to 200°C (400°F), gas mark 6.

Beat the eggs in a bowl, together with the cream, salt, pepper and a pinch of freshly grated nutmeg, and add to the pan. Mix well and turn the mixture into a greased earthenware baking dish. Sprinkle with the Parmesan cheese and bake for 30 minutes until the top is crisp and golden.

Note In Provence, gratins are traditionally cooked in a round earthenware baking dish known as a tian, but any ovenproof dish will do.

You can use rosemary or marjoram instead of sage, and grated Gruyère instead of Parmesan.

menu idea | gammon steaks with white beans | lemon tartlets

serve with | pink zinfandel

VEGETABLE PANCAKES
(PAILLASSONS DE LÉGUMES)

Serves 6

3 courgettes (zucchini)

3 carrots

3 waxy potatoes

½ celeriac (celery root)

juice of ½ lemon

2 tablespoons flour

2 eggs, beaten

1 tablespoon crème fraîche
or sour cream

nutmeg

3 tablespoons light
vegetable oil

30 g/1 oz butter

salt and freshly grated
black pepper

Rinse the courgettes (zucchini); peel the carrots and potatoes; peel and rinse the celeriac and sprinkle with lemon juice as this vegetable quickly discolours. Grate the vegetables using the medium-sized holes of the grater. Squeeze the juice from the vegetables with your hands or by pressing down firmly in a fine-mesh sieve. Put the grated vegetables in a bowl, add the flour, eggs, crème fraîche, a pinch of freshly grated nutmeg, salt and pepper, and mix well.

Form 6 pancakes or 12 smaller ones from the mixture. Heat half the oil and butter in a large frying pan and place half the pancakes (or the number your pan can hold) in the pan leaving space between them as they will spread a little during cooking. Cook over a low heat for 10 minutes, turn carefully with a spatula and cook for a further 10 minutes. Keep the first batch of pancakes warm and repeat the process with the rest of the oil and butter

Note You can add mixed herbs or grated cheese to the pancake mixture. Served with a green salad, the pancakes make a delicious light meal.

menu idea | rabbit with garlic and rosemary | chilled pears in redcurrant syrup
serve with | any dry light red

PEAS À LA FRANÇAISE
(PETITS POIS À LA FRANÇAISE)

Serves 6

2 kg/4 lb fresh peas
(unshelled weight)

20 small salad onions or
spring onions (scallions)

2-3 lettuces (Little Gem
or small Romaine)

60 g/2½ oz butter

1 sprig fresh tarragon

1 tablespoon granulated
sugar

200 ml/7 fl oz/¾ cup
water

salt and pepper

Shell the peas and peel the salad onions. If using spring onions, cut off the green part and discard, cut the white part into 2.5 cm/1-inch pieces. Discard any coarse outer leaves of the lettuces and shred the remaining leaves. Melt the butter in a deep frying pan and add the onions and shredded lettuce. Cover and leave to sweat over a very low heat for 5 minutes.

Add the peas, crushed tarragon leaves and sugar, season with salt and then add the measured water. Cover, and leave to simmer for 10-15 minutes after swirling the pan to mix the ingredients

If there is too much liquid when you are ready to serve, remove the lid and increase the heat to reduce its slightly. Serve immediately.

Note You can add sliced or diced carrot, turnip and potato at the same time as the onions.

menu idea | lamb casserole à la normande | redcurrant meringue tart
serve with | riesling, or a light dry red

PIPERADE

Serves 6

2 onions

100 g/3½ oz lightly smoked ham, Bayonne if possible

3 tablespoons olive oil

4 green (bell) peppers

1 kg/2 lb tomatoes

1 garlic clove

mild chilli pepper

6 eggs

salt and freshly ground black pepper

Peel and thinly slice the onions, and finely chop the ham. Heat 1 tablespoon of the olive oil in a deep pan and lightly fry the onions and ham over a medium heat. When the onions are more or less transparent, cover and leave to cook over a low heat for 20 minutes.

In the meantime, rinse the green (bell) peppers and remove their stalks, seeds and membrane. Cut into strips and fry in a separate pan in the rest of the olive oil until tender.

Peel the tomatoes by plunging into boiling water for 2 minutes to loosen the skins, remove the seeds and chop the flesh roughly. Peel and crush the garlic. When the onions have been simmering for 20 minutes, add the peppers, tomatoes and crushed garlic. Season with salt and a pinch of chilli pepper (or black pepper), mix well and cook over a very low heat until the liquid evaporates and you are left with a thick vegetable "compote".

Break the eggs into a bowl, beat a few times with a fork and pour over the compote in the pan. Mix in immediately and remove from the heat as soon as the eggs are cooked. Turn the piperade into a hot dish and serve as it is or, if you wish, surrounded by slices of pan-fried bacon.

Note You don't have to add the beaten eggs to the vegetables, they can be served separately scrambled or as an omelette.

menu idea | gazpacho | gâteau basque
serve with | a good dry red

OVEN-BAKED TOMATOES
(TOMATES CONFITES AU FOUR)

Serves 6

1.5 kg/3 lb tomatoes

3 teaspoons granulated sugar

3 tablespoons olive oil

1 sprig fresh thyme

salt and pepper

Preheat the oven to 150°C (300°F), gas mark 2.

Cut the tomatoes in half, remove the seeds and arrange the halves on a greased baking sheet. Season with salt and pepper, sprinkle with sugar and drizzle with olive oil.

Sprinkle with crushed thyme (use dried if you can't get fresh) and bake in the preheated oven for 1½-2 hours.

menu idea | spinach tart | floating islands

serve with | rosé, red zinfandel

STUFFED TOMATOES (TOMATES FARCIES)

Serves 6

6 large, firm tomatoes

625 g/1¼ lb cold, cooked meat (poultry, pork, veal or beef)

150 g/5 oz smoked bacon or uncooked ham

4 sprigs flat-leaf parsley

4 shallots

4 tablespoons olive oil

150 g/5 oz/2½ cups breadcrumbs made from 2- to 3-day-old bread

1 egg, beaten

200 ml/7 fl oz/¾ cup water

salt and freshly ground black pepper

Remove the top quarter of the tomatoes at the stalk end and set aside for "lids". Scoop out the flesh and strain through a sieve to collect the juice without the pips. Then remove the pips, chop the flesh and set aside. Season the inside of the tomatoes with salt.

Chop the cooked meat, bacon and parsley. Peel and thinly slice the shallots and soften in half the olive oil, in a deep frying pan. Add the chopped meat and parsley and stir continuously until the meat is lightly browned. Add the chopped tomato and season with salt and pepper.

Put the breadcrumbs in a bowl, add the tomato juice and leave to swell. Then add the mixture to the frying pan along with the beaten egg and mix well.

Preheat the oven to 180°C (350°F), gas mark 4.

Fill the tomatoes with the mixture, cover with their "lids", and arrange in an ovenproof dish. Pour the measured water into the dish and drizzle the tomatoes with the rest of the olive oil. Place in the oven for 45 minutes, checking to make sure the cooking liquid doesn't evaporate and adding a little more water if necessary.

Serve hot with rice or pasta shells, or warm as an entrée.

menu idea | rice salad à la romaine | Caen sablés

serve with | any full-bodied dry red

AUBERGINE (EGGPLANT) PURÉE
(CAVIAR D'AUBERGINES)

Serves 6

1.5 kg/3 lb aubergines
(eggplants)

1 garlic clove, peeled
and halved

For the mayonnaise:

1 egg yolk

1 teaspoon Dijon mustard

5 tablespoons olive oil

juice of 1 lemon

salt and freshly ground
black pepper

basil leaves

Preheat the oven to 180°C (350°F), gas mark 9.

Rinse the aubergines (eggplants) under running water and blot dry with absorbent kitchen paper. Remove the stalk and prick several times with the point of a sharp knife. Place on a baking sheet and cook in the preheated oven for 20 minutes, then turn and cook for a further 15 minutes.

Remove the aubergines from the oven and leave to cool. When they are cool enough to handle, cut them in half, scoop out the flesh and leave to drain in a sieve with the garlic for 2-3 hours.

Prepare a mayonnaise (see recipe p. 102) with the egg yolk, mustard and olive oil. Add the lemon juice and season with salt and pepper.

When the aubergine purée is nice and "dry" (i.e. has released all its moisture), mix with the mayonnaise. Garnish with chopped basil leaves and serve chilled or at room temperature.

Note The larger the aubergines, the more water they contain, which will affect the draining time.

Instead of mayonnaise, you can make the purée with olive oil and lemon juice, or with tahini (sesame paste) which gives the aubergines a slightly smoky flavour.

menu idea | bass in a salt crust | chocolate fondant
serve with | rosè, pink zinfandel or a light cabernet

SPINACH IN CREAM
(ÉPINARDS À LA CRÈME)

Serves 6

2 kg/4 lb fresh spinach
leaves

150 ml/5 fl oz/²⁄₃ cup
crème fraîche or double
(heavy) cream

For the Béchamel sauce:

3¹⁄₂ tablespoons plain
(all purpose) flour

25 g/1 oz butter

200 ml/7 fl oz/³⁄₄ cup milk

nutmeg

salt and freshly ground
black pepper

Cut off the stalks of the spinach, discard any discoloured or wilted leaves, and wash in plenty of cold water. Dry thoroughly in a salad spinner and shred finely. Put as much spinach as possible into a large pan, cover and cook over a low heat turning with a metal spoon and adding the rest of the spinach as it reduces. When all the spinach has reduced, continue cooking over a low heat until all the juices have evaporated.

While the spinach is cooking, make a Béchamel sauce with the flour, butter and milk (see recipe p. 112). Season with salt, pepper and a pinch of freshly grated nutmeg.

Add the Béchamel sauce and cream to the pan containing the spinach, allow to thicken slightly and serve immediately.

menu idea | duck à l'orange | raspberry delight
serve with | merlot, cabernet sauvignon

CAKES AND DESSERTS

AS A GENERAL RULE, PLAIN SHORTCRUST AND SWEET SHORTCRUST PASTRY IS BEST MADE BY HAND AND NOT IN A FOOD PROCESSOR, WHICH PRODUCES AN OVERLY ELASTIC TEXTURE. THE BEST WAY TO MAKE PASTRY IS TO MIX THE INGREDIENTS TOGETHER QUICKLY INTO A BALL OF DOUGH WITH A LIGHT TOUCH AND WITHOUT KNEADING. LET IT REST IN THE REFRIGERATOR; REMOVING IT 20 MINUTES BEFORE ROLLING. LINE THE BAKING TIN (PAN) WITH IT, RETURN TO THE REFRIGERATOR AND LEAVE TO CHILL WHILE YOU PREPARE THE FILLING. THIS ALL HELPS PREVENT THE PASTRY DRYING OUT WHILE BAKING. IF PREFERRED, USE HALF BUTTER/HALF LARD (CRISCO).

SHORTCRUST PASTRY (PÂTÉ BRISÉE)

Makes about 300 g/10 oz pastry
or a 25-cm/10-inch pastry base

200 g/7 oz/1½ cups plain
(all-purpose) flour

125 g/4 oz butter, well chilled

3½ tablespoons chilled water

pinch of salt

Rub the flour, salt and well-chilled butter together until the mixture forms a coarse but even crumbly texture. Add the measured water gradually while you bring the dough together into a ball. Chill in the refrigerator for at least 1 hour.

SWEET SHORTCRUST PASTRY

(PÂTÉ SABLÉE)

Makes about 300 g/10 oz pastry
or a 25-cm/10-inch pastry base

150 g/5 oz/1 cup plus 3 tablespoons
plain (all-purpose) flour

100 g/3½ oz butter

1 egg yolk

6 tablespoons icing sugar
(confectioners' sugar)

pinch of salt

Mix the flour, salt and well-chilled butter until the mixture forms a coarse but even crumbly mixture. Add the egg yolk and sugar and combine, first with a knife and then with the fingertips, into a soft dough. Chill in the refrigerator for at least 1 hour.

PUFF PASTRY (PÂTE FEUILLETÉE)

Makes 450 g/1 lb pastry or about 2 tarts
(You can freeze the other half)

250 g/9 oz/2 cups plain
(all-purpose) flour

1 tablespoon melted butter

100 ml/3½ fl oz/½ cup chilled water

1 teaspoon white wine vinegar

200 g/7 oz well-chilled butter

pinch of salt

Mix all the ingredients (except the chilled butter) by hand, or in a food processor. When you have a smooth and elastic dough, use your hands to bring it together in a ball and cut a cross in the surface with a knife.

Put the dough in a freezer bag and chill in the refrigerator for 3 hours. Dust your work surface with flour, and roll out each quarter of the cross so that the pastry looks like a four-pointed star. Soften the chilled butter by hitting it several times with the rolling pin, and spread it over the central part of the "star". Then bring the 4 points into the centre, folding them over the butter, to form a square. Chill in the refrigerator for 30 minutes so that the butter and pastry reach the same temperature.

Flour the work surface again and roll out the pastry as evenly as possible into the shape of a rectangle. Fold one third over to the centre, and then the other third over that. Give the pastry a quarter turn and roll it out into the same size rectangle as before. Fold into three once more, put it back in the freezer bag and chill in the refrigerator for

30 minutes. Repeat the process twice more with a 30-minute chilling period after each stage. The pastry is then ready to use but allow it to thaw out before attempting to roll it out to use.

RAISING AGENTS

Raising agents are used to lighten dough whose ingredients don't naturally contain leavens. There are two different types:

• baking powder, made from bicarbonate of soda and an acidic ingredient. This raising agent will only release its gases and cause the dough to rise at temperatures higher than room temperature, so baking powder only starts to work when the dough is baked in the oven.

• natural or baker's yeast is a fungus which causes fermentation. The carbon dioxide produced as a result of this process causes the dough to rise. Unlike baking powder, yeast is activated by exposure to moisture and moderate warmth. It is used exclusively for so-called "leavened" dough. Although you may be able to obtain fresh yeast in some specialist shops or from a bakery, it is now mainly sold dried in two forms: dried − activated with warm water and a little sugar; and "easy-blend" which is sifted in with the flour and the water added. Follow the maker's instructions on the pack for the best results. Yeast can become stale if kept overlong, once the pack has been opened, so it is important to check the date stamp.

BUCKWHEAT PANCAKE BATTER (GALETTES DE BLÉ NOIR)

Makes about 20 pancakes

2 eggs

400 ml/14 fl oz/1³/4 cups water

500 g/1 lb buckwheat flour

1 teaspoon salt

Beat the eggs with the measured water. Put the flour in a bowl and make a well in the centre. Gradually pour in the egg and water mixture stirring all the time. Add enough extra water, if necessary, to obtain a smooth, runny batter. Let stand for at least an hour and thin with a little water only if necessary. The batter should not be "watery".

WHEAT CRÊPE BATTER

(PÂTE À CRÊPES DE FROMENT)

Makes about 20 crêpes

250 g/9 oz/2 cups plain (all-purpose) flour

¹/2 teaspoon salt

2 tablespoons sugar

3 eggs

500 ml/17 fl oz/2 cups milk

50 g/2 oz butter

Mix the flour, salt and sugar in a bowl and make a well in the centre. Break the eggs into a separate large bowl and beat them with 200 ml/7 fl oz/³/4 cup of the milk. Pour this mixture into the flour and whisk vigorously to obtain a smooth batter without any lumps. Melt the butter. Gradually add the rest of the milk and the melted butter to the batter. Let stand for at least an hour.

BLINI BATTER

Makes about 12 blinis

7 g/¹/4 oz (1 sachet) dried yeast (or 7 g/¹/4 oz fresh yeast)

about 600 ml/1 pint/2¹/2 cups milk, warmed

250 g/9 oz/2 cups plain (all-purpose) flour

3 eggs, separated

125 ml/4 fl oz/¹/2 cup single (light) cream

salt

Prepare the yeast from maker's instructions on the pack. Put the flour and salt into a bowl and make a well in the centre. Using a fork, lightly beat the egg yolks egg with the yeast, then pour into the well. Mix together, gradually adding the rest of the warmed milk and cream. Leave to rise for an hour in a warm place, out of any draughts. Beat the egg whites until they form soft peaks and gently fold into the batter, which should be light and frothy with little bubbles on the surface. Let stand to rise again for 20 minutes.

BEATING EGG WHITES

Many recipes require you to separate the egg whites from the yolks and beat the whites until they form soft or stiff peaks, depending on the recipe: soft peaks can be folded into melted chocolate or puréed fruit without disintegrating, but stiff peaks are essential for meringue. The key to beating egg whites successfully is to make sure that your utensils are completely clean and free from grease. The egg whites should be at room temperature and there should be no sign of yolk.

PANCAKE BATTER

Makes about 12 pancakes

250 g/9 oz/2 cups plain (all-purpose) flour

1 teaspoon baking powder

¹/2 teaspoon salt

1 tablespoon sugar

1 egg plus 2 egg whites

125 ml/4 fl oz/¹/2 cup single (light) cream

2 tablespoons melted butter

400 ml/14 fl oz/1³/4 cups milk

butter for cooking

To serve: maple syrup

Mix the flour, baking powder, salt and sugar in a bowl. In a separate bowl, vigorously beat the egg yolk with the cream, melted butter and milk. Add to the flour and whisk to obtain a smooth batter. Let stand for 1 hour at room temperature.

Handy hints

• Make sure the frying pan is well greased when making crêpes. Wipe round the pan with a small wad of kitchen paper soaked in fat between making each crêpe.

• You can flavour batter with vanilla, orange flower water, finely grated lemon, orange or mandarin rind, or any type of liqueur.

• Wheat crêpes are best eaten with dry or sweet cider, depending on taste.

CONFECTIONERS' CUSTARD

(CRÈME PÂTISSIÈRE)

Makes 750 g/1½ lb

500 ml/17 fl oz/2 cups milk

1 vanilla pod, split

2 eggs plus 2 egg yolks

125 g/4 oz/ caster sugar (½ cup superfine)

3½ tablespoons plain (all-purpose) flour

4 tablespoons cornflour (cornstarch)

Pour the milk into a heavy-based pan, add the vanilla pod and bring gently to the boil. Let stand to infuse for 10 minutes. Remove the pod, scrape out the seeds with the point of a sharp knife and add them to the milk. In a separate bowl beat the egg yolks with the sugar until the mixture is pale and has doubled in volume: mix in the flour and cornflour, then gradually add the hot milk, beating continuously. Put back over the heat and allow to thicken, beating continuously to prevent the custard sticking to the bottom of the pan. Remove from the heat and continue to beat for 1 minute. You can add flavour with coffee (2-3 teaspoons instant coffee), 150 g/ 5 oz melted dark chocolate or a variety of liqueurs or spirits.

CHANTILLY CREAM (CRÈME CHANTILLY)

250 ml/9 fl oz whipping cream

3 tablespoons icing sugar (confectioners' sugar), sifted

vanilla extract (optional)

Chill the cream in the coldest part of the refrigerator for at least 2 hours. Put a large bowl in the refrigerator. Whip the cream by hand or with an electric mixer until it has doubled in volume and begun to thicken. Fold in the sugar, whipping continuously, and a few drops vanilla extract, if using. Do not over-beat or it can become "buttery". Refrigerate until ready to serve.

Handy hints

Commercial crèmes fraîche sold in the dairy sections of supermarkets, is thickened artificially with lactic fermenting agents which prevents it from being stiffly whipped. Whipping cream, on the other hand, is ideal for whipping, obviously, and is not so rich as double (heavy) cream. If you want a sharper tasting pouring cream, buy full-fat crème fraîche and dilute with a little milk.

After using a vanilla pod wipe it clean and insert in a screw-top jar filled with caster or icing sugar, so that you have a constant supply of vanilla-flavoured sugar.

CUSTARD CREAM (CRÈME ANGLAISE)

Makes 1 litre

750 ml/1¼ pints/3 cups milk

1 vanilla pod, split

8 egg yolks

125 g/4 oz/½ cup sugar

Pour the milk into a heavy-based pan, add the split vanilla pod and bring gently to the boil. Let stand to infuse for 10 minutes. Remove the pod, scrape out the seeds with the point of a sharp knife and add them to the milk.

Beat the egg yolks with the sugar until the mixture turns pale and doubles in volume, then gradually add the hot milk, beating continuously. Pour the mixture into the pan and thicken over a low heat, stirring continuously with a wooden spoon. Don't allow it to boil. The custard is ready when it clings to the back of the spoon. Remove from the heat, leave to cool and strain through a small-meshed sieve.

Instead of vanilla, you can flavour this custard with 150 g/5 oz of dark chocolate melted in the milk while it is warm but not hot; 2-3 teaspoons instant coffee dissolved in 2 tablespoons hot water or 2 tablespoons orange-flower water.

RED BERRY SAUCE

(COULIS DE FRUITS ROUGES)

500 g/1 lb red fruit (strawberries, raspberries, red currants...)

150-200 g/5-7 oz/¾-1 cup sugar (depending on the acidity of the fruit)

Put the fruit and sugar in a heavy-based pan over gentle heat until the sugar has melted and the fruit juices are beginning to run. Pass through a fine-meshed sieve.

CHOCOLATE SAUCE

(SAUCE AU CHOCOLAT)

125 g/4 oz best quality dark chocolate

150 ml/5 fl oz/⅔ cup milk

1 tablespoon crème fraîche or cream

Break the chocolate into small pieces, and melt in a bowl set over a pan of barely simmering water. Do not let the bowl touch the water. Stir until smooth, then gently add the milk and crème fraîche, or cream. Serve hot.

CARAMEL SAUCE

(SAUCE AU CARAMEL AU BEURRE SALÉ)

125 g/4 oz/½ cup sugar

1 tablespoon water

25 g/1 oz unsalted butter

100 ml/3½ fl oz/⅓-½ cup double (heavy) or single (light) cream

Melt the sugar in a small heavy-based pan. As soon as this has turned a pale amber colour, add the water and butter to stop caramelization. Blend in the cream and reheat without boiling. Serve hot or warm.

Note When adding water to hot melted sugar, protect your hands in case it spits.

GÂTEAU BATTU

Serves 6

2 sachets dried yeast

3½ tablespoons milk

250 g/9 oz/2 cups plain
(all purpose) flour

75 g/3 oz caster sugar
(7½ tablespoons superfine)

½ teaspoon salt

6 egg yolks

200 g/7 oz unsalted
butter, softened

2 egg whites

deep, preferably fluted,
well greased baking tin (pan)

Preheat the oven to 180°C (350°F), gas mark 4.

Mix the yeast with the warmed milk according to the maker's instructions on the pack. Blend the flour, sugar and salt together in a bowl and make a well in the centre. Add the egg yolks one by one, followed by the yeast then the softened butter. Mix together thoroughly. Beat two egg whites until they form stiff peaks and gently fold into the mixture.

Pour into the prepared baking tin and leave to rise until the mixture is level with the top of the tin. Bake for 45 minutes in the preheated or until a knife inserted into the centre of the cake comes out clean.

Remove from the oven, turn out onto a wire rack, and leave to cool.

Note Gâteau battu, a speciality from Picardy, is a cross between a sponge cake and a brioche. It is delicious served with cream or stewed fruit. Although it should ideally be baked in a special high-sided, fluted tin, you can use a brioche, kugelhopf or charlotte mould instead.

menu idea | watercress soup | lamb casserole à la normande
serve with | any chilled sweet dessert wine

PRUNE QUICHE
(FAR AUX PRUNES)

Serves 6

200 g/7 oz good quality
pitted prunes

100 ml/3½ fl oz/about
½ cup rum

4 eggs

125 g/4 oz/½ cup caster
sugar (½ cup superfine)

125 g/4 oz/scant cup plain
(all-purpose) flour

pinch of salt

300 ml/10 fl oz/1¼ cups
milk

60 g/2½ oz butter

quiche dish

Preheat the oven to 180°C (350°F), gas mark 4.

Put the prunes in a bowl, pour over the rum, and leave to soak.
Mix the eggs with the sugar. Gradually add the flour and salt,
then thin with sufficient milk to obtain a smooth batter.

Butter an ovenproof quiche dish. Drain the prunes and
arrange them in the dish. Cover with the batter, dot with
small knobs of butter and bake for about 40 minutes in the
preheated oven until the quiche is risen and a golden brown.
It will sink as it cools.

This dessert is best eaten at room temperature.

Note You can also soak the prunes in tea or orange flower
water instead of rum, if you prefer.

menu idea | crab soup | fish and prawn (shrimp) kebabs
serve with | white port, sauternes

KOUIGN-AMAN

1 sachet dried yeast

200 ml/7 fl oz/³/₄ cup warm water

300 g/10 oz/2½ cups plain (all-purpose) flour

½ teaspoon salt

175 g/6 oz butter

175g/6 oz/³/₄ cup sugar

deep baking tin

Mix the yeast with the measured water or according to the maker's instructions on the pack. Put the flour and salt in a bowl, make a well and add the yeast. Mix, then knead the dough by hand for about 10 minutes until smooth and elastic (you can also use an electric mixer fitted with a batter or dough paddle). Put the dough in a bowl, cover with a cloth and leave to rise in a warm place (22°C/72°F) for 1-2 hours.

When the dough has doubled in volume, place on a floured work surface and pull it apart to allow it to breathe. Shape it roughly into an oval and roll into a rectangle. Spread with 150 g/5 oz of the butter mixed with 150 g/5 oz/just over ½ cup of the sugar, stopping 2 cm/³/₄ inch from the edge. Fold down the top third of the dough and fold the bottom third on top to make 3 layers, roll out into a rectangle again. Repeat this once more but this time do not roll out. Refrigerate for 30 minutes.

Preheat the oven to 200°C (400°F), gas mark 6.

Remove the dough from the refrigerator and roll out again on the floured work surface, this time into a circle. Butter a round baking dish – preferably metal – and sprinkle it with the rest of the sugar. Place the dough in it and leave to rise for 30 minutes at room temperature.

Bake for 20-30 minutes in the oven until the cake is golden brown and has caramelised. Eat when cool.

Note Leftover Kouign-aman tastes just as good when reheated.

menu idea | melon surprise | roast lobster with tarragon butter
serve with | extra dry cider

TÔT-FAIT WITH PLUM BRANDY
(TÔT-FAIT À LA MIRABELLE)

Serves 6

125 g/4 oz/scant cup plain
(all-purpose) flour

150 g/5 oz caster sugar
(½ cup plus 2 tablespoons
superfine)

5 eggs

1 litre/1¾ pints/4 cups milk

100 ml/3½ fl oz/about
½ cup plum brandy

baking dish

Preheat the oven to 210°C (415°F), gas mark 6-7.

Blend the flour, sugar and eggs together in a bowl to obtain a
smooth batter. Gradually add the milk, then the brandy.

Pour the mixture into a generously buttered baking dish made
of earthenware or enamelled cast-iron. Bake for 30 minutes.

Note This simple cake is perfect for beginners.

menu idea | purple salad | sea bream à la Bercy
serve with | demi-sec champagne

CLAFOUTIS WITH BLACK CHERRIES
(CLAFOUTIS AUX CHERRIES NOIRES)

Serves 6

600 g/1 lb oz black
cherries, washed and
pitted

500 ml/17 fl oz/2 cups milk

125 g/4 oz butter

125 g/4 oz caster sugar
(½ cup superfine)

200 g/7 oz/1¾ cups plain
(all-purpose) flour

baking dish

Preheat the oven to 180°C (350°F), gas mark 4.

Arrange the prepared cherries in a buttered ovenproof earthenware dish.

Heat the milk with the butter over a low heat until the butter has melted. Mix the sugar, and flour in a separate bowl and add the hot milk gradually, stirring all the time to prevent lumps forming. The batter should have the consistency of single (light) cream.

Pour the batter over the cherries in the earthenware dish. Bake for about 40 minutes in the oven.

Leave to cool and serve warm or cold.

menu idea | asparagus à la flamande | chicken à la basquaise
serve with | cherry brandy

STRAWBERRY CHARLOTTE (CHARLOTTE AUX FRAISES)

Serves 6

100 ml/3½ fl oz/about ½ cup raspberry liqueur

30 boudoir biscuits (ladyfingers)

400 g/14 oz strawberries

5 gelatine leaves or 4 teaspoons powdered gelatine

200 ml/7 fl oz/¾ cup water

2 tablespoons caster (superfine) sugar

400 ml/14 fl oz/1¾ cups double (heavy) cream

vanilla extract

charlotte mould

Pour the liqueur into a small dish or bowl and add 3 tablespoons of water. Lightly and quickly soak the biscuits in the liquid one by one, sugar side up, and line the bottom and sides of the charlotte mould with them, liqueur-soaked side facing inwards. Set the remaining biscuits aside.

Lightly rinse and drain the strawberries. Slice them if they are very large. Soften the gelatine leaves in the measured water for 5 minutes then wring out (or make up the powdered gelatine according to the maker's instructions on the pack). Dissolve the caster sugar with 4 tablespoons of boiling water in a shallow bowl and dissolve the gelatine in this liquid. Leave to cool.

Whip the cream into soft peaks and stir in the gelatine and a few drops of vanilla extract. Fill the space in the centre of the lined mould with alternate layers of cream, strawberries and the remaining biscuits. Top with a layer of biscuits, flat side uppermost. Press down and cover with a flat dish weighed down with something heavy (e.g. soup cans). Chill overnight.

Turn out onto a dish and serve with Red Berry Sauce (see recipe p. 396).

Note For a perfect charlotte, arrange the boudoir biscuits at the bottom of the mould with great care to form a rosette or star. Brush them with egg white to stick them together instead of soaking them in the liqueur.

menu idea | gorgonzola pears | fresh tuna casserole
serve with | muscat beaumes-de-venise

GÂTEAU BRETON

Serves 6

1 whole egg, plus 4 egg yolks

200 g/7 oz caster sugar (1 cup superfine)

200 g/7 oz butter, softened

2 tablespoons rum

400 g/14 oz/3¼ cups plain (all-purpose) flour

large, shallow cake tin (pan)

Preheat the oven to 160°C (325°F), gas mark 3.

Beat the egg and egg yolks in a bowl with a fork. Add the sugar, softened butter, rum and flour in that order. Pour the mixture into a buttered shallow cake tin (pan). Brush the surface with milk and make a swirly pattern with a fork. Bake for 30 minutes until a nice golden brown and a testing needle comes out dry.

Serve cold.

Note This cake is ideal for serving at teatime and will keep well for several days.

menu idea | langoustines in court-bouillon | soft cheese tart
serve with | extra dry cider

CARAMEL PEAR CAKE
(GÂTEAU POIRES CARAMEL)

Serves 6

250 g/9 oz caster sugar
(1¼ cups superfine)

3 or 4 pears, depending
on size

4 eggs

pinch of salt

175 g/6 oz/1½ cups plain
(all-purpose) flour

1 teaspoon baking powder

175 g/6 oz unsalted butter

manqué mould or deep
sponge tin (cake pan)

Melt 5½ tablespoons of the sugar in a pan with a little water to obtain a light caramel and use it to coat the manqué mould.

Peel and halve the pears and remove the core and the pips. Arrange the pear halves in the mould with the rounded side resting against the caramel.

Preheat the oven to 180°C (350°F), gas mark 4.

Beat the eggs with the rest of the sugar and salt in a bowl until the mixture is pale coloured and frothy. Sift the flour and baking powder together and add small quantities alternately with the softened butter to the egg and sugar mixture. Pour the mixture over the pears and bake until golden brown and the surface bounces back when pressed, about 25 minutes.

Turn out while still hot before the cooling caramel sticks to the mould and makes this operation harder.

Note This recipe works well with other seasonal fruits, such as apples, apricots, peaches, pineapple and mangoes.

menu idea | pumpkin soup | rabbit with garlic and rosemary
serve with | poire Willems

412

GÀTEAU BASQUE

Serves 6

For the cake batter:

300 g/10 oz/2½ cups plain (all-purpose) flour

2 egg yolks, plus 1 whole egg

200 g/7 oz caster sugar (1 cup superfine)

pinch of salt

200 g/7 oz butter, softened

finely grated rind of 1 lemon

1 egg yolk, to glaze

For the confectioners' custard:

250 ml/9 fl oz/1 cup milk

2 egg yolks

25 g/1 oz/3½ tablespoons plain (all-purpose) flour

4 tablespoons caster (superfine) sugar

2 tablespoons rum

manqué mould or deep sponge tin (cake pan)

Make the batter by gently mixing the flour together with the egg yolks, egg, sugar, salt, softened butter and finely grated lemon rind. Stand for 1 hour.

In the meantime, prepare the confectioners' custard: bring the milk slowly to the boil. Mix the egg yolks with the flour and sugar in a bowl. Whisk the hot milk into the mixture, then pour back into the pan and slowly bring to the boil, stirring continuously. Allow to thicken for several minutes, stirring all the time to ensure the custard doesn't stick. Remove from the heat, leave to cool and add the rum.

Preheat the oven to 180°C (350°F), gas mark 4.

Pour ⅔ of the cake batter into the buttered manqué mould. Cover with confectioners' custard – stopping 1 cm/½ inch from the rim – and add the rest of the batter. Glaze the surface with 1 beaten egg yolk, make a swirly pattern with the point of a knife and bake for 40 minutes, until the top is golden brown and crispy.

menu idea | basque toro

serve with | muscat beaumes-de-venise

RUM BABA
(BABA AU RHUM)

Serves 6

For the dough:

7 g/¼ oz/1 sachet dried
yeast (or 20 g/¾ oz fresh
bakers' yeast)

150 ml/5 fl oz/⅔ cup milk

250 g/9 oz/2 cups plain
(all-purpose) flour

½ teaspoon salt

1 tablespoon caster
(superfine) sugar

4 eggs

125 g/4 oz butter

For the syrup:

¾ litre/1¼ pints/4 cups
water

400 g/14 oz caster sugar
(2 cups superfine)

150 ml/5 fl oz/⅔ cup rum

To decorate:
chantilly cream
(see recipe p. 396)

savarin mould

To prepare the dough: Make up the dried yeast with the milk according to the maker's instructions on the pack. If using fresh yeast, crumble the yeast into the warmed milk. Pour the flour into a bowl and make a well. Put the salt, sugar, eggs and yeast mixed with milk into the well and mix thoroughly. When the dough is smooth, blend in the softened butter. Knead by hand, lifting to stretch it, until it is smooth, elastic and has lost most of its stickiness. This may take about 15 minutes to "break up" the yeast. You can use an electric beater fitted with a dough hook to make this operation easier.

Generously butter a 26-cm/10-inch savarin or ring mould and half fill with the dough. Leave to rise in a warm place for about 1 hour. The mould should by then be almost full.

Preheat oven to 160°C (325°F), gas mark 3.

Bake for about 20 minutes and turn out onto a wire rack.

To make the syrup: Boil the measured water and sugar for 5 minutes, then remove from the heat and add the rum. Drizzle the hot syrup over the warm Baba, repeating several times until it has been completely absorbed. Leave to cool and chill until ready to serve.

Make up the chantilly cream to the recipe on p. 396, but as the syrup is very sweet, you may prefer to reduce the amount of sugar. Fill the hole in the middle of the Baba with the chantilly and serve immediately.

menu idea | crunchy vegetable salad | scallops with fennel
serve with | demi-sec champagne

CHEESECAKE

Serves 6

For the base:

200 g/7 oz Petit-Beurre biscuits

125 g/4 oz butter

50 g/2 oz Demerara sugar

pinch of salt

For the filling:

4 eggs

150 g/5 oz caster sugar (½ cup plus 2 tablespoons superfine)

1 tablespoon plain (all-purpose) flour

500 g/1 lb Petit-Suisse cheese, or well-strained soft white cheese

200 g/7 oz salted fromage frais

grated rind and juice of 1 lemon

shallow springform baking tin (pan)

To make the base: put the biscuits in a plastic bag and crush them with a rolling pin. Melt the butter. Mix the biscuit crumbs, butter, sugar and salt together and spread over the base of the springform tin. Press down the mixture with the bottom of a glass. Refrigerate while preparing the filling.

Preheat the oven to 140°C (275°F), gas mark 1.

Beat the eggs with the sugar and flour. Add the cheese, fromage frais, lemon rind and juice, mix well, and pour over the base. Bake for 1 hour. Turn off the oven and leave to cool completely in the oven. Chill before serving, preferably the following day.

Note A variety of American cheesecake is made with Graham crackers (not dissimilar to digestive biscuits) which make a deliciously crunchy base – and Philadelphia cream cheese. Seasonal fruit makes a good topping or you can serve this cheesecake with a sauce – the Red Berry Sauce (see recipe p. 396) would be particularly good.

menu idea | artichokes à la grecque | lamb stew garnished with spring vegetables

serve with | muscat de Rivesaltes

CHOCOLATE REFRIGERATOR CAKE

Serves 6

300 g/10 oz best quality dark chocolate

5 tablespoons milk

125 g/4 oz butter

100 g/3½ oz icing sugar (scant cup confectioners' sugar)

¼ teaspoon vanilla extract

1 packet Petit-Beurre or Rich Tea biscuits (cookies)

loaf tin (pan)

Break the chocolate into pieces and melt with the milk in a double boiler or in a bowl set over a pan of barely simmering water. Do not let the bowl touch the water, otherwise the chocolate will "fudge" and refuse to melt. Stir well to obtain a smooth cream.

Remove the top of the double boiler or the bowl from the pan and blend in the butter, sugar and a few drops of vanilla extract.

Break up the biscuits into rough, even pieces and add to the mixture. (Do not completely crush into crumbs.) Mix gently to obtain a smooth mixture, pack into a loaf tin, and level with a spatula.

Chill overnight in the refrigerator and turn out carefully. Serve with chantilly cream (see recipe p. 396) or vanilla ice cream.

Note You can also use 150 g/5 oz of Cornflakes or Rice Krispies instead of biscuits.

menu idea | chilled tomato soup | rice salad à la romaine

serve with | muscat beaumes-de-venise

FRUITCAKE

Serves 6

75 g/3 oz candied fruit

75 g/3oz raisins or sultanas (golden raisins)

100 ml/3½ fl oz/½ cup rum

175 g/6 oz butter

200 g/7 oz caster sugar (1 cup superfine)

250 g/8 oz/1¾ cups plain (all-purpose) flour

1 teaspoon baking powder

2 eggs

75 g/3 oz split almonds

To decorate: 6 glacé cherries and 1 angelica stick

cake tin

Finely dice the candied fruit and macerate with the raisins in the rum.

Preheat the oven to 160°C (325°F), gas mark 3.

Beat the butter with the sugar until pale in colour, then alternately add the flour sifted with the baking powder, then the eggs, one by one. Gently mix in the rum with the currants, candied fruit and almonds.

Pour the batter into a buttered cake tin and decorate the top with cherries and small pieces of angelica. Bake for 1¼ hours. The cake is cooked when a knife inserted into the centre of the cake comes out clean. Turn off the oven and leave to stand for 15 minutes with the door ajar. Then turn out onto a wire rack to cool.

Note Dried fruit – apricots, dates or figs chopped into small pieces – or chocolate chips can be used instead of the candied fruit.

menu idea | split-pea soup | vegetable pancakes
serve with | muscat beaumes-de-venise

ORANGE SAVARIN (SAVARIN À L'ORANGE)

Serves 6

For the dough:

1 sachet dried yeast
(or 15 g/½ oz fresh bakers'
yeast)

100 ml/3½ fl oz/½ cup milk

150 g/5 oz/1¼ cups plain
(all-purpose) flour

1 tablespoon sugar

2 eggs

75 g/3 oz butter, softened

For the syrup:

2–3 oranges

75 g/3 oz sugar

200 ml/7 fl oz/¾ cup
weak tea

To decorate:

4 oranges

2 tablespoons orange
flower water (optional)

savarin mould

To prepare the dough: make up the dried yeast in the warmed milk according to maker's instructions on the pack or crumble the yeast into the warmed milk. Put the flour in a bowl and make a well. Put the sugar, eggs and the yeast mixture in the well and mix well. When the dough is smooth, blend in the softened butter. Knead by hand, lifting to stretch it, until it is smooth, elastic and has lost its stickiness. You can use an electric beater fitted with a dough hook to make this easier.

Generously butter a 26-cm/10-inch savarin or ring mould and half fill with the dough. Leave to rise in a warm place for about 1 hour. The mould should by then be almost full.

Preheat the oven to 160°C (325°F), gas mark 3. Bake the savarin for about 20 minutes, then turn out onto a rack to cool.

To make the syrup: squeeze 2 of the oranges and add the sugar and tea to the orange juice to obtain 500 ml/17 fl oz/ 2 cups of liquid. Top up with juice from the third orange if necessary. Bring to the boil. Gradually drizzle the hot syrup over the savarin until it is completely absorbed.

To decorate: peel the oranges and cut into quarters, removing as much pith and membrane as possible. Flavour them with the orange flower water and leave to macerate in the refrigerator. Fill the centre of the savarin with the orange quarters just before serving.

Note You can add grapefruit or mandarin segments to the orange quarters.

menu idea | autumn salad | paupiettes of sole in dill sauce
serve with | muscat de Rivesaltes

CHESTNUT DÉLICIEUX
(DÉLICIEUX AUX MARRONS)

Serves 6

3 eggs

150 g/5 oz unsalted butter, softened

300 g/10 oz sweetened chestnut cream (see note)

85 g/3 oz/¾ cup self-raising flour

1 teaspoon baking powder

3½ tablespoons rum

1 teaspoon vanilla extract

manqué mould or deep sponge tin (cake pan)

Preheat the oven to 160°C (325°F), gas mark 3.

Beat the eggs and softened butter together. Add the chestnut cream and continue beating. Mix in the flour and baking powder, followed by the rum and vanilla extract.

Pour the dough into a buttered manqué mould and bake in the preheated oven for 45 minutes. Turn off the oven. Leave the cake to cool with the door ajar, then turn out onto a rack to cool completely.

Note Chestnut cream is a sweetened chestnut purée often flavoured with vanilla. It must not be confused with unsweetened chestnut purée.

For a richer, more stylish cake, ice with 100 g/3½ oz of dark chocolate (70-75% solids) melted with 2 tablespoons of crème fraîche (or double cream) and a knob of unsalted butter.

menu idea | onion soup with garlic | fillets of duck breast with ceps
serve with | port

MOCHA BISCUIT CAKE
(MOKA AUX PETITS-BEURRE)

Serves 6

75 g/3 oz icing sugar
(²/₃ cup confectioners'
sugar)

150 g/5 oz unsalted butter,
softened

2 egg yolks

1 teaspoon instant coffee

300 ml/10 fl oz/1¼ cups
warm black coffee

40 Petit-Beurre biscuits

150 g/5 oz best quality
dark chocolate

2 tablespoons milk

rectangular dish, or cake tin
(pan)

Beat the sugar, 125 g/4 oz of the butter, the egg yolks and instant coffee powder to obtain a smooth mixture.

Pour the black coffee into a dish and lightly soak the biscuits in it. (Do not leave the biscuits soaking or they will become too soft to handle.) Arrange them in a dish to form a rectangle with 2 biscuits side by side widthways and 4 biscuits lengthways (as in the photograph). Build 5 layers of biscuits, spreading a little coffee/butter cream between each layer, finishing with a layer of biscuits. Refrigerate while preparing the topping.

Break the chocolate into pieces in a bowl, add the milk and set the bowl over a pan of barely simmering water. Do not let the bowl touch the water. Stir until the chocolate is melted and smooth, remove from the heat and blend in the rest of butter. Mix well to obtain a smooth cream and leave to cool. Spread this cream over the surface of the mocha biscuit cake using a spatula and put back in the refrigerator until ready to serve.

Note This cake is best eaten a day or two after it's been made. You can use a little coffee extract instead of instant coffee and add a dash of whisky or brandy to the coffee used to soak the biscuits. If you're in a rush, you can simply dust the cake with cocoa.

menu idea | purple salad | blue trout
serve with | sparkling wine

428

CHOCOLATE FONDANT
(FONDANT AU CHOCOLAT)

Serves 6

200 g/7 oz best quality
dark chocolate

200 g/7 oz butter

125 g/4 oz caster sugar
($\frac{1}{2}$ cup superfine)

1 heaped tablespoon plain
(all-purpose) flour

4 eggs

manqué mould or deep
sponge tin (cake pan)

Preheat the oven to 150°C (300°F), gas mark 2.

Butter the manqué mould, line with greaseproof paper and butter again. Break the chocolate into small pieces and put in a bowl set over a pan of barely simmering water. Do not let the bowl touch the water. Add the diced butter and stir until melted. Remove from the heat and add the sugar, flour and eggs in that order, mixing well after adding each ingredient.

Pour the mixture into the mould and bake in the preheated oven for about 40 minutes. Remove from the oven and leave to cool. Turn out when cold and peel off the greaseproof paper.

Note Use good quality chocolate – about 70% solids. You can melt the chocolate in the microwave, following the manufacturer's instructions.

Take care when baking the cake that the oven doesn't get too hot, otherwise the cake will dry out during cooking.

menu idea | melon surprise | guinea fowl with vanilla
serve with | demi-sec champagne

CAEN SABLÉS
(PETITS SABLÉS DE CAEN)

Makes about 30 biscuits

3 eggs

250 g/9 oz/2 cups plain
(all-purpose) flour

150 g/5 oz caster sugar
(³/₄ cup superfine)

250 g/9 oz unsalted
butter, softened

finely grated rind of
1 unwaxed lemon

pinch of salt

Hard boil the eggs for 10 minutes. Cool rapidly under cold water and remove the shells. Cut each egg in half and remove the yolks and crush with a fork.

Mix the flour with the sugar, softened butter, egg yolks and the finely grated lemon rind. Form into a ball, cover, and refrigerate for 1 hour.

Preheat the oven to 180°C (350°F), gas mark 4.

Roll out this dough to a thickness of ¹/₂ cm/¹/₄ inch and cut into circles with a pastry cutter or small glass. Arrange on buttered, floured baking sheets and bake in the preheated oven for 6-7 minutes without letting them brown. (You may have to swap round the shelves to ensure the sablés colour evenly.) Leave to cool on a wire rack.

menu idea | salmon tartare | lamb casserole à la normande

serve with | port

NANCY MACAROONS
(MACARONS DE NANCY)

Makes about 30 macaroons

200 g/7 oz/2 cups ground almonds

200 g/7 oz caster sugar (1 cup superfine)

2 egg whites

2 tablespoons mild honey

several drops of bitter almond extract

Thoroughly mix all the ingredients together in a terrine and chill for 3 hours.

Preheat the oven to 120°C (250°F), gas mark ½.

Using a wooden spoon, pile small walnut-size rounds of this dough onto a baking sheet lined with buttered greaseproof paper, flatten slightly, and bake in the preheated oven for 20-30 minutes until the macaroons are golden brown.

Leave to cool and peel off the paper. Store the macaroons in an airtight container to keep them soft.

Note You can use grated coconut instead of ground almonds to make coconut rocks.

menu idea | gorgonzola pears | seared salmon steaks
serve with | marsala

FRENCH DOUGHNUTS (MERVEILLES)

Makes 500 g/1 lb merveilles

325 g/11 oz/2¾ cups plain (all-purpose) flour

4 eggs

5 tablespoons caster sugar

75 g/3 oz butter

finely grated rind of 1 lemon

generous pinch of salt

icing sugar, for dusting (confectioners' sugar)

light oil, for frying

deep fryer

Put the flour in a bowl and add the rest of the ingredients. Knead lightly with the fingertips until the dough is smooth and pliable. Shape into a ball, sprinkle with flour and refrigerate for at least 1 hour.

Roll out the dough on a floured work surface and cut it into strips, then rectangles. Heat the oil (see below) then fry the fritters in several batches for a few minutes until golden brown, turning them with a skimmer. Place them on absorbent kitchen paper to drain, then sprinkle with icing sugar.

Note Drop a small piece of dough into the oil to check it is the right temperature: it will be surrounded by small bubbles if the oil is hot enough. The oil should never smoke during cooking.

In the Lyons region, these fritters are also called "bugnes" and sometimes "beignets de carnaval" (carnival fritters).

menu idea | Provençal tomato soup | salt cod brandade
serve with | port, madeira, marsala

436

CANNELÉS

Makes 6-8 cannelés

500 ml/17 fl oz/2 cups milk

½ vanilla pod, split open

50 g/2 oz butter plus 50 g/
2 oz to butter the moulds

100 g/3½ oz/scant cup
plain (all-purpose) flour

250 g/9 oz caster sugar
(1¼ cups superfine)

2 whole eggs, plus 2 egg
yolks

1 tablespoon rum

pinch of salt

Cannelé moulds, or dariole
moulds – ramekins will do
at a pinch

Bring the milk slowly to the boil with the half vanilla pod and 50 g/2 oz butter. In the meantime, mix the flour and sugar together, then blend in the eggs and egg yolks. Pour the boiling milk over this mixture stirring continuously to obtain a smooth, runny batter. Leave to cool and add the rum. Strain to remove the vanilla seeds and chill for 1 hour.

Preheat the oven to 180°C (350°F), gas mark 4.

Half fill the generously buttered moulds with the chilled batter. Place on a baking sheet and bake for 1 hour. The cannelés should be crispy and caramelised on the outside and soft inside. Turn out while still hot.

Note Cannelés are tricky to make: butter the moulds very carefully, using a brush, if possible. If they begin to overflow, lower the oven temperature. You can use small ramekins or dariole moulds instead of the fluted cannelé moulds, but the end result will be noticeably different.

menu idea | aubergine (eggplant) purée | red mullet with three (bell) pepper purée
serve with | sauternes

APPLE RABOTES
(RABOTES AUX POMMES)

Serves 6

2 egg yolks

250 g/9 oz butter, softened

200 g/7 oz caster sugar (1 cup superfine)

500 g/1 lb plain (all-purpose) flour

6 medium cooking apples

juice of 1 lemon

1 cinnamon stick

1 clove

For the glaze:

1 egg yolk mixed with 2 tablespoons milk

Mix the egg yolks with the softened butter and 100 g/3½ oz/ ½ cup of the sugar. Add the flour and salt. Knead quickly into a ball and stand for 1 hour.

In the meantime, peel and core the apples (keeping them whole) and cook for 10 minutes over a low heat with 100 g/ 3½ oz/½ cup sugar, lemon juice, spices and enough water to cover them. Leave to cool.

Preheat the oven to 180°C (350° F), gas mark 4.

Roll out the dough and cut into 6 squares large enough to enclose the apples. Place an apple in the middle of each square and wrap them in the pastry, taking care to seal the edges tightly with the glaze. Place on a buttered baking sheet and brush them with the rest of the glaze. Bake in the preheated oven for about 20-30 minutes, depending on the size of the apples. A very thin skewer passed through the pastry into the apple will tell you if they are cooked.

Serve the rabotes warm with double (heavy) cream, ice cream or custard.

Note You can use pears instead of apples for this recipe.

menu idea | fruity duck salad | blanquette de veau
serve with | dry cider

CRÊPES SUZETTE

Serves 6

For the batter:

200 g/7 oz/1½ cups plain (all-purpose) flour

3 eggs, beaten

pinch of salt

5 tablespoons caster (superfine) sugar

450 ml/15 fl oz/1¾ cups milk

60 g/2½ oz butter, melted

grated rind of ½ orange

For the orange cream:

150 g/5 oz icing sugar (1¼ cups confectioners sugar)

150 g/5 oz unsalted butter, softened

3 tablespoons Cointreau

grated rind of ½ orange

1 tablespoon caster sugar

To prepare the crêpe batter: mix the flour with the beaten eggs and salt in a bowl. Add the sugar and 100 ml/3½ fl oz/½ cup of milk. Mix well to prevent lumps forming. Slowly add the rest of the milk, melted butter and orange rind. Chill for 2 hours.

Dry-fry the crêpes by warming a non-stick crêpe pan and pouring in a small quantity of the batter, tilting in all directions to ensure that it spreads in a thin film. Cook over a fairly high heat until the crêpe slides when you shake the pan. Turn over and cook the other side for a couple of minutes: you'll soon acquire the knack of making very thin crêpes. Pile the crêpes on a plate under foil as they are cooked to keep them soft.

To prepare the orange cream: mix the icing sugar with the softened butter and flavour with the liqueur and orange rind. Spread a thin layer of cream over each crêpe. Fold into 4 and arrange in a fan shape in an ovenproof dish. Cover with foil.

Preheat the oven to 150°C (300F), gas mark 2.

Ten minutes before serving, remove the foil, and reheat in the oven. When you bring the crêpes to the table, sprinkle them with sugar, pour out a spoonful of warmed liqueur (30°C/86°F), light it then drizzle it over the crêpes until the flames go out.

Note For really succulent crêpes, make sure you cook the batter over a fairly high heat. If you don't have a non-stick crêpe pan, grease your pan with a wad of kitchen paper soaked in melted butter. Grand-Marnier or Curaçao works just as well as Cointreau in this recipe.

menu idea | artichokes à la grecque | quails roasted in muscat

serve with | white port

CURRANT CRAMIQUE (CRAMIQUE AUX RAISINS)

Serves 6

7 g/¹⁄₄ oz freeze-dried yeast or 15 g/¹⁄₂ oz bakers' yeast

100 ml/3¹⁄₂ fl oz/¹⁄₂ cup warm milk

1 teaspoon salt

500 g/1 lb/3¹⁄₂ cups plain (all-purpose) flour

3 eggs, lightly beaten

150 g/5 oz unsalted butter, softened and diced

150 g/5 oz/1¹⁄₄ cups currants, rinsed in boiling water

1 teaspoon cinnamon

150 g/5 oz/generous ¹⁄₂ cup pearl sugar (see note)

loaf tin

For the glaze:

1 egg yolk mixed with 2 tablespoons milk

loaf tin

To prepare the dough: make up the dried yeast in the warmed milk according to the maker's instructions on the pack, or crumble the yeast into the warmed milk and leave to rise.

Sift the salt and flour in a large bowl, make a well in the centre and pour in the yeast mixture. Add the eggs and mix thoroughly. Knead the dough vigorously, then mix in the diced butter, scalded currants, cinnamon and 100 g/3¹⁄₂ oz/¹⁄₂ cup of the sugar. Cover the bowl with a clean cloth and leave to rise in a warm place for at least 2 hours.

Preheat the oven to 190°C (375F), gas mark 5.

Butter a loaf tin. Break the dough and shape into an oval the same size as the tin. Place in the tin, cut a cross in the top to allow the dough to rise and brush the surface with the glaze. Sprinkle with the rest of the sugar and leave to rise again until the dough has completely filled the tin.

Bake the cramique for about 30 minutes. Turn out while still hot and leave to cool on a wire rack.

Note Pearl sugar, a coarse type of sugar also known as decorative or sanding sugar, is used for sprinkling over the top of baked goods. As an alternative use cubed sugar broken into pieces with a small hammer.

menu idea | cream of carrot soup | quiche lorraine

serve with | port or madeira

GÂCHE VENDÉENNE

Makes 1 large gâche

15 g/½ oz fresh bakers' yeast (or 7 g/¼ oz dried yeast)

100 ml/3½ fl oz/½ cup warm milk

2 eggs

150 g/5 oz caster sugar (¾ cup superfine)

2 tablespoons crème fraîche, or sour cream

125 g/4 oz unsalted butter, softened

1 tablespoon orange flower water

500 g/1 lb/3½ cups plain (all-purpose) flour

½ teaspoon salt

To decorate:

1 egg, to glaze

candied fruit or angelica

icing (confectioners') sugar

Make up the dried yeast in the warmed milk according to the maker's instructions on the pack, or crumble the yeast into the warmed milk and leave to rise.

Beat the 2 eggs with the sugar. Add the crème fraîche or cream, softened butter, orange flower water, yeast mixture and finally the flour sifted with the salt. Knead energetically for about 10 minutes until the dough is pliable and no longer sticks to your fingers. Put into a bowl covered with a clean cloth and leave to rise in a warm place for 2 hours.

Knead again, taking care to remove all the air bubbles. Shape into an oval loaf and leave to rise again for several hours in a warm place.

Preheat the oven to 180ºC (350º F), gas mark 4.

Glaze the gâche with beaten egg and decorate with candied fruit. Place on a greased baking sheet and bake for 1 hour until firm and golden. Leave to cool and sprinkle with icing sugar.

Note This cake is best eaten the day after baking.

menu idea | mouclade

serve with | port or madeira

KUGELHOPF

Serves 6

7 g/¹/₄ oz freeze-dried yeast or 12 g/³/₈ oz fresh bakers' yeast

3¹/₂ tablespoons warm milk

250 g/9 oz/2 cups plain (all-purpose) flour

¹/₂ teaspoon salt

3 eggs, beaten

175 g/6 oz unsalted butter, softened

3 tablespoons caster sugar (superfine)

about 20 whole blanched almonds

100 g/3¹/₂ oz/³/₄ cup raisins

icing (confectioners') sugar, to decorate

kugelhopf mould

Make up the dried yeast in the warmed milk according to the maker's instructions on the pack, or crumble the yeast into the warmed milk and leave to rise.

Sift the flour and salt into a large bowl, make a well in the centre and add the yeast mixture and eggs. Knead for at least 10 minutes with an electric beater fitted with dough hooks, or by hand, to obtain smooth elastic dough. Add the softened butter and sugar in small quantities, ensuring that they're well blended before adding more. Continue mixing for 5 minutes until the dough is smooth and shiny and stands away from the sides of the bowl. Cover the bowl with a clean cloth and leave to rise in a warm place for 2 hours.

When the dough has risen, "knock it back", working it as little as possible. Cover the bowl with clingfilm (plastic wrap) and refrigerate for 24 hours.

Preheat the oven to 190°C (375F), gas mark 5.

Butter the kugelhopf mould and put an almond in each cavity. Mix the raisins into the dough and half fill the mould with it. Leave to rise for 45 minutes in a warm place and when the dough is level with the top of the mould, bake for 30 minutes. Don't let the Kugelhopf overcook, otherwise it will be too dry.

Turn out onto a wire rack and dust with a little icing sugar before serving.

Note Kugelhopf is best eaten the day after baking.

menu idea | pumpkin soup | gammon steaks with white beans
serve with | gewurztraminer

SUGAR TART
(TARTE AU SUCRE)

Serves 6

For the dough:

1 sachet dried yeast

100 ml/3½ fl oz/½ cup warmed milk

250 g/9 oz/2 cups plain (all-purpose) flour

1 tablespoon sugar

pinch of salt

1 egg

125 g/4 oz unsalted butter

For the filling:

1 egg

1 heaped tablespoon sugar

1 teaspoon cinnamon

100 g/3½ oz/½ cup light Vergeoise sugar or soft brown sugar

quiche dish

Make up the yeast in the warmed milk according to the maker's instructions. Put the flour in a bowl and make a well in the centre. Add the sugar, salt, egg and yeast mixture and mix well with the flour. Knead the mixture to obtain a smooth, elastic dough. Add the butter and work thoroughly into the dough until completely blended. Shape into a ball and leave to rise in a warm place until the dough has doubled in volume.

Roll out the dough and line the bottom of a large buttered quiche dish.

To make the filling: beat the egg with the sugar and cinnamon. Spread this mixture over the surface of the dough and sprinkle liberally with the brown sugar. Leave to rise in a warm place for a further hour.

Preheat the oven to 180°C (350°F), gas mark 4 and bake the tart for about 30 minutes or until it is crisp and golden. Serve warm.

Note This speciality from northern France is usually eaten at teatime or at breakfast with a cup of coffee. It is also delicious served with fromage frais mixed with honey. You can also add 75 g/3 oz/¾ cup flaked (slivered) or chopped almonds to the filling.

menu idea | cream of cauliflower soup | poached smoked haddock
serve with | white port

SOFT CHEESE TART
(TARTE AU FROMAGE BLANC)

Serves 6

250 g/9 oz shortcrust pastry (see recipe p. 392)

200 g/7 oz caster sugar (1 cup superfine)

3 eggs, separated

2 tablespoons plain (all-purpose) flour

500 g/1 lb fromage frais

2 tablespoons thick crème fraîche (or sour cream)

100 g/3½ oz/¾ cup raisins soaked in tea

grated rind of 1 lemon

manqué mould or large quiche tin

Butter a manqué mould or quiche tin, preferably one that has a detachable base. Roll out the pastry and use to line the mould. Put in the freezer for 1 hour. Place the mould in a cold oven and turn the oven control to 160°C (325°F), gas mark 3 to begin baking. When this temperature has been reached, take the mould from the oven, but do not switch off the oven.

In the meantime, whip the sugar and egg yolks together in a bowl. Add the flour, fromage frais, crème fraîche or cream, drained raisins and grated lemon rind. Beat the egg whites until they form stiff peaks and gently fold into the mixture. Pour this filling into the pre-cooked pastry base and place the dish on the lowest shelf of the oven. Bake for a further 30 minutes at 160°C (325°F), gas mark 3, or until golden and firm but not rock solid as it will continue to cook in its own heat for a while. Remove from the mould while still warm and leave to cool on a wire rack.

Note Instead of fromage frais you can use mascarpone or sieved ricotta cheese.

menu idea | Scandinavian salad | marinated herrings
serve with | muscat beaumes-de-venise

APPLE UPSIDE-DOWN TART
(TARTE DES DEMOISELLES TATIN)

Serves 6

12 sugar lumps

100 ml/3½ fl oz/½ cup water

8 apples (Braeburn, Cox's Orange Pippin, etc.)

150 g/5 oz unsalted butter

100 g/3½ oz/½ cup sugar

1 teaspoon cinnamon

250 g/9 oz shortcrust pastry (see recipe p. 392)

manqué mould or solid-base quiche tin

Make a caramel by heating the sugar lumps with the measured water. When it has turned a pale golden colour, pour it into the bottom of a metal manqué mould or solid-base quiche tin.

Peel, core and cut the apples into thick slices (2-cm/¾ inch). Melt the butter in a large frying pan and gently fry the apples for 1–2 minutes on each side until golden. Arrange the slices in concentric circles on top of the caramel in the mould. Sprinkle with the cinnamon and sugar.

Preheat the oven to 180°C (350°F), gas mark 4.

Roll out the pastry into a circle slightly larger than the circumference of the mould, lay the sheet of pastry over the apples and gently fold in the edges between the apples and the sides of the mould. Make a small hole in the centre to allow steam to escape. Place in the preheated oven and bake for 30 minutes.

Remove from the oven and immediately, but carefully, turn the tart out upside-down onto a serving dish. Leave to cool.

Note If you like a crunchy caramel topping, prepare some more caramel with 12 sugar lumps and pour over the tart just before serving.

menu idea | gorgonzola pears | skate with capers
serve with | cider or madeira

RHUBARB TART
(TARTE À LA RHUBARB)

Serves 6

300 g/10 oz shortcrust pastry (see recipe p. 392)

1 kg/2 lb rhubarb

50 g/2 oz/½ cup flaked (slivered) almonds

2 tablespoons fine semolina

1 teaspoon cinnamon

6 tablespoons soft brown sugar

metal quiche dish

quiche tin

Roll out the pastry on a floured work surface and line a metal quiche tin. Place in the freezer.

Preheat the oven to 180°C (350°F), gas mark 4.

Peel the rhubarb if necessary, wash and dry carefully, then cut into chunks. Scatter the flaked almonds, semolina, cinnamon and half the sugar over the pastry base. Arrange the chunks of rhubarb on top and sprinkle with the rest of the sugar. Bake for 45 minutes on the lowest shelf of the oven.

Serve warm, or cold, dusted with icing sugar.

Note To save time, or when fresh rhubarb isn't in season, you can use frozen rhubarb. The taste of orange goes very well with rhubarb, so you can use the grated zest of 1 orange instead of cinnamon. If the rhubarb is too tart, replace half with 2 ripe bananas and leave out the flaked almonds. This interesting combination will make a sweeter tart.

menu idea | sorrel soup | sardines stuffed with Swiss chard
serve with | demi-sec champagne

LEMON TARTLETS
(TARTELETTES AU CITRON)

Serves 6

250 g/9 oz sweet
shortcrust pastry
(see recipe p. 392)

3 lemons, preferably
unwaxed

250 g/9 oz/1¼ cups sugar

4 eggs

100 g/3½ oz unsalted
butter, softened

1 tablespoon icing
(confectioners') sugar

metal tartlet moulds

Roll out the pastry on a floured work surface, cut into rounds and use to line the bottom of the tartlet moulds. Place in the refrigerator.

Grate the rind of 1 washed lemon and squeeze the juice from all 3 lemons. Put the rind in a small pan with the sugar and eggs and thicken over a low heat. Put this cream through a fine-meshed sieve to remove any rind. Gradually stir in the butter, bit by bit, and the lemon juice and set aside to cool.

Preheat the oven to 160°C (325°F), gas mark 3.

Remove the pastry bases from the refrigerator and fill ³/₄ full with the lemon mixture. Bake for 25 minutes until light golden in colour. Remove the tartlets from the oven, dust with icing sugar, and then return to the oven for a further 5 minutes.

Note Use loose-base moulds as they are easier to turn out. To make orange tartlets, use 2 oranges instead of the 3 lemons and reduce the sugar by 4 tablespoons.

menu idea | green pea soup | shepherd's pie
serve with | zinfandel

FIG TART
(TARTE FINE AUX FIGUES)

Serves 6

250 g/9 oz puff pastry
(see recipe p. 392), or
ready-made frozen puff
pastry

12 fresh figs, washed
and cut in half

2 egg yolks

4 tablespoon crème
fraîche (or sour cream)

75 g/3 oz/1 cup ground
almonds

2 tablespoons caster
(superfine) sugar

vanilla extract

1 teaspoon cinnamon
powder

125 g/4 oz/½ cup
granulated sugar

square baking tin

Thaw out the puff pastry if using frozen ready-made.

Preheat oven to 220°C (425°F), gas mark 7.

Roll out the pastry on a floured work surface and use to line
the baking tin. Prick the base with a fork and bake in the
preheated oven for 10 minutes. Remove from the oven but
do not switch it off.

Arrange the fig halves cut side up over the pre-cooked pastry
base. Beat the egg yolks, crème fraîche or cream, ground
almonds, caster sugar, a few drops of vanilla extract and the
cinnamon together. Pour this mixture over the figs, put the
tart back in the oven and bake for a further 10 minutes.
Remove from the oven – again keeping it switched on – and
dust the tart with granulated sugar. Return the tart to the
oven to caramelize for a further 5 minutes.

Note This tart works just as well with apricots or plums.

menu idea | aubergine mould (eggplant mold) | roast monkfish (anglerfish)
serve with | port, madeira, vin santo

REDCURRANT MERINGUE TART
(TARTE AUX GROSEILLES MERINGUÉE)

Serves 6

250 g/9 oz sweet
shortcrust pastry
(see recipe p. 392)

400 g/14 oz redcurrants

3 egg whites

6 tablespoons caster
(superfine) sugar

90 g/3¼ oz icing sugar
(¾ cup confectioners'
sugar)

metal quiche tin

Roll out the pastry and use to line the quiche tin. Put in the freezer for 1 hour.

Preheat the oven 220°C (425°F), gas mark 7.

Bake the pastry base for 10 minutes in the preheated oven. Remove the pastry base and reduce the oven temperature to 100°C (200°F), gas mark ¼. In the meantime, strip the redcurrants from their stalks, wash and drain them.

Beat the egg whites until they form very stiff peaks, adding both types of sugar halfway through beating. Divide between 2 bowls. Gently mix the redcurrants with the first half and spread over the pastry base. Cover with the meringue in the second bowl. Bake for 1 hr in the cool oven. Eat warm or cold.

Note Leave the oven door ajar while you're filling the pastry base, so that the oven will be cool enough to bake the meringue without burning it. The set meringue should be hard and dry. You can also add 50 g/2 oz/½ cup of coarsely chopped hazelnuts.

menu idea | watercress soup | paupiettes of sole in dill sauce
serve with | pink champagne

HONEY AND WALNUT TART
(TARTE AU MIEL ET AUX NOIX)

Serves 6

300 g/10 oz sweet shortcrust pastry (see recipe p. 392)

150 g/5 oz/1½ cups shelled walnut halves, coarsely chopped

50 g/2 oz unsalted butter, softened

50 g/2 oz/⅓ cup soft brown sugar

4 tablespoons honey

150 ml/5 fl oz/⅔ cup whipping cream

metal quiche tin

Preheat the oven to 200°C (400°F), gas mark 6.

Roll out the dough on a floured work surface and use to line the quiche tin. Chill in the refrigerator.

Using a fork, mix the coarsely chopped walnuts with the butter and sugar. Add the honey and cream and spread this mixture over the pastry base. Bake for 40 minutes in the preheated oven. Serve cold.

Note This tart will keep for several days. It's actually better prepared the day before.

Pick a full-flavoured honey, such as heather, chestnut or mountain honey, which will bring out the flavour of the walnuts. Maple syrup can be used instead of honey.

menu idea | split-pea soup | mountain salad
serve with | banyuls

PLUM CRUMBLE TART
(TARTE AUX QUETSCHES AUX STREUSELS)

Serves 6

For the pastry:

90 g/3 oz unsalted butter

1 egg yolk

2 tablespoons soft brown sugar

3 pinches of cinnamon

pinch of salt

175 g/6 oz/scant 1½ cups plain (all-purpose) flour

For the filling and topping:

500 g/1 lb quetsch plums or damsons

75 g/3oz/⅔ cup plain (all-purpose) flour

100 g/3½ oz/½ cup sugar

50 g/2 oz well-chilled unsalted butter

metal baking tin

To prepare the pastry: mix the butter, egg yolk, brown sugar, cinnamon and salt in a bowl. Add the flour and knead to obtain a pliable dough. Chill for 1 hour in the refrigerator.

Wash and halve the plums, discard the pits.

Preheat the oven to 200°C (400°F), gas mark 6.

Roll out the dough on a floured work surface and use to line the baking tin. Arrange the plum halves over the pastry base.

To make the topping: put the flour, sugar and butter in a bowl and blend together using two knives until the mixture resembles coarse crumbs. Sprinkle over the plums, place the tart in the oven and bake for 30 minutes.

Note Originally from Alsace, this tart is served warm, dusted with cinnamon and icing sugar. You can also serve it with crème fraîche, yogurt, whipped cream or vanilla ice-cream. To save time, you can substitute the crumble mixture with 75 g/3 oz/½ cup of chopped mixed nuts mixed with 75 g/ 3 oz/½ cup of soft brown sugar.

menu idea | autumn salad | guinea fowl with vanilla
serve with | port, madeira

TWELFTH-NIGHT CAKE (GALETTE DES ROIS)

Serves 6

400 g/14 oz puff pastry
(see recipe p. 392)

For the frangipane:

50 g/2 oz unsalted butter

50 g/2 oz icing sugar
(scant ½ cup confectioners'
sugar)

50 g/2 oz/⅔ cup ground
almonds

1 tablespoon plain
(all-purpose) flour

1 egg

1 tablespoon rum

bitter almond extract

For the glaze:

1 egg yolk mixed with
2 tablespoons milk,
to glaze

icing sugar

lucky charm

To make the frangipane: whisk the butter until soft and creamy. Add the icing sugar, ground almonds, flour and egg in that order to obtain a smooth, light cream. Flavour with rum and a few drops of almond extract and set aside to rest.

Preheat the oven to 220°C (425°F), Gas Mark 7.

Divide the puff pastry in half. Roll out one half on a floured work surface, cut out a 25-cm/10-inch circle and place it on a baking sheet.

Spread the frangipane cream over the top, stopping 2 cm/ ¾ inch from the edge, position the lucky charm and brush a little glaze around it. Brush a little water round the pastry edge. Roll out the other half of the dough, cut out a circle the same size and place it carefully on top of the first. Press the edges tightly together with a fork so that they won't come apart. Brush the rest of the glaze over the cake and make a wavy pattern radiating out from the centre with the tip of a knife.

Place in the oven and bake for 10 minutes, then lower the temperature to 180°C (350°F), gas mark 4 and bake for a further 20 minutes. Take the cake from the oven 5 minutes before the end of the cooking time, dust with icing sugar and put back in the oven until the icing sugar melts and the pastry has a glossy sheen. Remove from the oven and allow to cool for 15 minutes before serving.

Note Make sure you remember to put the lucky charm inside the cake.

menu idea | pumpkin soup | beef cooked in red wine
serve with | dry cider

FIADONE

6 eggs, separated

**150 g/5 oz caster sugar
(³⁄₄ cup superfine sugar)**

**400 g/14 oz Brocciu
cheese, or ricotta**

**grated rind and juice of
1 lemon**

manqué mould, or deep
ovenproof dish

Preheat the oven to 180°C (350°F), gas mark 4.

Beat the egg yolks in a bowl with the sugar until the mixture
becomes pale and frothy. Add the cheese, grated lemon rind
and juice. Mix these ingredients together to obtain a smooth
mixture. In a separate bowl, beat the egg whites until they
form stiff peaks and gently fold them into the cheese mixture.

Pour into a buttered manqué mould and bake for 30 minutes.
Serve warm or cold.

Note This dessert is a speciality from Corsica where it's
flavoured with citron zest. You can also add several drops
of bergamot oil.

menu idea | baked lasagne
serve with | marsala

RICE PUDDING – FRENCH STYLE (TEURGOULE)

Serves 6

150 g/5 oz/¾ cup short-grain rice

2 litres/3½ pints/8 cups full-cream milk

125 g/4 oz/½ cup sugar

1 teaspoon ground cinnamon

¼ teaspoon salt

earthenware or ceramic ovenproof baking dish

Rinse the rice in cold water. Add to a pan of boiling water and strain as soon as it comes back to the boil.

Preheat the oven to 150°C (300°F), gas mark 2.

Heat the milk with the sugar, cinnamon and salt in a pan. Add the rice and remove from the heat. Stir well and transfer the contents to an ovenproof earthenware or ceramic baking dish with a lid. Place in the oven and cook for 2½ hours or until the surface of the Teurgoule is golden brown and caramelized. Serve warm or cold.

Note Use Italian risotto rice – such as Carnaroli or Arborio – which retains its shape well, even after prolonged cooking, and use best-quality milk.

menu idea | melon surprise | sole with herbs
serve with | muscat beaumes-de-venise

CRÉMETS

Serves 6

750 g/1½ lb fromage frais

300 ml/10 fl oz/1¼ cups whipping cream

2 egg whites

muslin (cheesecloth) squares

small perforated moulds

Stir the fromage frais to ensure there are no lumps and drain off any whey.

Stiffly whip the cream but do not let it go "solid". Beat the egg whites until they form stiff peaks. Gently fold the whipped cream into the cheese and blend well. Again, gently fold the egg whites into this mixture to obtain a smooth mousse.

Line some small perforated moulds with muslin and fill each one with the cheese mousse. Fold the muslin over the top and leave to drain on a plate in the refrigerator overnight.

Turn out on individual plates and serve with sugar and seasonal fruit.

Note Crémets, which are a speciality of Angers, can also be served with raspberry coulis (see Red berry sauce p. 396).

menu idea | vichyssoise | gammon steaks with white beans
serve with | demi-sec champagne

LEMON MOUSSE
(MOUSSE AU CITRON)

Serves 6

4 lemons, preferably unwaxed

6 eggs, separated

300 g/10 oz caster sugar (1½ cups superfine sugar)

Grate the rind of 1 washed and scrubbed lemon or pare the zest into thin strips with a vegetable peeler. Put in a small bowl and cover with clingfilm (plastic wrap) to keep it from drying out. Squeeze the juice from all 4 lemons.

Whisk the egg yolks with the sugar until the mixture becomes pale and frothy. Add the lemon juice and mix well. Pour into a pan over a low heat, stirring continuously until it thickens: don't allow to boil. Leave aside to cool.

Beat the egg whites until they form stiff peaks and gently fold them into the cooled lemon cream. Pour into stemmed glasses or a large bowl. Serve well chilled and sprinkled with grated lemon rind or strips of zest.

Note Buy plump, unwaxed lemons as these are sweeter.

menu idea | carrot and cumin salad | rabbit with mustard
serve with | muscat beaumes-de-venise

DARK CHOCOLATE MOUSSE
(MOUSSE AU CHOCOLAT NOIR)

Serves 6

200 g/7 oz best quality,
dark chocolate (not
unsweetened)

4 tablespoons water

5 eggs, separated

3 tablespoons sugar

150 ml/5 fl oz/²⁄₃ cup
whipping cream

Break the chocolate into small pieces, place in a bowl and add the measured water. Use a double boiler if you have one, otherwise set the bowl over a pan of barely simmering water, but do not let the bowl touch the water, and stir until melted.

Beat the egg yolks with the sugar until the mixture is pale and frothy. Add the melted chocolate.

Stiffly whip the cream, but do not let it go "solid", and gently fold it into the chocolate mixture. Beat the egg whites until they form stiff peaks and gradually fold them into the mousse a little at a time, mixing the chocolate mixture from top to bottom in a gentle circular motion. Pour the mousse into a bowl and chill in the refrigerator for at least 4 hours.

Note You can melt the chocolate in a little coffee. You can also leave the mousse overnight in the freezer and serve it as a frozen dessert.

menu idea | mushroom salad with yogurt | lamb casserole à la normande
serve with | banyuls

MONT-BLANC

Serves 6

500 g/1 lb chestnuts
(see note)

500 ml/17 fl oz/2 cups milk

1 vanilla pod

4 tablespoons caster sugar

250 ml/9 fl oz/1 cup
Chantilly cream (see
recipe p. 396)

To decorate: small pieces
of marrons glacés

Split the flat side of the chestnut shells with a sharp knife. Put them in a pan of cold water and bring to the boil over a low heat. Take the chestnuts from the hot water in small batches and remove the shells, which should peel away easily.

Put the peeled chestnuts in a pan with the milk, the vanilla pod, split lengthways, and the sugar. Simmer over a very low heat for 30–40 minutes: the chestnuts should have absorbed almost all the milk. Put them through the medium blade of a vegetable mill, or through a potato ricer, and collect the "vermicelli" in a large serving bowl. Chill for several hours.

Just before serving, make the Chantilly cream. Make a well in the middle of the chestnut purée and fill with Chantilly cream. Decorate with small pieces of marrons glacés.

Note To save time, you can use vacuum-packed peeled chestnuts or a jar of water-packed chestnuts.

You can add 2 tablespoons of dark rum to the chestnut purée or serve the Mont-blanc with cherries in eau-de-vie and chocolate sauce.

menu idea | cheese soufflé | scallops with fennel
serve with | crémant

CRÈME CATALANE

Serves 6

8 egg yolks

100 g/3½ oz caster sugar
(½ cup superfine sugar)

2 tablespoons cornflour
(cornstarch)

1 litre/1¾ pints/4 cups milk

1 unwaxed lemon

½ teaspoon ground
cinnamon

ramekins or small dishes

Whisk the egg yolks with 2 tablespoons of the sugar in a large mixing bowl, then add the cornflour mixed with a little milk. Set aside.

Bring the rest of the milk slowly to the boil in a pan with 4 tablespoons of the sugar, the lemon rind removed in one long strip, and the cinnamon. Infuse for 5 minutes, then put through a fine-meshed sieve.

Pour both mixtures into a clean pan and thicken over a low heat for about 5 minutes, stirring continuously. Pour the cream mixture into shallow ramekins or earthenware dishes, leave to cool and refrigerate. Just before serving, sprinkle the rest of the sugar over the top of the desserts and caramelize under the grill or with a kitchen blow torch.

Note If you don't have any small individual dishes, pour the cream into a large shallow serving dish.

menu idea | stuffed aubergines (eggplants) à l'orientale | shepherd's pie
serve with | muscat beaumes-de-venise

FLOATING ISLANDS
(ŒUFS À LA NEIGE)

Serves 6

600 ml/1 pint/2½ cups
milk, plus a little extra

5 eggs, separated

6 tablespoons caster
(superfine) sugar

1 vanilla pod

For the caramel:

25 sugar lumps

Bring the milk to the boil in a large pan over a low heat.

In the meantime, beat the egg whites with 2 tablespoons of the sugar until they form stiff peaks. Shaping them with a tablespoon or serving spoon, drop 6 pear-sized portions of the egg white into the boiling milk and poach for 30 seconds on each side. Drain them on kitchen paper or a clean cloth. Strain the milk through a fine-meshed sieve and top up with more if necessary to make 500 ml/17 fl oz/2½ cups of liquid.

Make a custard cream with the rest of the ingredients (see recipe p. 396) and leave to cool. Pour the custard cream into a large deep dish and "float" the egg whites on top, then refrigerate.

Just before serving, decorate the floating islands with strands of crisp caramel. The caramel is made with the sugar lumps and a little water in a small pan over medium heat. When the syrup has turned golden brown, stop it cooking by plunging the bottom of the pan into cold water. Wait a few seconds, then trickle the caramel over the "islands". Serve immediately before the caramel dissolves.

Note You can flavour the custard by infusing 3 sprigs of fresh lavender instead of the vanilla.

menu idea | black pudding and apple salad | goat's cheese tart
serve with | muscat beaumes-de-venise

EGG CUSTARD
(ŒUFS AU LAIT)

Serves 6

750 ml/1¼ pints/3 cups milk

½ vanilla pod

5 eggs

75 g/3 oz/⅓ cup sugar

soufflé mould or ramekins

Bring the milk to the boil with the half vanilla pod split lengthways. Infuse for 5 minutes, then remove the vanilla pod, scrape out the seeds with the point of a sharp knife and add them to the milk.

Preheat the oven to 150°C (300F), gas mark 2.

Whisk the eggs with the sugar in a bowl. Gradually add the hot milk, stirring continuously. Put through a fine-meshed sieve and pour this custard into an 18-cm/7-inch ovenproof soufflé mould placed within a larger container. Boil some water and pour into the outside container to come about half way up the soufflé mould. Place in the preheated oven for 45 minutes. Remove from the oven and leave to cool.

Note These egg custards can be made in individual ramekins, but they will take less time to cook (about 15 minutes).

menu idea | warm chestnut salad | salmon trout fillets with mushrooms
serve with | muscat d'alsace

CRÈME BRÛLÉE

Serves 6

2 whole eggs

8 egg yolks

175 g/6 oz caster sugar
(1 scant cup superfine
sugar)

few drops pure vanilla
extract

900 ml/1½ pints/3½ cups
whipping cream

75 g/3 oz/½ cup soft
brown sugar

baking dish or ramekins

Preheat the oven to 130°C (250°F), gas mark ½.

Carefully mix the whole eggs, egg yolks, sugar and vanilla without whisking to avoid forming any froth or air bubbles. Gradually blend in the cream. Pour the mixture into a baking dish or small individual ramekins placed on a baking sheet and cook in the preheated oven for about 40 minutes.

Open the oven door slightly, leave to cool, then chill in the refrigerator, preferably overnight. An hour before serving, sprinkle brown sugar over the chilled crème brûlées and put them under a hot preheated grill (broiler) or use a kitchen blow-torch. Watch them carefully as the sugar melts and caramelizes and remove as soon as the caramel has turned a deep brown. Stand at room temperature, then chill for ½ hour before serving.

Note You can also prepare the crisp caramel topping just before serving if you want to create a contrast in temperature between the cold custard and the hot caramel.

You can flavour crème brûlées with a host of different ingredients including lemon zest, coffee essence, various liqueurs and almond essence.

menu idea | cabbage and bacon soup | grilled goat's cheeses
serve with | demi-sec champagne

ALMOND BLANCMANGE
(BLANC-MANGER AU LAIT D'AMANDES)

Serves 6

15 g/¹/₂ oz gelatine taken from 2 packets

200 ml/7 fl oz/³/₄ cup water

750 ml/1¹/₄ pints/3 cups milk

1¹/₂ teaspoons almond extract

4 egg yolks

125 g/4 oz/¹/₂ cup sugar

1 teaspoon cornflour (cornstarch)

2 tablespoons orange flower water

200 ml/7 fl oz/³/₄ cup whipping cream

charlotte mould

Dissolve the gelatine in the measured water according to the instructions on the packet. Make a Custard cream (see recipe p. 396) with the milk, 1 teaspoon of the almond extract, egg yolks, sugar and cornflour. Stir the gelatine into the custard cream while it is still hot and flavour with the remaining ¹/₂ teaspoon of almond extract and the orange flower water. Cool rapidly in a basin of iced water.

Whip the cream until it forms soft peaks and gently fold into the chilled custard when the latter begins to thicken. Pour the mixture into the mould and leave to set in the refrigerator for at least 12 hours, or overnight.

When ready to serve, dip the mould in hot water for a few moments to loosen the blancmange and then turn out onto a serving dish.

Serve with red berry sauce (see recipe p. 396) or apricots in ginger (see recipe p. 504).

Note You can decorate the blancmange with fresh shelled almonds when in season.

menu idea | vichyssoise | red mullet with three (bell) pepper purée
serve with | demi-sec champagne

TIRAMISU

Serves 6

150 ml/5 fl oz/²⁄₃ cup strong coffee

2 tablespoons Marsala

24 boudoir sponge biscuits (ladyfingers)

3 eggs, separated

4 tablespoons sugar

400 g/14 oz mascarpone cheese

3½ tablespoons cocoa powder

Pour the coffee and 1 tablespoon of the Marsala into a small deep dish. Lightly and quickly soak half the sponge fingers in this liquid and arrange them in a single layer over the bottom of a serving dish.

Beat the egg yolks and sugar together until pale and frothy, then add the cheese and the rest of the Marsala. Blend together thoroughly. Beat the egg whites until they form stiff peaks, then gently fold them into the mixture. Spread half of this cream over the layer of sponge fingers.

Soak the remaining sponge fingers and arrange in a layer on the cream layer, then top with the remaining cream. Smooth the surface, cover with clingfilm (plastic wrap) and place the dish in the refrigerator for at least 12 hours, preferably overnight. Dust with the cocoa powder before serving.

Note Mascarpone is a white creamy cheese that can be bought from Italian delicatessens and large supermarkets.

The boudoir sponge biscuits (ladyfingers) absorb liquid very quickly so the assembling of this dessert will be easier if they are soaked in two batches.

menu idea | mushroom salad with yogurt | beef and onion stew
serve with | muscat beaumes-de-venise

RASPBERRY DELIGHT
(MOUSSE DÉLICIEUSE)

Serves 6

150 ml/5 fl oz/⅔ cup whipping cream

1 egg white

5 tablespoons caster (superfine) sugar

400 g/14 oz raspberries

500 g/1 lb fromage frais

Whip the cream to soft peaks, then beat the egg white until it forms stiff peaks, folding in 1 tablespoon of the sugar while it is still soft.

Crush two-thirds of the raspberries.

Stir the fromage frais in a separate bowl until smooth, then gently blend in the whipped cream, egg white and finally the crushed raspberries. Pour the mousse into a large bowl or stemmed glasses and decorate the top with the remaining whole raspberries. Chill at least 3 hours before serving.

Note You use strawberries, blueberries, mango or fresh diced pineapple instead of raspberries. You can also combine several types of fruits: blueberries, blackberries, strawberries, melon, peaches and redcurrants.

menu idea | gazpacho | lamb curry
serve with | crémant

POACHED PEARS WITH BLACKCURRANTS
(POIRES POCHÉES AUX GRAINS DE CASSIS)

Serves 6

100 g/3¹/₂ oz/¹/₂ cup sugar

100 ml/3¹/₂ fl oz/¹/₂ cup blackcurrant liqueur

250 ml/9 fl oz/1 cup water

6 large pears

1 jar blackcurrant jelly

200 ml/7 fl oz/³/₄ cup red Burgundy

150 g/5 oz/1¹/₄ cups fresh blackcurrants

Put the sugar and blackcurrant liqueur in a pan with the measured water and bring to the boil.

Peel the pears but leave whole and poach in the syrup for 10 minutes, 5 minutes on each side. Remove the pears with a slotted spoon and arrange in a serving dish.

Mix the blackcurrant jelly into the cooking syrup, bring to the boil and reduce for 10 minutes, to obtain a thickish syrup. Remove from the heat, add the wine and pour over the pears. Leave to cool and sprinkle with fresh blackcurrants.

Note Delicious served chilled with vanilla ice cream or Chantilly cream (see recipe p. 396).

menu idea | dandelion leaf and bacon salad | lamb chops
serve with | pear liqueur or rosé

CHILLED PEARS WITH REDCURRANT SYRUP
(SOUPE GLACÉE DE POIRES AUX GROSEILLES)

Serves 6

500 g/1 lb redcurrants

100 ml/3½ fl oz/½ cup water

150 g/5 oz/¾ cup sugar

250 ml/9 fl oz/1 cup Riesling

1 kg/2 lb small pears

rose petals (from unsprayed bushes)

Rinse the redcurrants, put in a small pan with the measured water and cook gently until the currants begin to break. Strain the juice through a sieve, pressing the fruit well down.

Mix the redcurrant juice, sugar and wine together in a small pan. Peel and halve the pears, removing the core and pips, and cook gently in the redcurrant juice until they are tender – the cooking time will vary depending on the size and variety of the pears. Leave to cool and then chill in the refrigerator.

Decorate with rose petals to serve.

menu idea | stuffed artichoke hearts | squid tourte

serve with | pear liqueur or rosé

PEACHES IN RED WINE
(SOUPE DE PÊCHES AU VIN ROUGE)

Serves 6

6 large peaches

6 tablespoons sugar

350 ml/12 fl oz/1½ cups red Bordeaux

12 sugar lumps

1 cinnamon stick
(or 1 teaspoon ground cinnamon)

Peel and halve the peaches, remove the stone (pit) and sprinkle with sugar. Leave to macerate for 1 hour.

Put the red wine, sugar lumps and cinnamon stick in a pan, and boil for 10 minutes. Add the peaches along with their syrup and poach for 15 minutes. When the fruit is cooked, strain carefully − keeping the liquid − and place 2 peach halves in each individual glass bowl.

Reduce the cooking liquid by half, leave to cool, and pour over the peaches.

Chill in the refrigerator until ready to serve.

Note Choose ripe, unblemished peaches, allowing two per person if they are a bit on the small side. A useful tip for peeling peaches: plunge the fruit into boiling water and then immediately into a bowl of iced water − the skin will come away easily.

menu idea | spinach salad with goat's cheese | seared salmon steaks
serve with | any light dry red or rosé

RHUBARB AND ORANGE COMPOTE
(COMPOTE DE RHUBARBE À L'ORANGE)

Serves 6

3 oranges
750 g/1½ lb rhubarb
200 g/7 oz/1 cup sugar
100 ml/3½ fl oz/½ cup water

To serve: 1 large carton whipping cream, freshly grated (or ground) ginger and 1 packet ginger snap biscuits

Remove the rind of the oranges with a zester or vegetable peeler and cut into thin strips. Blanch the rind for 5 minutes in boiling water to remove the bitterness. Squeeze the juice from the oranges.

Rinse the rhubarb, peeling and/or removing the "strings" as necessary, and cut into small chunks. Put the rhubarb in a pan with the orange juice and 150 g/5 oz/¾ cup sugar, and cook over a medium heat for 20 minutes.

Bring the rest of the sugar and measured water to the boil in another pan and add the strips of orange rind. When the rind is translucent and the syrup nice and thick, remove from the heat and leave to one side.

Leave the compote to cool and, just before serving, decorate with the pieces of the crystallized orange peel.

Serve warm or cold with ginger snap biscuits and whipped cream flavoured with ginger.

Note If time is at a premium, simply cook the rhubarb with a jar of thick-cut orange marmalade.

menu idea | cream of courgette (zucchini) soup with parsley | scrambled eggs with truffles
serve with | muscat beaumes-de-venise

APRICOTS IN GINGER
(ABRICOTS AU GINGEMBRE)

Serves 6

1 kg/2 lb apricots

about 2.5-cm/1-inch piece
fresh ginger

100 g/3½ oz/½ cup sugar,
less if the apricots are
very sweet

65 g/2½ oz flaked almonds
(⅔ cup slivered almonds)

Halve the apricots and remove the stone (pit). Peel and grate the ginger. Put the apricot halves in a pan, sprinkle with sugar and grated ginger, mix, and leave to macerate for 2 hours.

Place the pan on an extremely low heat, cover, and cook for 30 minutes or until the fruit is soft. Remove from the heat and leave to cool.

Just before serving, lightly toast the almonds in a non-stick frying pan and sprinkle on the compote. Serve at room temperature.

Note You can use fresh, whole blanched almonds instead of flaked almonds or serve the compote with macaroons.

menu idea | pissaladière | beef and onion stew
serve with | muscat de Rivesaltes

QUETSCH PLUMS IN SYRUP
(SOUPE DE QUETSCHES)

Serves 6

1 kg/2 lb quetsch plums,
or damsons

500 ml/17 fl oz/2 cups
fruity, white Alsace wine

100 g/3½ oz/½ cup brown
sugar

grated rind of 1 lemon

1 teaspoon ground mixed
spice

Wash the plums, cut in half and discard the stone (pit).

Put the wine, sugar, lemon rind and mixed spice into a pan
and bring to the boil. Add the plums and leave to simmer over
a low heat for 10–15 minutes.

Remove from the heat and leave to cool. Serve chilled.

Note This dessert is also delicious served warm with ice cream
flavoured with cinnamon or hazelnuts.

menu idea | cream of carrot soup | tajine of lamb with aubergines (eggplants)
serve with | madeira, tokay, port

AUTUMN-FRUIT COMPOTE
(FRUITS D'AUTOMNE RÔTIS)

Serves 6

750 g/1½ lb slightly sharp apples (Bramley, Granny Smith, Blenheim Orange, Cox's Orange Pippin...)

750 g/1½ lb ripe pears

1 large, ripe quince (or plums, prunes, figs)

65 g/2½ oz butter

150 g/5 oz/⅔ cup soft brown sugar

1 vanilla pod, split lengthways with seeds removed

To serve: thick crème fraîche

Peel and core all the fruit. Cut into quarters and then halve each quarter.

Melt the butter in a very large frying pan, add the fruit and stir with a wooden spatula to ensure it is well coated with butter. Sprinkle with the soft brown sugar and add the vanilla pod. Cook over a medium heat, shaking the pan occasionally and turning the fruit carefully with the spatula until it is nicely browned and caramelized.

Serve hot with thick crème fraîche, sour cream, yogurt or whipped cream.

Note You can flambé this dessert to serve – simply pour 70 ml/2½ fl oz/¼ cup Calvados or brandy over the compote and set alight.

menu idea | carrot and cumin salad | fillets of duck breast with ceps
serve with | gewurztraminer

APPLE CRUMBLE
(CRUMBLE AUX POMMES)

Serves 6

6-7 cooking apples

125-175 g/4-6 oz/¹/₂-³/₄ cup sugar, to taste

lemon juice, to taste

For the crumble (crisp):

250 g/8 oz/1³/₄ cups plain (all-purpose) flour

150 g/5 oz/²/₃ cup granulated sugar

75 g/3 oz butter

ovenproof dish, greased

Peel and core the apples and chop roughly. Place the apple pieces and the sugar together with lemon juice in a pan and stew lightly to soften the apples but not too much – the pieces should hold their shape. Remove the pieces from the pan with a slotted spoon and place in the prepared dish, leaving the cooking liquid behind.

Preheat the oven to 180°C (350°F), gas mark 4.

To make the crumble: put the flour and sugar in a mixing bowl, stir together, and rub in the fat lightly with your fingertips until the mixture resembles breadcrumbs and just begins to form lumps. Cover the apples completely with the crumble mixture.

Place the dish on a baking sheet and bake in the preheated oven for 40-50 minutes, until the top is crisp and golden.

Note Make the crumble by hand rather than using a food processor as this will give it a lighter texture.

If you have time, chill the crumble mixture in the refrigerator before covering the fruit.

menu idea | crunchy vegetable salad | roast rabbit with garlic and rosemary
serve with | cider

SPICED FRUIT CRUMBLE (CRUMBLE ÉPICÉ)

Serves 6

1 kg/2 lb red plums

250 g/9 oz/2 cups prunes

1 orange

2.5-cm/1-inch piece ginger

2 cloves

1 cinnamon stick

For the crumble:

150 g/5 oz/1¼ cups plain (all-purpose) flour

100 g/3½ oz/1 cup ground almonds

100 g/3½ oz/½ cup soft brown or muscovado sugar

125 g/4½ oz butter

To serve: sour cream or thick, creamy yogurt

ovenproof dish, greased

Wash and stone (pit) the plums and prunes. Rinse the orange, remove a strip of rind with a zester or vegetable peeler, and squeeze the juice. Peel and grate the ginger. Put the fruit, ginger, spices, orange rind and juice in a pan. Add a little water and cook over medium heat for 15 minutes.

Preheat the oven to 180°C (350°F), gas mark 4.

To make the crumble: put the flour, ground almonds and sugar in a mixing bowl, stir together, and rub in the fat lightly with your fingertips until the mixture resembles breadcrumbs and is just beginning to form lumps. Do not work too long as the oil in the ground almonds will start to "run".

Remove the spices from the fruit compote and turn into the baking dish. Cover the fruit completely with the crumble mixture and bake in the preheated oven for 25-30 minutes, or until the top is crisp and golden.

Serve with sour cream or thick, creamy yogurt.

Note If you don't have a cinnamon stick or fresh ginger, you can use ½ teaspoon each of these spices in their ground form.

menu idea | split-pea soup | lamb chops
serve with | gewurztraminer

QUICK ICE CREAM
(GLACE MINUTE)

Serves 6

250 g/9 oz fromage frais

400 g/14 oz frozen raspberries or strawberries

7½ tablespoons caster (superfine) sugar

Put the fromage frais in the freezer for 15 minutes so that is really cold.

Process the frozen raspberries (do not defrost) with the sugar and fromage frais in an electric blender, turn into individual bowls and serve immediately.

Note This deliciously smooth ice cream must be prepared quickly but, when mixed, it can be put in the freezer until you are ready to serve dessert.

menu idea | mussel salad with curry sauce | oven-baked chicken with garlic

serve with | rosé

YULE LOG (BÛCHE DE NOËL)

Serves 6

For the base:

75 g/3 oz best quality dark chocolate (not unsweet-ened), broken into pieces

50g/2 oz butter

4 eggs, separated

100 g/3½ oz/½ cup caster (superfine) sugar

75 g/3 oz plain (all-purpose) flour

For the cream filling:

200 ml/7 fl oz/¾ cup whipping cream

3 tablespoons rum

1 teaspoon vanilla extract

300 g/10 oz chestnut purée

For the frosting:

150 ml/5 fl oz/⅔ cup whipping cream

150 g/5 oz best-quality dark chocolate, not unsweetened, broken into pieces

Swiss roll (jelly roll) baking tin, greased and lined with greased baking paper

Preheat the oven to 180°C (350°F), gas mark 4.

To make the base: melt the chocolate with the butter in a bowl over a pan of barely simmering water (not allowing the bowl to touch the water). Stir until smooth then remove the bowl and put to one side. Replace with another bowl containing the egg yolks and sugar, and beat until the mixture is light and frothy. Remove from the heat and mix in the flour, then the melted chocolate. In a separate bowl, beat the egg whites to stiff peaks and fold carefully into the chocolate mixture. Spread evenly in the Swiss roll tin and bake for 15 minutes or until risen and springy when pressed. Cool for a short while, then turn out onto a clean, damp dish towel, peeling off the baking paper.

To make the cream filling: whip the cream and add the rum and vanilla extract to the chestnut purée. Beat the purée until it has a smooth, creamy texture and then carefully mix in the whipped cream. Spread over the cold base and roll up like a Swiss roll, using the dish towel to help you. Wrap in clingfilm (plastic wrap) and chill in the refrigerator for at least 24 hours.

To make the frosting: bring the cream slowly to the boil, remove from the heat and add the chocolate. Stir until smooth with a wooden spatula and leave to cool. Chill in the refrigerator for 1 hour, then beat to a mousse-like consistency. Unwrap the Yule Log and place on a wire cake rack. Cover evenly with the chocolate icing, making "bark" striations with a fork. Return to the refrigerator until ready to serve.

Note The Yule log will have a richer texture if you drizzle a little rum mixed with water over the warm base.

menu idea | Landes-style smoked duck salad | escalopes of foie gras with apples
serve with | demi-sec champagne

APPENDICES

CONVERSION TABLES

THE OVEN TEMPERATURES GIVEN IN THIS BOOK ARE BASED ON A STANDARD OVEN. COOKING TIMES SHOULD BE ADJUSTED IF USING A FAN-ASSISTED OR MINIATURE OVEN. FOR BEST RESULTS CONSULT THE MANUFACTURERS GUIDELINES.

THE CONVERSIONS GIVEN IN THE RECIPES ARE APPROXIMATE ONLY. ALWAYS USE EITHER THE METRIC OR IMPERIAL SET OF MEASUREMENTS IN EACH RECIPE, NEVER MIX THE TWO SYSTEMS. ALL CUP AND SPOON MEASUREMENTS ARE LEVEL, UNLESS OTHERWISE STATED.

OVEN TEMPERATURES

	°C	°F	gas mark
cool	140	275	1
cool	150	300	2
moderate	170	325	3
moderate	180	350	4
moderate/hot	190	375	5
moderate/hot	200	400	6
hot	220°	425	7
hot	230	450	8
very hot	240	475	9

DRY WEIGHT

metric	imperial	metric	imperial
10 g	½ oz	200 g	7 oz
25 g	1 oz	250 g	9 oz
50 g	2 oz	300 g	10 oz
75 g	3 oz	350 g	12 oz
100 g	3½ oz	400 g	14 oz
125 g	4 oz	500 g	1 lb
150 g	5 oz	750 g	1½ lb
175 g	6 oz	1 kg	2 lb

HANDY MEASURES

The following ingredients measured in level tablespoons give approximately 1 oz/25 g

Ingredient	no. of tablespoons
cocoa powder	4
currants/sultanas (golden raisins)/raisins	4
desiccated (dry unsweetened) coconut	5
flour/cornflour(cornstarch)	3
ground almonds/hazelnuts/walnuts	4
honey/syrup/jam (jelly)	1
rice	2
salt	1
sugar: granulated/caster (superfine)	2
sugar: icing/demerara	3

LIQUIDS

metric	imperial	US cups
50 ml	2 fl oz	¼ cup
100 ml	3½ fl oz	scant ½ cup
125 ml	4 fl oz	½ cup
150 ml	5 fl oz	⅔ cup
200 ml	7 fl oz	¾ cup
250 ml	9 fl oz	1 cup
300 ml	10 fl oz	1¼ cups
350 ml	12 fl oz	1½ cups
400 ml	14 fl oz	1¾ cups
500 ml	17 fl oz	2 cups
600 ml	1 pint	2½ cups
750 ml	1¼ pints	3 cups
1 litre	1¾ pints	4 cups

GLOSSARY

Al dente Italian term, used for pasta or rice or vegetables. The food should still be firm to bite into when removed from the heat.

Andalouse, à l' A garnish made with (bell) peppers, aubergines, tomatoes and rice.

Armoricaine, à l' Sauce made with white wine, tomato and fish, lobster or crayfish stock.

Bain-marie (Mary's bath) refers to the cooking method of placing a pan of food in another pan with water in it to stabilize the heat reaching the food.

Basquaise, à la Basque garnish of tomatoes, (bell) peppers, garlic and cured Bayonne ham.

Bibbelskäse Fresh cow's milk cheese, seasoned with horseradish and fresh herbs.

Bordelaise, à la Dishes cooked in a sauce made with red wine, shallots and bone marrow (Bordeaux).

Boulangère, à la ('in the style of the baker's wife') Food cooked in the oven and garnished with potatoes and thinly sliced onions.

Brocciu Corsican ewe's or goat's milk cheese with an oily texture.

Carbonade flamande A Flemish dish of beef and onions stewed slowly in beer.

Carré Frais Rich, creamy cow's milk cheese from Normandy.

Caudière A French seafood stew or soup based on mussels and onions.

Clafoutis A traditional dessert from the Limousin region of France. It is made by pouring pancake batter over fruit in a pie or flan dish and baking in the oven.

Cocotte, en Eggs cooked in individual ramekin dishes set in a bain-marie and placed in the oven.

Court-bouillon A spiced aromatic liquor or stock used mainly for cooking fish and shellfish. Wine and vinegar may sometimes be added to the court-bouillon, which is usually prepared in advance and allowed to cool.

Cramique Brioche bread with currants or raisins. It is served warm with butter.

Crémet Cream cheese mixed with whisked egg-whites and whipped cream (Anjou, Nantes region).

Crêpe Savoury or sweet thin pancake.

Crudités Raw vegetables, thinly sliced or grated, served as a starter or, with a dip, as a snack. Popular crudités include carrots, celeriac, cucumber, sweet (bell) peppers, red cabbage, celery, fennel, tomatoes, mushrooms and radishes.

Dariole Small, steep-sided cylindrical moulds, used to make pastries and cakes.

Daube Meat stewed slowly with onions in a red wine and herb stock. Daube à la normande includes Normandy products (e.g. apples, cider). Daube provençale adds olives to the stock.

Flambé Spirits are poured over the dish and set alight.

Flamiche A tart filled with strong cheese, leeks or other vegetables (northern France).

Forestière, à la A garnish of wild mushrooms, potatoes and bacon cooked in butter.

Fumet A liquid obtained by reducing a stock or cooking liquid that is added to a sauce to enhance its flavour or give extra body.

Gâche Vendéenne A kind of half-risen, sometimes twisted brioche.

Gâteau battu (beaten cake) Like Pannetone, this Picardy speciality is a rich cake with a texture resembling brioche in the shape of a chef's hat.

Gratin dauphinois Seasoned, sliced potatoes baked in cream and crusted on top.

Grecque, à la A vegetable dish cooked in a concentrated tomato, olive-oil and lemon-juice marinade.

Kouign-aman A large, flat cake from Brittany whose name means 'bread and butter'. It is made from bread dough enriched with butter or double (heavy) cream, baked in the oven and caramelized with sugar.

Kugelhopf A yeast cake from Alsace, of Austrian origin, containing raisins or currants and cooked in a special high crownlike mould.

Lyonnaise, à la Dishes characterized by the use of chopped onions glazed in butter, sometimes with vinegar and chopped parsley.

Meunière (à la) A method of cooking that can be used for all types of fish. The fish is coated in seasoned flour, fried in butter and served with some more melted butter with the addition of a squeeze of lemon juice and a few freshly chopped herbs.

Mouclade Mussels cooked in white wine with parsley and shallots served in their own sauce with fresh cream, egg yolk and butter.

Neige Describes preparations involving whisked egg whites. Oeufs à la neige - a dessert of stiffly whipped egg whites poached in milk and served in a thin, caramelized vanilla custard.

Noilly Prat Dry French vermouth.

Orientale, à l' A dish containing rice, sweet (bell) peppers, tomatoes, aubergines (eggplants), saffron or various other ingredients.

Paillasson A thin pancake made with shredded potatoes or other vegetables.

Papeton A purée made with aubergines (eggplants) and eggs and cooked in a mould, originally in the shape of a papal crown (Avignon).

Paupiette A thin slice or escalope of meat filled with savory stuffing, rolled up, and braised.

Peas à la française A garnish prepared with onion and lettuce.

Pineau des Charentes Sweetish aperitif made by stopping fermentation with the addition of brandy. It varies in colour and style depending on the maker.

Piperade A fondue of sweet (bell) peppers and tomatoes flavoured with onions and garlic. Often served with omelette or scrambled eggs and hot cured ham (Basque region).

Pissaladière An open, pizza-style onion tart topped with anchovies and black olives (Nice).

Pistou A Provençal sauce made from fresh basil crushed with garlic and olive oil.

Pot-au-feu A stew made with beef, onions, carrots, turnips, celery and leeks. The stock is served first, then the meat and vegetables

Potée A meat and vegetable stew with regional variations. Named after the earthenware pot in which it was traditionally cooked.

Provençale, à la Garnishes inspired by Provençal cuisine, including tomatoes, garlic and olive oil.

Ratatouille A Provençal dish consisting of aubergines (eggplants), courgettes (zucchini), garlic, sweet (bell) peppers and tomatoes, simmered in olive oil and flavoured with aromatic herbs.

Romaine, à la A term used to describe dishes inspired by Roman cuisine, usually including eggs with spinach, anchovies, and Parmesan cheese.

Saint-Florentin A French wheel-shaped cow's-milk cheese with soft curd and reddish-brown washed rind.

Saint-Marcellin A small, cylindrical cow's-milk cheese from the Dauphiné. A soft cheese with a mild flavour and a natural, thin blue mould rind.

Rouille A pungent Provençal sauce to serve with bouillabaisse, made from chillies, garlic and oil.

Tapenade Tapenade is a paste made of black olives, capers, anchovies, mustard, basil and parsley. It can be used on crostini or bruschette, with pasta and in sauces, as a marinade for meat and also for adding to casseroles and stews.

Tian A vegetable or potato gratin, named after the round, open earthenware baking or serving dish (tian) in which it is traditionally served (Provence).

Tôt-fait This term is used for two kinds of cake. It can be a type of pound cake, often flavoured with lemon. It also refers to a cake made from sugar and flour mixed with milk and eggs, then melted butter and flavoured with vanilla. Cooked in a shallow dish this latter is eaten hot before it collapses.

Unilaterale, à l' Fillet of fish grilled on one side only.

Vergeoise Soft brown sugar (beet or cane) used in Northern France for making pastries and sprinkling on pancakes and waffles.

Top left: kouign-aman; top right: mouclade
Bottom left: pot-au-feu; bottom right: ratatouille

LIST OF RECIPES

MEAT AND POULTRY

FISH

CAKES AND DESSERTS

THEMATIC INDEX

CAKES AND DESSERTS

ALPHABETICAL INDEX

ACKNOWLEDGEMENTS

SHOPPING & TABLE DESIGN

Tables, wallpaper, table linen

Agapè - pages: 11, 13, 15, 17, 21, 29, 33, 37, 43, 47, 49, 65, 67, 85, 105, 107, 115, 117, 119, 121, 123, 125, 129, 131, 133, 135, 139, 151, 153, 157, 159, 161, 163, 165, 167, 169, 171, 175, 177, 179, 181, 183, 189, 191, 197, 201, 203, 205, 207, 213, 229, 245, 247, 251, 253, 255, 257, 259, 263, 267, 269, 277, 279, 281, 283, 285, 287, 291, 301, 303, 305, 307, 309, 311, 313, 315, 317, 325, 331, 333, 335, 337, 341, 343, 349, 351, 353, 355, 357, 359, 361, 363, 365, 367, 369, 371, 375, 377, 379, 383, 385, 387, 389, 399, 401, 403, 411, 421, 425, 429, 433, 435, 439, 441, 445, 447, 449, 453, 455, 457, 459, 461, 463, 465, 467, 471, 473, 475, 479, 485, 487, 489, 491, 493, 497, 499, 503, 505, 507, 511, 513, 515, 517.

Farrow & Ball - pages: 19, 25, 31, 39, 41, 57, 63, 69, 71, 73, 75, 77, 81, 91, 93, 97, 155, 173, 185, 187, 193, 431, 495, 509.

Jeannine Cros - pages: 27, 35, 51, 59, 79, 87, 89, 223, 225, 227, 231, 233, 235, 237, 241, 249, 265, 271, 275, 283, 289, 293, 295, 409, 415, 483.

Nana Ki - pages: 95, 99, 109, 137, 141, 419, 437, 477.

Zero One One - pages: 327, 329, 423, 427, 451, 501.

Place settings and cutlery

Agapè - pages: 19, 31, 33, 35, 37, 47, 67, 71, 73, 81, 83, 99, 107, 115, 129, 131, 133, 141, 155, 157, 159, 163, 171, 175, 201, 203, 231, 247, 255, 285, 289, 311, 315, 333, 343, 363, 367, 379, 389, 399, 413, 423, 431, 461, 467, 477, 479, 501, 503, 505, 507, 511, 513.

La Samaritaine - pages: 57, 463.

Zero One One - pages: 85, 359, 473.

Glassware, crockery, cookware and other items

Agapè - pages: 11, 17, 19, 21, 25, 27, 29, 31, 35, 41, 45, 49, 51, 59, 63, 65, 71, 73, 75, 77, 79, 81, 85, 89, 91, 93, 95, 97, 107, 109, 129, 131, 133, 137, 151, 153, 155, 157, 163, 165, 169, 173, 175, 181, 183, 185, 187, 189, 197, 205, 231, 237, 241, 247, 249, 253, 255, 271, 281, 285, 289, 291, 301, 305, 307, 309, 311, 313, 315, 325, 343, 351, 353, 355, 357, 361, 365, 375, 379, 387, 389, 407, 409, 415, 423, 425, 427, 433, 441, 447, 451, 455, 457, 471, 473, 477, 479, 483, 487, 489, 495, 499, 501, 503, 509, 517.

Astier de Villatte - pages: 43, 191, 269, 337, 389.

Gargantua - pages: 449, 507.

La Samaritaine - pages: 47, 83, 87, 99, 125, 135, 139, 159, 179, 193, 231, 241, 245, 257, 267, 275, 303, 307, 335, 339, 349, 367, 373, 385, 405, 419, 431, 439, 463, 481, 491, 497, 515.

Le Bon Marché - pages: 413, 485, 493.

Lô Sushi - pages: 7, 53, 101, 111, 143, 215, 297, 319, 357, 391, 519.

Zero One One - pages: 67, 229.

Delphine and David would like to thank Sandra for her patience and help. The editor would like to thank Léone for her invaluable assistance.

ADDRESS BOOK

Agapè (vintage tableware)
91 Avenue Jean-Baptiste-Clément 92100 Boulogne, France +44-(0)1 47 12 04 88 www.agapedeco.com

Astier de Villatte (hand-made glass and tableware)
173 Rue St Honoré 75001 Paris, France +44-(0)1 42 60 74 13

Farrow & Ball (wallpaper)
www.farrowandball.com

La Samaritaine
19 Rue de la Monnaie 75001 Paris, France +44-(0)1 40 41 20 20
www.lasamaritaine.com

Le Bon Marché
24 Rue de Sèvres 75007 Paris, France +44-(0)1 44 39 80 00
www.lebonmarche.fr

Lô Sushi (restaurant)
1 Rue du Pont-Neuf 75001 Paris, France +44-(0)1 42 33 09 09

Nana Ki (fabrics and table linen)
5 Rue Condé 75006 Paris, France +44-(0)1 55 42 95 26

Zero One One
2 Rue Marengo 75001 Paris, France +44-(0)1 42 27 00 11

Design and layout of recipes: Delphine de Montalier

Editor: Élisabeth Darets
Art and publishing editors: Emmanuel Le Vallois, Fabienne Travers and Sophie Coupard
Production: Laurence Ledru
Proofreading: Jean-Pierre Leblan

© Marabout (Hachette Livre), 2004
This edition published by Hachette Illustrated UK,
Octopus Publishing Group Ltd., 2-4 Heron Quays, London E14 4JP

English translation by Sue Rose and Wendy Allatson for
JMS Books LLP (email: moseleystrachan@aol.co.uk)
Translation © Octopus Publishing Group Ltd.

A CIP catalogue for this book is available from the British Library

ISBN-13: 978-1-84430-139-3

ISBN-10: 1-84430-139-7

Printed by Toppan Printing Co., (HK) Ltd.